A
MOUNTAIN
BOYHOOD

AT THAT INSTANT THE BEAR CAME TO LIFE.

[Page 30]

A MOUNTAIN BOYHOOD

By JOE MILLS

Illustrated by
ENOS B. COMSTOCK

Introduction and Notes by
JAMES H. PICKERING

University of Nebraska Press
Lincoln and London

Introduction and Notes copyright © 1988 by the
University of Nebraska Press

First Bison Book printing: 1988
Most recent printing indicated by the first digit below:
1   2   3   4   5   6   7   8   9   10

Library of Congress Cataloging-in-Publication Data
Mills, Joe, 1880–1935.
   A mountain boyhood.
   Reprint. Originally published: New York: J.H. Sears, 1926.
   "Bison book."
   1. Mills, Joe, 1880–1935—Childhood and youth.
2. Pioneers—Colorado—Biography. 3. Estes Park
Region (Colo.)—Social life and customs. 4. Natural
History—Colorado. 5. Colorado—Biography. 6. Longs
Peak (Colo.) 7. Rocky Mountain Naitonal Park (Colo.)—
History. I. Pickering, James H. II. Title.
F781.M46A3   1988   978.8'69031'0924   87-30202
ISBN 0-8032-3126-1
ISBN 0-8032-8154-4 (pbk.)

This Bison Book reproduces the 1926 edition published by
the J. H. Sears & Company, Inc., New York. To this edition
an introduction with five photographs, notes for the entire
volume, and a map have been added.

TO

THE ONE WHO MADE THIS
BOYHOOD POSSIBLE

MY WIFE

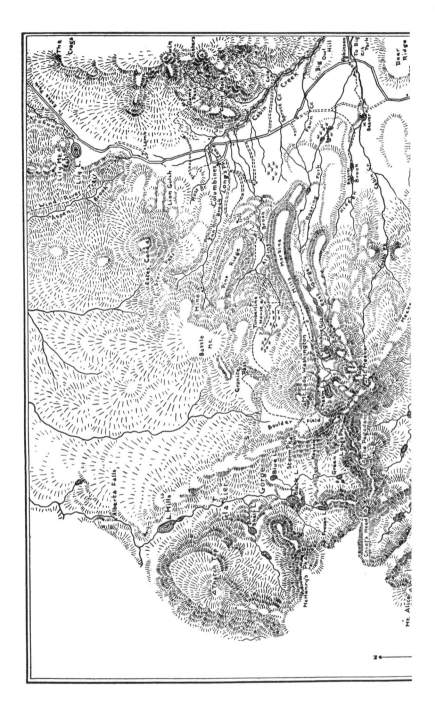

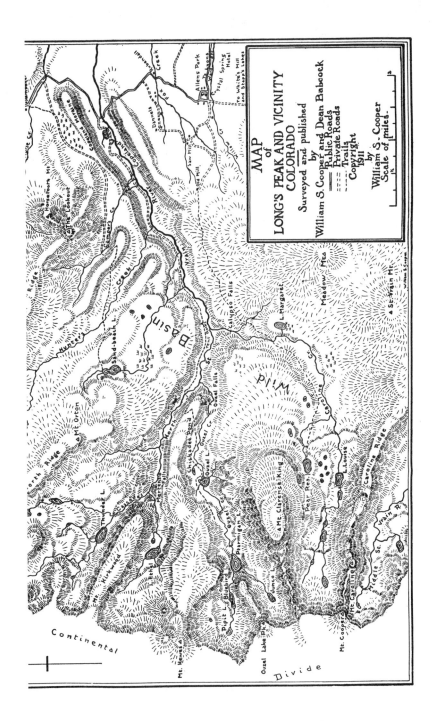

MAP
of
LONG'S PEAK AND VICINITY
COLORADO
Surveyed and published
by
William S. Cooper and Dean Babcock
Public Roads ————
Private Roads ====
Trails ------
Copyright
1911
by
William S. Cooper
Scale of miles

INTRODUCTION

by James H. Pickering

Though initially published in *Boys' Life*, the official magazine of American scouting,[1] Joe Mills's *A Mountain Boyhood* is a good deal more than simply a book for boys. To be sure, *A Mountain Boyhood* faithfully adheres to the requirements of the genre with its episodes of exploration and adventuring and its ample wilderness lore of the how-to-do it variety. What makes Mills's book memorable and gives it lasting importance, however, is that for all its romantic coloring *A Mountain Boyhood* provides the best single sustained account we have of life in Estes Park, Colorado, and the surrounding region during the first decade of the twentieth century. That the area Joe Mills writes about is now embraced by Rocky Mountain National Park should make this new edition of particular interest to all those who over the years have made Estes Park one of America's most visited and popular mountain resorts.

As even the most casual visitor soon discovers, the name Mills is one that has been long and intimately connected with the history and topography of Estes Park and its adjacent wilderness. It repeats itself in Mills Lake, one of the most scenic and visited lakes in Rocky Mountain National Park, and in Mills Moraine and Mills Glacier, two landmark features on the rugged eastern slope of Longs Peak. The name is also permanently affixed to a bronze historical marker on Colorado's "Peak-to-Peak" Highway 7, nine miles south of the town of Estes Park, locating the site of a homestead cabin erected in 1885–86.[2] With the single exception of Joe Mills Mountain in Odessa Gorge, however, all of these places commemorate the life and career of Joe Mills's older brother Enos Abijah Mills (1870–1922), the celebrated writer-naturalist, mountain guide, and innkeeper, whose persistent lobbying efforts in the years after 1909 proved to be a major, if not decisive, factor in the creation of Rocky Mountain National Park in 1915.

Such achievements were hard-won and well-deserved and earned Enos Mills a national and international reputation. Moreover, as has become increasingly clear in recent years, the achievements of Enos Mills, though centered in Colorado, are part of the larger story of a developing national consciousness concerning the American wilderness and how that wilderness can best be preserved and protected for future generations. Joe Mills understood and accepted the recognition bestowed upon his older brother, both during Enos Mills's own lifetime and in the years following his death in 1922. Despite the fact that he had considerable achievements of his own, Joe Mills was content to live in the shadow of the man who became known as the "father of Rocky Mountain National Park." As is so often the case, however, the verdict of history is in many respects an ironic one, for the interests and careers of the brothers Mills were very much alike. Both were dedicated disciples of the conservation ethic of John Muir, both espoused the virtues of outdoor mountain life, and both developed a special, contagious enthusiasm for the rugged yet largely unsettled valley at the foot of Longs Peak where they made their home. Both built homestead cabins with their own hands, both became largely self-taught naturalists, guides, authors, and lecturers, and both played leading roles in developing Estes Park into a summer playground for the nation. The story of Enos Mills has been told many times. Joe Mills's story, on the other hand, has been largely forgotten. The republication of *A Mountain Boyhood* provides an appropriate occasion to correct the imbalance.

To do so has required a great deal of help and I should like to acknowledge and thank the following individuals: Lennie Bemiss, Estes Park Library; Bridget Bower, Earlham College; Paul T. Bryant, Radford University; Francis R. Burdette, South Bend [Indiana] Public Library; Melvin E. Busch and Betty Hedlund, Estes Park Area Historical Museum; Donald Brown, Rocky Mountain National Park; Ellen K. Brown, Kent Keeth, William

Menefee, and Virginia Ming, Baylor University; Ann Cantrell, Long Beach, California; Harvey L. Carter, Colorado Springs, Colorado; Carol Collins, South Bend, Indiana; Ceil Damschroder, Fort Collins, Colorado; David S. Cooper, Nyack, New York; Stephen Dahl and Ann Hiflinger, Colorado State University; Mrs. Alex Early, Fort Worth Public Library; Ola May Earnest, Linn County [Kansas] Historical and Genealogical Society; David Eisen, Mishawaka-Penn [Indiana] Public Library; Walter B. Franklin, Jr., Boulder, Colorado; Clayton F. Freiheit, Denver; James B. Gallagher, East Lansing, Michigan; Eleanor M. Gehres, Denver Public Library; Thomas D. Hamm, Indiana University; Patricia Cairns Kemp, Grand Lake, Colorado; Ruth Kjos, Kelseyville, California; James X. Kroll, Denver, Colorado; Eric L. Mundell, Indiana Historical Society; Marilyn M. Nobbe, Morrison-Reeves Library, Richmond, Indiana; Donald J. Orth, United States Board on Geographic Names, Reston, Virginia; Robert and Elsie Peirce, Haggerstown, Indiana; Johnny Lou Pettey, Hot Sulphur Springs, Colorado; Cheryl Lamb Replogle, Elkhart, Indiana; Patrick J. Sartorius, Phoenix, Arizona; Deborah S. Smith, Wayne County, Indiana; Barbara A. Snedden, Des Moines, Iowa; Cassandra Volpe, University of Colorado; and Brigid Welch, M. D. Anderson Library, University of Houston.

Enoch Josiah Mills (1880–1935), or Joe Mills as he came to be known, was born and raised on the family farm, some five miles south of the town of Pleasanton in Linn County, Kansas. He was the youngest of the ten children of Enos Mills, Sr. (1834–1910) and his wife, the former Ann Lamb (1837–1923),[3] who had arrived in Linn County from Iowa in the spring of 1857. For the Mills family and their neighbors the early years in Linn County were difficult ones. In the aftermath of the Kansas-Nebraska Act of 1854, which permitted the residents of the two territories to decide whether or not to organize themselves as slave states, the prairies of eastern Kansas had become the fulcrum of the struggle between opposing forces. Violence, often instigated by marauding bands of proslavery "Border Ruffians" from neighboring Missouri, was widespread and families with strong Quaker antislavery beliefs, like the Millses, were particularly vulnerable.

Seven years of turbulence, culminating in the Battle of Mine Creek between Union and Confederate armies in October 1864, sorely tried the mettle of Linn County's pioneer families, most of whom, like the Millses and their relatives and neighbors the Lambs, asked for little more than the opportunity to farm and raise their families. Fortitude and hard work were at last rewarded, and though prairie farming was never easy in the boom-bust years following the Civil War, the Mills family not only survived but managed to achieve a measure of prosperity.

Joe Mills's introduction to Colorado and the allure of the West came early in the form of the stories his parents told about their brief trip to Breckenridge in the spring of 1860 in search of gold. Though their mountain adventures yielded nothing but memories, they were sufficient to stir the imaginations of their sons and to set in motion a series of events that would in time lead both Enos and Joe to Estes Park. Enos was the first to go. By the time he was fourteen it was clear that a congenital childhood illness (vaguely described as a digestive disorder, though at least one source mentions tuberculosis) rendered him unsuited for the daily rigors of farm life. The mountains offered a more healthy alternative, and so in 1884 Enos Mills went alone by way of Kansas City and Denver to Estes Park. There, under the tutelage and watchful eye of the Reverend Elkanah J. Lamb (1832–1915), his father's older cousin who operated a guest ranch at the foot of Longs Peak, Enos built a homestead cabin and began to educate himself about the ways of the mountains.

Joe Mills, by contrast, had to bide his time. Endowed with a healthy and robust constitution, the younger son was needed at home on the farm. There he remained, attending local schools, until the fall of 1898, when he entered Kansas Normal College in nearby Fort Scott. Other than its proximity to home, which no doubt reduced the expense, Joe Mills's reasons for attending KNS are not clear. What did become clear during his first and only year in Fort Scott, however, was that Joe Mills was a gifted collegiate athlete. Those abilities, once discovered, were to shape much of his subsequent career.

Having apparently won the assent of his parents that he was ready to explore a larger world, Joe Mills left Kansas in 1899 to enroll at Colorado Agricultural College (now Colorado State University) in Fort Collins. Whatever his academic success there,[4] Joe Mills's successes on the athletic field were little short of phenomenal. Moreover, for someone athletically inclined, his timing could not have been more perfect. His arrival in Fort Collins coincided with the decision of the college to reinstitute intercollegiate football after a five-year absence, to reorganize the Athletic Association as a support group, and to open a new football field, all of which greatly raised the level of enthusiasm for intercollegiate sports among students and faculty alike. In an era in which college football was played without pads and helmets and commonly accepted rules, and was characterized by frequent instances of dubious sportsmanship, direct faculty participation (in 1899 "five [CAC] teachers were used to make an eleven"), and semiprofessional coaches,[5] Joe Mills nonetheless excelled. This fact becomes all the more remarkable given his slight stature (he weighed only 129 pounds), for the dominant football strategy of the day featured variations of the now-outlawed formation known as the "wedge" and placed a decided emphasis on size and brute strength.

During his three years at Fort Collins, 1899 to 1902, Joe "Nuck" Mills played halfback and quarterback on the football team, shortstop and centerfield on the baseball team, guard on the basketball team, and in addition ran track. Despite his size, Joe Mills had the distinction in 1900 and again in 1901 of playing "on every C. A. C. team through every college contest."[6] "Enoch Mills, our little quarterback, is a 'corker,'" bragged the *Rocky Mountain Collegian* following the completion of the 1900 season: "Although he has not the weight to smash through interference, he can trip them up in a very amusing but effective manner. Quick, lithe, and with an eye that is always on the ball, together with his speed, makes him a star player."[7] Though the Aggie team of 1901 had a record of only three wins and two losses, it managed to outscore its five opponents by a margin of 158 points to 38 points. The season concluded satisfactorily enough with an 80 to 0 Thanksgiving Day rout of a team made up of soldiers from Fort Russell, Wyoming, in a game mercifully halted after fifteen minutes of the second half.

After three years of study in Fort Collins, Joe Mills suc-

E. J. MILLS,
Athletic Director.

Joe Mills in his University of Denver uniform, 1903. Reproduced from the
1910 Baylor University *Round-Up.* Courtesy of The Texas Collection,
Baylor University, Waco, Texas.

cumbed to the attractions of the nearby mountains. From the late spring of 1902 to the early fall of 1903, he made his home in Estes Park, and it is to this period that the majority of the reminiscences in *A Mountain Boyhood* properly belong. These were, as we shall see, among the most interesting and happy days of Joe Mills's life. Nevertheless, they could not last. In the fall of 1903, Mills abandoned his outdoor life and entered the University of Denver. Though his official "Record Sheet" for the school year 1903–4 records only two courses each semester—a year-long sequence in economics and separate courses in social science and English—they were apparently sufficient for him to earn a degree.[8] Once again, however, Joe Mills was called upon to demonstrate his prowess as an athlete, and again he rose to the occasion. Mills quarterbacked the 1903 Denver football team during a season described in retrospect as "a struggle for recognition" and served as player-manager of a basketball team that won three of its four regular season games.

Though the University of Denver had high hopes for the 1904 football team on which Joe Mills was expected to play as captain and quarterback, he decided not to return.[9] Instead, he accepted a coaching position in Texas at Fort Worth University. As it soon became clear, Joe Mills had a gift for mentoring the young, and within a brief span of years his success in the collegiate coaching ranks earned him a considerable and growing reputation. In Texas, as in Colorado, Joe Mills also starred on the football field. As player-coach at Fort Worth University he earned "all-Southwestern" honors as a quarterback for the 1904 season.

Mills remained at Fort Worth University until February 1907 and then accepted a similar post as "physical director" across town at Polytechnic College, an institution that, though short-lived, was then undergoing a period of impressive expansion. While living in Fort Worth, Mills roomed at the local YMCA, where he captained and played on its basketball team, twice winner of the state championship. The highlight of these years, however, was unquestionably his courtship of a young woman named Ethel M. Steere (1884–1970), a schoolteacher and the daughter of a local attorney.[10] Joe Mills and Ethel Steere were married in Fort Worth in May 1908. That fall, after rejecting no less than five coaching offers from other states as well as an offer to play professional baseball, Joe Mills transferred his allegiance to Baylor University in Waco.

Mills arrived in Waco in September amidst high expectations. An article on the front page of the September 12th edition of *The Lariat,* entitled "Athletics at Baylor," began by assuring its readers that "Baylor University is committed to the support and encouragement of clean athletics. That physical exercise and training is as essential to a well-rounded character as is the drill in English grammar or the study of ethics is plain to every thinking man or woman." The article then went on to extol the new athletic director and coach as "one of the most vigorous athletic men and elegant gentlemen in all the country."[11] Mills developed his agenda for Baylor athletics with surprising speed and thoroughness. He raised money for adequate equipment and instruction and oversaw the creation of a council to bring athletics under firm academic control. His football and basketball teams performed well on the field. But, despite his obvious successes at Baylor, Joe Mills did not stay. In March 1911, he announced his intention to resign that coming June to return to Colorado in order to "engage in business." Joe intimated to the student paper that his reasons for leaving were primarily financial ones.[12] No doubt money was an issue, for his Baylor salary could not have been large. But the greatest reason was unquestionably the pull of the mountains themselves. In his heart of hearts Joe Mills had never left Estes Park and now, in 1911, he was prepared to return.

On his first visit to Estes Park a dozen years earlier, in the spring or summer of 1899,[13] Joe Mills had entered upon a world that had changed relatively little since that day some forty years before when Joel Estes and his son had become its first known white visitors. To be sure, thanks to the publication of a variety of guidebooks, travel narratives, and magazine sketches—mostly promotional in nature—Estes Park was becoming an increasingly well known place to vacation and recreate among scenery widely said to rival the Swiss Alps. Visitors in 1899 had their choice of accommodations. They could stay at one of the picturesque if unpretentious guest "ranches" operated during the summer months by such early Estes Park pioneers as Elkanah Lamb, Abner Sprague, William James, Alexander MacGregor, and Horace Ferguson. They could also stay at the more lavishly appointed and expensive fifty-room English Hotel with its wrap-around porch and artificial lake built by the Earl of Dunraven in 1877 near the site of Joel Estes's original ranch and outbuildings. Then as now, many summer visitors simply preferred to pitch a tent and camp along the banks of the Big Thompson or Fall rivers or along one of their tributary streams. For most visitors Estes Park proved a seductive place. Many of those who came returned year after year and by 1900 a number of these annual visitors had built their own cabins as summer vacation homes. As far as "civilization" was concerned, however, the site of the future village of Estes Park consisted of little more than John Cleave's eight-by-ten frame post office, his nearby home, and a building housing the local school. All this was about to change, and change dramatically, in the decade that followed.

Part of this change was the inevitable result of Estes Park's growing popularity and increasing accessibility as a summer resort. But the major reason, particularly during the second half of the decade, had to do with the purchase, subdivision, and rapid development of two large tracts of prime real estate that had long been in private hands. The first of these was the hundred and sixty acre homestead of John Cleave at the junction of the Big Thompson and Fall rivers. It was purchased in March 1905 by Cornelius H. Bond (1854–1931) and four partners for $8,000. Bond and his associates wasted no time. On August 24th of that year they formed the Estes Park Town Company, which had the land surveyed and subdivided for sale. Twenty-five-foot lots fronting Elkhorn Avenue sold for a mere fifty dollars and as a result new businesses—including a photography studio, a shoe repair shop, a bakery, a barber shop, a laundry, a butcher shop, and a livery stable—sprang up almost overnight. A year later, in 1906, Josie Hupp opened at the corner of what is now Elkhorn and Moraine avenues the twenty-three-room Hupp Hotel, featuring steam heat and hot and cold running water.

The second major transfer of property involved the residual

Estes Park village in 1903, from the southeast. Courtesy of the Denver Public Library, Western History Department.

holdings of the Earl of Dunraven and the English Company, some six thousand acres in all, which Freelan O. Stanley (1849–1940) and his partner Burton D. Sanborn, a Greeley developer, purchased for about $80,000 in 1907. Stanley, a native of Newton, Massachusetts, and the inventor of the Stanley Steamer automobile, had come to Estes Park in 1903 to regain his health and stayed on to play a major role in the town's development. His first project was to undertake the building of the magnificent red-roofed Stanley Hotel overlooking the village. With its opening in June 1909, luxurious and thoroughly modern accommodations for the gentry had come to Estes Park.

Other developments quickly followed: the opening of a new road up the Big Thompson Canyon connecting Estes Park and Loveland in 1903; the formation of the Estes Park Protective and Improvement Association, an informal forum in which to air and resolve community issues (fittingly enough, with F. O. Stanley as president and C. H. Bond as secretary), and the construction of a new schoolhouse in 1906; the beginning of a volunteer fire department and the establishment of an automobile stage line between Estes Park and Loveland in 1907; the organization of the Estes Park Bank, the Estes Park Water Company, the Estes Park Light and Power Company, a local telephone exchange with twenty-five subscribers, the building of the first church, and the publication of a new, if short-lived, newspaper, *The Mountaineer*, in 1908. Though none could rival the Stanley in size or appointments, the decade also saw a proliferation of new resort hotels in response to an ever-increasing number of summer visitors: the Wind River Lodge (on the current site of the YMCA of the Rockies) in 1902; Horseshoe Inn (originally conceived by Frank Lloyd Wright) in 1909; Moraine Park Lodge, Sprague's Lodge, Fern Lake Lodge, and Stanley Manor (an impressive year-round facility next to the Stanley Hotel) in 1910; and the Brinwood Hotel in Moraine Park in 1911.[14] The permanent year-round population expanded accordingly: from 125 in 1890 to 218 in 1900, and to 396 in 1910. To make matters even more interesting, after 1909 there was also, thanks to the crusading activities of Enos Mills, a rising tide of excitement over prospects for a new national park.

In 1899, when Joe Mills arrived, this period of remarkable growth and development was just beginning. Though he noted, and lamented, the lack of wild game (the result of thirty years of unrestricted hunting), the world that the nineteen-year-old Mills encountered in Estes Park was still largely unspoiled. This was particularly true of his immediate destination, the sequestered upland valley at the base of Longs Peak, some eight miles south and fifteen hundred feet above John Cleave's post office, where Elkanah Lamb had been living since 1875 and where his older brother Enos had erected his homestead cabin in 1885–86. Here indeed was a world apart, a place whose heavily wooded slopes of lodgepole pine were intermixed with stands of shimmering green aspen and willow. Longs Peak Valley, as this pastoral amphitheater was then known, was bounded on the west by the majestic 14,255-foot Longs Peak and its near neighbors Mount Meeker and Mount Lady Washington, and on the east by the crests of Twin Sisters Mountain, a series of jagged knobs, pinnacles, and projections. To the north was the hydrographic divide between the St. Vrain and Big Thompson rivers known as Lamb's Notch (the site of Parson Lamb's "Mountain Home"); while to the south the retreating declension of an ancient moraine swept downward toward the densely forested watershed of Wild Basin. In 1899 it would have been difficult indeed to find a more idyllic spot to fire the imagination or enthusiasm of a young man of nineteen venturing into the mountains for the very first time.

Though it goes unacknowledged in *A Mountain Boyhood,* one of the chief attractions of Estes Park for Joe was the opportunity to be reunited with his older brother. The years 1899 to 1907, in fact, marked the halcyon days of the relationship between Joe and Enos Mills, particularly the period in 1902–3 when both brothers made their home in Longs Peak Valley. Enos, the self-taught naturalist and guide, had much to teach his younger brother, and Joe Mills, unschooled in the ways of the mountains, had much to learn. For Enos Mills especially, these were important years. In 1902 he finally succeeded in purchasing Longs Peak House from Carlyle Lamb. Renamed Longs Peak Inn and enlarged to meet the needs of an expanding number of summer visitors, it became the base of operations for his own distinctive approach to mountain hospitality and "nature guiding." Interestingly enough, three of Enos Mills's most famous achievements as a mountaineer belong to this period as well. In February 1903 he made the first recorded winter ascent of Longs Peak, and that same month crossed the Continental Divide to Grand Lake on snowshoes by way of the Flattop Mountain trail, an undertaking that had previously been considered impossible. Four months later, in June, he then repeated Elkanah Lamb's perilous feat of 1871 by descending the East Face of Longs Peak, crossing the steep snowfield known as "Lamb's Slide," and emerging on the shore of Chasm Lake some three thousand feet below. To these years belong as well many, if not most, of the reminiscences that Joe Mills recorded in *A Mountain Boyhood,* including the building of his homestead cabin on the lower slope of Twin Sisters Mountain overlooking Longs Peak Valley.

Joe's willingness to help in running Longs Peak Inn during the summer months was no doubt critical to the success of Enos Mills's new venture,[15] especially since Enos's increasing agenda of public activities required his absence even during the height of the tourist season. Joe not only became one of his brother's carefully selected and personally trained group of mountain guides[16] but during the summers of 1906 and 1907, and perhaps earlier, was given control over management of the Inn. During one of these absences, in early June 1906 with Enos lecturing in St. Paul and Joe in charge, the main building at the Inn and its new dining room burned to the ground. When Joe Mills returned to the Inn for the 1908 season, it was in the company of "a beautiful bride." "We all welcomed the happy couple warmly," Charles Hewes recalled, "and they spent a glorious honeymoon before the rush of the season came on."[17]

Just when Joe Mills actually cut the logging road to the site and began work on his cabin is not clear, but it was complete and occupied by March 23, 1906, when it was visited by a writer for the *Denver Times:*

> The cabin of another brother is also most interesting, and a walk
> to its romantic site is one of the easy first tramps of guests at the

[Longs Peak] inn. It is built of logs and is placed between the jagged rocks on one of the cliffs on the side of one of "the Sisters," twin
mountains which form part of the shelter for the beautiful meadow land of the inn park.

The brother, Mr. Enoch Mills, is a university athlete, and his
picturesque cabin with its great cobblestone fireplace, is lined with
college and athletic trophies.

The view from the rocks which shelter this cabin in its eagle-
nest-perch is glorious indeed.[18]

Because of the pressure of his duties in Waco, Joe Mills abandoned his homestead without ever staking a formal claim. The
cabin beneath Cabin Rock continued to stand, however, until
1968, when it was accidentally set on fire. The "great cobblestone fireplace" alone remains to mark the site.

Unfortunately, the cordial working relationship between Enos
and Joe Mills did not last. Though their quarrel and final part-
ing of the ways no doubt had much to do with all-too-familiar
sibling rivalries and the feelings that often come to define mentor relationships, its public manifestation was apparently a dispute over the building of Timberline House, an overnight way
station for those climbing Longs Peak, located in Jim's Grove
below the Boulder Field some three and a half miles from the
Inn.[19] Reconciliation, if it was tried at all, proved useless, and
after 1908 Enos and Joe Mills, together with their families, were
content to go their separate ways. When their paths did cross, it
was likely to be on opposing sides of controversial issues. So deep
were the feelings that, in spite of the fact that Joe Mills returned
to Colorado to live in 1911, it was not until late January of 1916
that he could bring himself to visit his old haunts in Longs Peak
Valley.[20]

However disappointing and painful his estrangement from
Enos must have been, it did not dampen Joe Mills's enthusiasm
for Colorado or for Estes Park. Their honeymoon season of 1908
made a convert of Ethel Steere Mills as well, and when Joe decided to give up his athletic directorship at Baylor, Colorado
inevitably became their choice for a new home. Joe Mills's ap-
prenticeship experience as manager at Longs Peak Inn had

The Forks Hotel, Drake, Colorado, c. 1911. Courtesy of the Denver Public Library, Western History Department.

clearly been a satisfying one, for his first foray into private business in the summer of 1911 was as manager of the Forks Hotel, located at the hamlet of Drake in the Big Thompson Canyon halfway between Loveland and Estes Park. Why he chose Drake and its small two-story tourist hotel is not clear other than that it was close to Estes Park and available for lease. In terms of the future it gave Joe and Ethel the opportunity to see whether or not they enjoyed the mountain resort business with its short but hectic summer season. The Forks, as it turned out, was a good choice. Built in 1899 or 1900 by Frank Bartholf, who was for many years the largest landowner in Larimer County, the Forks Hotel had become a popular stopping place for tourists as soon as the new road up the Big Thompson to Estes Park was opened in 1903.[21]

Though Joe and Ethel Mills apparently did well enough at the Forks to confirm their newly chosen occupation,[22] their stay in Drake was relatively brief. These were nonetheless happy years, for they coincided with the birth in September 1911 of their first child, Eleanor Ann Mills.[23] Understandably, however, Joe wanted to establish a more permanent arrangement for the family, one whose destiny he himself could in some measure control. If he and Ethel were going to preside over a resort, its location should be in Estes Park. Moreover, since he had watched Enos rebuild Longs Peak Inn to his own distinctive specifications after the 1906 fire, it is hardly surprising that Joe Mills would want to design and build a place of his own.

He did not wait long. On September 13, 1913, the *Estes Park Trail* made the announcement on Mills's behalf: "A letter from Mr. Enoch Mills says that he has decided to leave the Forks and that next season he will be in Estes Park. Mr. Mills has made a fine record as a hotel man since he has had the hotel at the Forks and he will be a valuable acquisition to the Park. All his old customers and many new ones will cordially welcome him."[24] The site Joe Mills selected was a twenty-one-acre tract on the northern side of Prospect Mountain overlooking the village of Estes Park and encompassing a particularly fine view. The land was obtained from F. O. Stanley on January 14, 1914, and with the aid of a construction loan of six thousand dollars Mills began to build the twenty-room frame hotel he would call the Crags. Despite the delay caused by the unprecedented snowfall during the winter of 1913–14, which by May 1914 had reached a total of more than twenty feet, actual construction progressed rapidly. "Met Joe Mills in the village," Charles Hewes noted in his journal on April 8, 1914, "and he says he will have his hotel built and open for business by the 15th of June. It is in a very sightly place and shall make him a beautiful home."[25] Mills's prediction was not too far off. The Crags was formally opened on July 4, 1914, and at once "was filled to overflowing."[26] The day featured a picnic for local residents at the foot of Prospect Mountain, and "after the baskets were emptied, the Rev. E. J. Lamb gave an enthusiastic address appropriate to the occasion on 'Pioneer Days of Estes Park.'"[27] Two weeks later a new road past the Crags was finished and the first full season of Joe Mills's proprietorship was well underway.

For the next twenty-one seasons Joe and Ethel Mills presided over the Crags Hotel, which quickly took its place among Estes Park's most popular summer resorts. Much of its success was due to the popularity of the proprietors themselves and to the very personal role Joe and Ethel together played in seeing to it that their guests were well taken care of and entertained. Weekly picnics and trout fries on the side of Prospect Mountain, with Joe Mills slicing watermelon, mental telepathy stunts and guest lectures by firelight in the main parlor of the lodge, visits to the local "picture show" and day trips to various scenic spots around the area, and fishing expeditions to Lawn Lake and elsewhere ("Mr. Mills reported that they caught more wind than fish")— all were designed to prevent guests from spending a "slow time."[28] The highlight of that first season was undoubtedly the visit by Clarence S. Darrow, "the prominent lawyer and defender of trade unions" who stayed at both Longs Peak Inn and the Crags.[29] Many of the guests quickly assumed the status of "regulars," returning to "the house on the hill," as the Crags became known, season after season. A certain sign of their success was the fact that the Crags was enlarged in 1917 and again in 1923–24 to accommodate a growing tourist business.[30]

Estes Park remained the home of Joe and Ethel Mills until the

The Crags Hotel ("The House on the Hill"), c. 1925. Courtesy of the Estes Park Area Historical Museum.

years 1918–24, when he once again returned to the helm of intercollegiate athletics.[31] This time the call came from the University of Colorado in nearby Boulder, where he was asked to assume the position of athletic director and head football coach. The times were difficult. These were war years when many of the best athletes were away in the army. The opening of practice for the fall 1918 football season had to be delayed an entire month because the Boulder campus was being used as an army training site, and though school finally got underway on October 1, classes had to be called off and the University closed briefly in November because of an influenza epidemic that ultimately claimed nineteen lives. Joe Mills's 1918 football team finished with a 2–3–1 record, not bad under the circumstances. But when his football fortunes did not improve in 1919 (Colorado's record was 2–3–0), Mills resigned, offering the statement that "his work in Estes Park demanded all his time." In "A Tribute to Mills," a writer for the *Silver and Gold* on January 20, 1920, editorialized that the university was losing "one of the greatest boosters it ever had. . . . This year he remained as chief mentor of the Silver and Gold in spite of the call of his work in Estes Park."[32]

Joe Mills's announcement, and the student paper's tribute, proved premature. The University urged Mills to stay on as basketball and track coach. At length, he agreed, perhaps in part because of such expressions of personal support but, most immediately, because these new coaching responsibilities dovetailed nicely with the tourist season in Estes Park. It proved a wise decision, for the four years that followed proved to be the high point of Joe Mills's coaching career. His 1919, 1920, and 1921 basketball teams won conference championships. His track teams were champions from 1920 through 1924. His 1921 golf team, the first ever to take part in intercollegiate play among Rocky Mountain Conference schools, also brought home a championship for Colorado's Silver and Gold.

At Colorado, as at Baylor, Joe Mills crusaded for better sports facilities. This time his pleas did not go unanswered. On Homecoming Day of 1924, Dr. George Norlin, Colorado's president, dedicated a new University gymnasium and football stadium.

Coach Mills of the University of Colorado.
Reproduced from the 1919 *Coloradoan.*

Ironically, however, by this time Joe Mills had resigned permanently from the University of Colorado.

In many respects, the ability to alternate with the seasons between Boulder and Estes Park must have been an ideal arrangement. Basketball practice did not begin until after the Crags had been closed down for the winter and the end of the track season coincided almost exactly with the arrival of the first tourists in Estes Park. Nevertheless, by the spring of 1924 Joe Mills had decided that it was time to move on to other things. He would continue, of course, to own and operate the Crags. But otherwise, he told the *Rocky Mountain News,* what he really wanted to do was to write: "Mills gave as his reasons for resignation the fact that he wishes to devote his time to writing and the composition of short stories for the Red and Blue books, for which magazines he has contributed in other years, and now is under contract to furnish a series of stories dealing with animals and mountain life for both of these books.[33]

Joe Mills's interest in writing was not new. It dated back at least to his days at Baylor,[34] and continued to develop in the decade that followed. It is difficult, however, to reconstruct with certainty this phase of his career. With the exception of the novel entitled *The Comeback* and *A Mountain Boyhood,* both of which were published by J. H. Sears and Company in 1926; an historical essay on "Early Range Days," which he contributed to *Colorado: Short Studies of Its Past and Present* in 1927;[35] and about a dozen articles and stories published in such places as *Country Life in America, St. Nicholas, Outing, Trail and Timberline, Blue Book Magazine,* the *Estes Park Trail, Saturday Evening Post,* and *Nature Notes from Rocky Mountain National Park,*[36] the full range and extent of Joe Mills's authorship can only be inferred.

Not surprisingly, most of the articles and stories that can be identified are ephemeral and easily forgotten. In this respect, *The Comeback* and *A Mountain Boyhood,* the two book-length projects that occupied Mills's attention during the period immediately following his resignation from the University of Colorado, are clearly different. Published in book form within months of one another in 1926, *The Comeback* and *A Mountain Boyhood,* rooted as they are in Estes Park and the surrounding area, are both clearly labors of love. Both are also, taken on their own terms, interesting and successful books.

The Comeback is a dog story of the sort popularized in the first decades of the century by Ernest Thompson Seton (1860–1946) and his contemporaries, who pioneered a new kind of realistic animal story, one based on the scientific observation of how real animals behave in their natural habitats. Writing during a period of intense new interest in the wilderness and wildlife, Seton and fellow naturalists like the venerable John Burroughs (1837–1921) rejected as "nature faking" and "sham naturalism" attempts to humanize and sentimentalize animals by attributing to them human traits and human moral dilemmas.[37] What they sought instead was a balance between literature and natural history in which the dramas of animal life were anchored squarely in the "facts" of observed behavior. Though such a balance was difficult to achieve and sustain, and Seton himself was not always successful, it was his stories and essays, comprising some twenty-odd volumes, that provided an example to be emulated by a whole generation of would-be nature writers.

Joe Mills was one of those emulators. *The Comeback,* consciously or not, finds its source and authority in Seton's famous wolf story, "Lobo, the King of Currumpaw," which appeared in the November 1894 issue of *Scribner's Magazine* and then became part of Seton's widely heralded first collection, *Wild Animals I Have Known* (1898).[38] Seton's story was based on his own true-life experiences in the Currumpaw Valley of eastern New Mexico, where he had tried in vain for four months to outwit and trap "the gigantic leader of a remarkable pack of gray wolves that had ravaged the Currumpaw Valley for a number of years." In *The Comeback* Joe Mills goes Seton one better by writing an animal story that not only features in "Three-toes" a worthy successor to Seton's wily and elusive protagonist but also includes a collie named Jane, who for a time joins "Three-toes" in his mountain lair and mothers a new and dangerous breed of predator. Set along the eastern slope of the Rockies from the St. Vrain and Poudre river area of Colorado northward to Laramie in Wyoming, *The Comeback* tells the story of a man named Jim Hunter, who, like Seton, accepts the invitation of local cattlemen to rid the district of a dangerous marauder, a cross between wolf and coyote. Hunter, we are told, is no mere "wolfer" or bounty-hunter: "The standing reward offered mattered little. It was the lure of the outdoors that called him. The habits of the wild animals made a fascinating study. The riders called him 'a naturalist,' but Hunter made no claim along that line. He was happy rambling through the wilds with the collie as his lone companion."[39] The search for "Three-toes," followed by the search for "Three-toes," Hunter's collie Jane, and their pups, makes up the basic plot of Mills's story. Like Seton's Lobo, "Three-toes" is no threat to man himself. His essential crime is that by following his natural instinct for survival and preying on cattle he successfully challenges man's supremacy over nature and threatens his economic system. For this reason "Three-toes" must be destroyed. By and large, Mills manages to avoid sentimentality and to treat his subject in an honest and fairly objective and scientific way. As he pursues his quarry, Hunter comes to understand "Three-toes" and Jane on their own terms by using his powers of observation. He also becomes aware of his own limitations as a human being and of the mutuality of all living things. Mills even manages to handle convincingly Jane's shifting and conflicting loyalty to her master and her primitive and instinctive ties to the wolf. To be sure, there is pathos in the final death of both animals, but in the case of "Three-toes," at least, the death of a natural predator must be regarded as an inevitable, if regrettable, part of the life cycle of the natural world.

A Mountain Boyhood is a nature story of a different sort. It is, by turns, a successful and most palatable brew of autobiographical reminiscence, western travelogue, action adventure story, local and regional history, and nature essay mixed together with a strong dose of campcraft, woodlore, and character-building advice. What gives the book its special charm and character and much of its appeal for readers young and old, however, is the author's success in presenting through the history and geography of a *particular* time and place the *timeless* metaphor of the wilderness frontier and all that it has come to suggest to the popular mind about the quintessential values of American life.

To some extent, of course, *Boys' Life* and its vast middle-class adolescent readership determined and shaped the kind of book that Mills could write. As the house organ after 1911 of the newly formed Boy Scouts of America, *Boys' Life* specialized in character building and the transmittal of practical skills. The fare of each issue generally consisted of historical or "true life" adventure stories, articles focusing on various aspects of out-of-doors living, biographical sketches of successful men worthy of emulation, and regular monthly columns by such campcraft experts as Dan Beard (1850–1941), author of the best-selling *American Boy's Handy Book* (1882), whose forte was how-to articles emphasizing practical gadgetry. It is fairly easy to see and understand in retrospect how each of these imperatives influenced Joe Mills's book. What is remarkable is that Mills was able not only to meet his editors' demands but to transcend them.

Mills's major concession to *Boys' Life* involves the identity of his protagonist, the voice that tells the story. Mills himself had been almost twenty when he first visited Estes Park in 1899, and he was well into his twenties, a man with a coaching career, when he gained most of his first-hand knowledge of the region. The narrator of *A Mountain Boyhood,* on the other hand, is very much a boy. Emotionally honest and full of the energy of youth, he has the happy capacity to greet the world and each new experience with enthusiasm and fresh perceptions and, not infrequently, with awe and wonder. The protagonist is not, that is, Joe Mills himself, but rather an idealized version of the boy Joe Mills might have been had he arrived in Estes Park, like his brother Enos, as a boy of fourteen or fifteen. The choice of narrator turns out to be a most fortuitous one. His contagious boyish enthusiasm, coupled with the force of conviction that first-person narrative always carries with it, provides *A Mountain Boyhood* with one of its most appealing qualities.

What undoubtedly most attracted the editors of *Boys' Life* to Joe Mills's book, however, was the subject matter itself, for outdoor living and wilderness adventuring occupied a high priority in the agenda of American Scouting. The passing of the frontier, which Mills himself laments, encouraged many Americans to look upon the wilderness with new eyes. By the final decade of the nineteenth century, and certainly by 1900, what was once only an obstacle to be overcome and exploited had become widely regarded as a unique and potent factor in the development of American institutions and American values.[40] Without a wilderness, of course, there could be no pioneering. That fact alone gave the wilderness new meaning and value. One important response to such discoveries was the wilderness conservation and preservation movement that sought to establish within forest preserves and national parks a kind of perpetual wilderness where Americans could renew contact with their pioneer heritage. Another was the American Boy Scout movement. By the turn of the century the majority of American youths no longer grew up, as Joe Mills himself had done, in a rural environment. Rather, they were city boys, the products of a new urbanized and industrialized age, cut off from the wilderness and its transforming values. A crucial reason for the dramatic popular growth and increasing momentum of American Scouting following its incorporation in 1910 was precisely because it offered, as Roderick Nash has noted, "a solution to the disturbing phenomenon of a civilization that seemed to be tearing itself away from the frontier roots that many felt to be the source of greatness."[41]

A Mountain Boyhood, with its emphasis on mountain adventuring, nature lore and campcraft, quite obviously fits the American Boy Scout program. Every episode that the narrator recounts—whether observing, studying, and tracking wild game; crossing Flattop Mountain on snowshoes in midwinter to attend a housewarming in the wilderness beyond Grand Lake; or setting up camp in Wild Basin and living off the land—is calculated to educate the adolescent reader in the ways of the wilderness. Its lessons, moreover, are clear. Wilderness living and exploration are not just fun; they serve to test one's strength and hardiness and to develop judgment and resourcefulness. They foster self-reliance, independence, mental preparedness, moral and physical courage, and a whole range of common-sense skills not only associated with the traditional pioneering experience but deemed essential for success in the everyday modern world. Not surprisingly, given Joe Mills's own athletic predilections, mountain climbing provides the ultimate yardstick for forming good habits and building character: "climbing tests a man's judgment, his physical endurance, and tries his soul. It brings out his true character. The veneer of convention wears through inside a few miles of trail work and reveals the individual precisely as he is, often to his shame, but usually to his glory."

The wilderness world that Mills sets before his reader is a most attractive one. It is the kind of Robinson Crusoe world that every boy dreams of being able to claim as his own: a world largely devoid of parental restraint and interference, and without the problems, perplexities, and responsibilities of adult life. It is also a place in which one can recreate the vanished world of the frontier, a world, Mills tells us, of "adventure, hazard always, mystery, offtimes, romance, life." The latter appeal is clearly established in the book's opening chapter, "Going West," where the narrator expresses his "lifelong regret" that "my boyhood came after the gold rushes were over; the buffalo bands had passed for the last time; the Indian fighting ended." Though such exciting events "were still fresh in the memory of my parents," it is the fate of his own generation, the generation born in the 1880s, to become the first not to have direct and immediate access to the frontier experience. One of the chief attractions of the mountain wilderness about Estes Park, in fact, is that it still offers "faraway places where few men had ever been" and a chance to recapture and relive the "early frontier period [that] passed before my birth."

Though it certainly is not without flaws, *A Mountain Boyhood,* after more than sixty years, still makes for memorable and interesting reading. In this respect it defies the fate of all but a small handful of books written explicitly for an adolescent audience. What makes *A Mountain Boyhood* different and distinctive, and justifies a new edition, is the care and attention that its author pays to the delineation of time and place. Most boys' books are set in a land of make-believe where the setting, however appropriate, is as fictive as the adventures that unfold there. This is not true of Joe Mills's Estes Park. To be sure, the rugged mountain wilderness he portrays has, in retrospect, been somewhat softened, romanticized, and domesticated, for Joe Mills belonged to a generation that had come to realize that the wilderness must be saved and preserved. Nevertheless, as the explanatory notes prepared for this new edition plainly suggest, the world of *A Mountain Boyhood,* with one or two minor exceptions, is a world that can be historically and geographically documented. Joe Mills was writing about a world he both knew and loved, and he well understood that the full awareness and appreciation of any landscape is invariably deepened and enriched when it is mixed with the traditions and memories of the past. To read Mills's book is to be able to retrace, if at times only indirectly by way of casual reference or allusion, the history of Estes Park from its first discovery in 1859 down to the time of the book's publication. For this reason, if for no other, *A Mountain Boyhood* deserves a place of its own among the local and regional histories of Colorado's Front Range.

When he was not looking after tourists or attending to the needs of his own growing family,[42] giving occasional lectures,[43] or writing, Joe Mills was actively engaged in civic affairs as one of Estes Park's leading citizens. The easy popularity that he enjoyed among his fellow resort owners and the residents of Estes Park made him a natural target for civic projects. People liked Joe Mills and they respected his ability to get things done. As a result, it was perhaps inevitable that Mills would come to play an active role in the two major controversial issues involving Rocky Mountain National Park that occupied the attention of the Estes Park region for more than a dozen years. Unfortunately, his role in these controversies brought Joe Mills once more into direct opposition to the strongly held views of his brother Enos and of his sister-in-law Esther Burnell Mills (1889–1946).[44]

The first of these was the dispute over the right of the new National Park administration to regulate transportation within the park; the second, and related, issue was over whether or not the State of Colorado should formally cede jurisdiction over the roads within the park to the U.S. government. The cede jurisdiction issue was a particularly complicated one, and before it could be finally resolved in February 1929 it attracted the attention not only of the citizens of Colorado but of the nation at large.[45]

The controversy over the establishment of policies regulating transportation within Rocky Mountain National Park was, perhaps, inevitable, for as the number of annual visitors grew they soon outstripped the park's capacity to accommodate the flow of automobile traffic. Fifty-one thousand people entered the park in 1916, the year following its dedication. In 1917, that number jumped to 120,000, and officials boasted that Rocky Mountain drew more people "than the combined tourist patronage of Yellowstone, Yosemite, Glacier, and Crater Lake Parks."[46] Two years later, despite World War I, the total reached nearly 170,000. A logical response—but an immediate source of contention—was the attempt by Superintendent Claude L. Way in the spring of 1919 to reduce the number of vehicles in the park by entering into an exclusive franchise agreement with Roe Emery's Rocky Mountain Park Transportation Company. This agreement, which was awarded without public discussion or competitive bids, effectively banned from the park independent rent-car (or "jitney") drivers who made their summer livings by transporting visitors to and from hotels or taking them on sightseeing excursions. Such entrepreneurs not only helped to keep the roads congested but, it was charged, not infrequently inflicted upon their customers poor service and high prices. The franchise agreement with Roe Emery, who had pioneered motor bus transportation at Glacier National Park, seemed to offer a reasonable solution to a growing problem.

It did not appear at all reasonable, however, to Enos Mills of Longs Peak Inn and to several other Estes Park hotel men, most notably F. O. Stanley, whose touring cars were among those directly affected. Mills, who could not resist a fight where matters of principle were concerned, quickly made himself the center of opposition. For him it was purely and simply a question of an illegal monopoly established and maintained by arrogant and indifferent bureaucrats interfering with the exercise of public rights.[47] In August 1919, in order to establish a test case over the park's right to establish such a concessions policy, Enos Mills openly, and with advanced warning, defied the ban by sending a car into the park. As the 1919 summer season drew to a close, however, the rent-car controversy appeared to die down, and park

officials and local resort owners attempted to use the interlude
to mediate the issue. One such attempt involved Joe Mills, a firm
supporter of the Park Service and its administrative policies, who
was appointed by the Hotel Men's Association of Estes Park to
canvas its membership for complaints or suggestions regarding
the concessions policy.[48]

Enos Mills sued Claude Way in the United States District
Court of Colorado for interfering with "his common rights as a
citizen of the State of Colorado in traveling over the Park roads."
Despite two rounds of court decisions that upheld the Park Service's right to regulate and denied Mills's claim of vested rights,
the issue continued to smolder without final resolution. It gradually became part of a larger legal issue involving a suit by the
State of Colorado challenging the right of the federal government to regulate traffic over roads that had never been formally
ceded to the jurisdiction of the United States. This so-called "Cede
Jurisdiction" controversy dragged on past the untimely death of
Enos Mills in September 1922 in a series of inconclusive court
cases that reached their climax in January 1926, when the State
of Colorado, threatened with the loss of major federal appropri-
ations for road maintenance and construction within the park,
dropped its litigation. This placed the issue squarely in the hands
of the Colorado legislature, which was called upon to debate a
bill ceding to the federal government final jurisdiction over all
state roads within the park. The high drama that ensued, which
fully engaged the attention of the state press and brought forth
lobbying groups up and down the Front Range, was filled with
heated accusations of government intimidation and federal "en-
croachment on the rights and property of States."

Once again the Mills family had a role to play. Joe Mills, acting in an official capacity as vice-president and later president
of the Estes Park Chamber of Commerce, wrote letters to members of the Colorado legislature and to the newspapers and took
part in a series of debates in Estes Park, Boulder, and Greeley
defending the proposed legislation on the basis of economic
self-interest ("it will make available government resources to
develop roads in an area the state will be unable to finance for
fifty years") and because it promised to open up the scenic re-

sources of Colorado. He later appeared at hearings of the Colorado House and Senate, and it was there that he found his views directly opposed by his brother's widow, Esther Mills, who had taken over not only the management of Longs Peak Inn but Enos Mills's causes as well. According to the *Boulder News-Herald,* which covered her appearance before a hearing of the State House of Representatives in February 1927, "Mrs. Mills, proprietor of Long's [sic] Peak Inn, flayed the autocratic, discriminating, monopoly granting policies of the National Park Service."[49] The issue continued to be contested until February 1929, when political fervor gave way to economic realities—in the form of some $500,000 in federal road appropriations—and the cede bill was passed by both legislative houses and signed into law.

These years of political controversy, coupled as they were with the beginnings of the Great Depression, made the life of an Estes Park resort owner far from easy. Though business had greatly increased with the establishment of the park in 1915, and especially during the early 1920s when eastern railways began booking regular excursion trips to the park, the cede jurisdiction issue brought an end to the influx of new capital and economic development came to a virtual halt. "At present," Charles Hewes noted in his December 1928 year-end summary, "the region, particularly the Estes Park region, has the reputation of being literally and actually broke on account of money, of [there] being too many resorts, hotels, and business places—there is not enough business to support them all. . . ."[50] Two years later resort and hotel business was once again reported on the decline and during the Great Depression itself establishments like the Crags were forced to lower their prices by some forty percent in order to compete for what remained of the summer trade.

Despite such economic uncertainties, life for Joe and Ethel Mills continued to be an active and happy affair. Joe's civic work on behalf of the Estes Park Chamber of Commerce occupied much of his spare time during the middle and late 1920s, and the 1930s found him busy on a state-wide basis working on behalf of major new road legislation benefiting the entire Estes Park region. "Joe Mills deserved a vacation if anybody in this region did," begins

a congratulatory editorial in the March 22, 1935, edition of the
Estes Park Trail:

> But with a man like Joe Mills, work for the good of the commu-
> nity comes ahead of personal desires, personal needs, and even
> ahead of personal health. . . .
>
> Because he has worked so quietly and effectively, many of us
> have not realized what a competent, loyal worker we have in Joe
> Mills. Not many communities are fortunate enough to have such
> an able man working for them, and Estes Park should take some
> steps to let Joe know that his efforts in behalf of community af-
> fairs are appreciated. Many thanks, Joe Mills![51]

For a man now in his mid-fifties such retrospectives were
highly appropriate and timely. Mills's family and friends used
the occasion of his fifty-fourth birthday to hold a special dinner
party at the Crags on the evening of July 21, 1934. It was a most
festive event, attended by his two children, Eleanor Ann and
Mark; by Dorr Yeager, chief naturalist at Rocky Mountain National Park, who had become his son-in-law some two months
before;[52] and by a number of Joe and Ethel's key employees and
close friends. In honor of the event Ethel Mills prepared one of
her "famous iced angel food cakes," cleverly decorated to sum-
marize Joe Mills's full and varied career. A description in the
Estes Park Trail noted:

> Mr. Mills arrived in Estes Park on a bicycle in 1899 (in time to
> see the Bear Lake fire) and the fact and method of his arrival were
> symbolized by a miniature bike and spruce tree on the top-most
> layer. . . .
>
> On the lower tier of the cake were models of various animal
> characters of his stories and novels, including bear, elk, deer, wild
> horses, coyotes, sheep and wolves. About the base of this beauti-
> ful "sweet-food mountain" were symbols of his varied activities
> since coming to the park which include such divergent businesses
> as being guide, naturalist, lecturer, university athletic director,
> football coach, photographer, movie cameraman, radio broad-

caster, reporter, golf champion, president of the country club, and
president of the chamber of commerce.[53]

Such a happy time would not be repeated. A little more than
a year later, on October 3, 1935, Joe Mills was dead, the victim
of a bizarre accident six days before in which his car collided
head-on with a street car on the outskirts of Denver. "Since late
Friday afternoon, when the staggering report of the possibly fatal accident reached the village," the *Estes Park Trail* reported
in its front page story, "the question on the lips of every man and
woman was, 'How is Joe Mills?' The final report of his death left
Estes Park grief-stricken and subdued, slowly comprehending
the significance of the irreparable loss of Joe Mills."[54] Two days
later, on October 5, 1935, Charles Hewes recorded in his journal:

> Today, in Denver, was held the funeral of Joe Mills, who was to-
> tally injured a week ago yesterday by his car colliding with a street
> car in Denver. He never regained consciousness. Joe was the man
> who gave me a job when I first came to Estes Park in 1907, as a
> flunky at Longs Peak Inn, where he was the manager. He was a
> fine and active man, and no one in this community will be missed
> as much as he, for he was our most active agent in Regional mat-
> ters, and popular with everybody.[55]

The *Estes Park Trail* echoes Hewes's sentiments with is own
nunc dimittis:

> Through the impressionable years of boyhood, through the in-
> spired ambitious years of youth and young manhood, and through
> the courageous, determined years of manhood Joe Mills has been
> a part of Estes Park, Estes Park a part of him. He loved the region
> with a silent, unobtrusive love that was truly food for the inner
> man, and he was moved to further and develop it by motives of the
> highest altruism.[56]

Ethel Mills, with the help of her son Mark, continued to operate the Crags through the years of World War II. In April 1945,
however, she leased the hotel for the coming summer season to

Henry Lynch, the former manager of the Stanley Hotel and a long-time summer resident of Estes Park. A year later, the Crags was sold and the grand old hotel on Prospect Mountain passed out of the hands of the Mills family.[57] Estes Park, however, did not forget Joe Mills. In late December of 1948, David H. Canfield, superintendent of Rocky Mountain National Park, filed a formal request with the Park Service's Board of Geographic Names to rename "a minor peak, elevation 11,903 feet, lying slightly southeast of and immediately adjacent to Odessa Lake" Joe Mills Mountain. In support of his request, which was duly promulgated in April 1949, Canfield wrote that it would serve

> to commemorate the name of Joe Mills who came to the Estes Park region in 1898 and, until his death in 1935, gave his full energies to the preservation of the scenic splendor of the area. He climbed peaks within the national park, explored and photographed the area for years. Mr. Mills pioneered the movement for setting aside the national park area, and after its creation, gave the Federal Government his staunch cooperation in its administration. A naturalist, author, and lecturer, he made known the beauty of the country and contributed to its fame.[58]

Of Joe Mills nothing more need be said.

NOTES

1. *A Mountain Boyhood* was serialized in *Boys' Life* in eight monthly installments as follows: vol. 16 (June 1926): 13–15, 54–55; 16 (July 1926): 14–15; 16 (August 1926): 17–18, 46–47; 16 (September 1926): 10–11; 16 (October 1926): 14–15, 55; 16 (December 1926): 34, 38, 90; 17 (January 1927): 28–29, 43; 17 (February 1927): 20–21, 60. It was published in book form by J. H. Sears and Company, 40 West 57th Street, New York, on November 2, 1926. The first, June 1926 installment was accompanied by Mills's own photographs: "Longs Peak from Wild Basin," "Parson Lamb's Ranch in Winter," "The Land of My Dreams" (a scenic view of Estes Park from the top of Park Hill).

2. The homestead cabin at the foot of Longs Peak built by Enos Mills in 1885–86 is now maintained as a museum. The historical marker was erected in 1982.

3. Four of the first five Mills children did not survive early childhood: Augusta E. (1856–59), Elkana (1857–59), Mary E. (1858–60), and Ruth (died at birth in March 1862). In addition to Enos and Joe, the surviving children included Marie Naomi (b. 1861), Sarah (1863–1922), Rhoda Ellen (b. 1865), Sabina Belle (b. 1867), and Horace (b. 1874). Enos Mills, Sr., his wife, and several of their children are buried in the Lamb family cemetery located in Potosi Township some two miles south and east of Pleasanton. It was established by Ann Mills's father, Josiah Lamb, in November 1857.

4. Colorado State's original student records were kept in very large leatherbound books. After being microfilmed, these books were sealed at the State Archives. Unfortunately, the microfilm copy is of poor quality. What we can learn from it is that Enoch Mills entered Colorado Agricultural College on March 17, 1899. He attended the third term of a preparatory year and the first term only of a sub-freshman year (two programs which, "by providing instruction approximating grades seven through twelve, enabled otherwise unqualified students to gain admission to the College," according to historian James Hansen; the first term only of the sophomore year; and all three terms of the junior year. Unfortunately, the extant records do not provide the dates those years were recorded or any additional information. In 1899 the student body numbered 345 (of which 251 were men). By 1902 total enrollment had increased to 448. See James C. Hansen, *Democracy's College in the Centennial State: A History of Colorado State University* (Fort Collins: Colorado State University, 1977), p. 144.

5. *Rocky Mountain Collegian*, vol. 11, Dec. 10, 1901, p. 1. The rough and tumble semiprofessional spirit of the times is more than evident in the following editorial account in the *Rocky Mountain Collegian*, the student newspaper, of the disputed CAC game with Wyoming in 1900: "They say that [George] Toomey, our coach, was the cause of it all and that it was agreed that he should not play. This is ABSOLUTELY FALSE; nothing was said at any time about Mr. Toomey's not playing and, moreover, they played THEIR coach, McMurray; why should they object to our playing Toomey? . . . That Mr. Toomey made some fine end runs we admit, but that he did all the playing we deny. In making this claim Laramie forgets that after they had broken Mr. Toomey's collar bone and he had been carried from the field, we made TWO of our THREE touchdowns." Quoted in Hansen, *Democracy's College,* pp. 141–42. On another occasion "The game of football between the Agricultural col-

lege and state Normal teams [before a crowd estimated at five hundred] ended in the middle of the second half by the refusal of the college to play, the score standing 10 to 0 in favor of the Normals [when Newall, the Aggie's captain, simply walked off the field with the ball following a dispute]." *Denver Post,* vol. 9, Oct. 7, 1900, p. 18.

6. The details of Joe Mills's athletic career at CAC as well as at the University of Denver and Fort Worth University (below) are found in the 1909 edition of *The Round-Up,* the Baylor University yearbook. It is also possible to trace the successes of his CAC years in the pages of the *Rocky Mountain Collegian.* For example, the May 29, 1902, issue of the *Collegian* (vol. 11, p. 25) notes that in the annual College Field Day held on May 7th Joe Mills finished second in the fifty-yard dash, second in the running broad jump, second in the hundred-yard dash, and second in the high hurdles. Information on CAC athletics during the period is also found in Hansen's *Democracy's College,* pp. 125–28; 141–43.

7. *Rocky Mountain Collegian,* vol. 10, Dec. 1900, p. 24. According to the 1903 edition of the *Silver Spruce,* the junior annual (Fort Collins: State Agricultural College, 1903, n.p.): "'Nuck' Mills is a star player of the first Team. He is light but makes up for it by his quickness and agility. . . . He has the reputation of being the best quarter back in the state."

8. Mills's University of Denver transcript for 1903–4 is the only available official record of his attendance. It lists only the courses taken and the credits and grades earned. According to the October 4, 1935, edition of the *Rocky Mountain News* (p. 8), however, Joe Mills "took his degree at the University of Denver."

9. Information on Joe Mills's University of Denver athletic career, including two photographs, are found in the 1905 yearbook *Kynewisbok,* 7 (University of Denver: May 1904), pp. 219–25.

10. Ethel Steere was the youngest of twelve children of George W. Steere. She was educated at Fort Worth University. She apparently took her degree in 1903, for she is listed in the 1904–5 city directory as a "substitute teacher" and from 1905 to 1908 as a "teacher." At the time of her marriage to Joe Mills, her father is listed as city recorder and as secretary of the Fort Worth Public Library.

11. "Athletics in Baylor," *The Lariat,* vol. 8, Sept. 12, 1908, p. 1. The *Lariat's* initial announcement of Mills's appointment the preceding April was equally laudatory: "Since his coming to Texas, no single man in the South has been more active in athletics than has Enoch J. Mills, and it is safe to say that no coach south of the Mason and Dixon line has accomplished as much in the development of his charges, when the facilities and quality of material furnished him are considered. . . . In

short, from whatever viewpoint he is considered, the impression is given of the most essential qualities of an all around athlete, and one who has brain-power to impart his knowledge and skill to his proteges, and at the same time hold their respect, admiration, and personal friendship." *The Lariat,* vol. 8, April 25, 1908, p. 1. An equally laudatory news story announced Mills's departure from Fort Worth. It was headlined: "Baylor Gets Coach Mills. Famous Athletic Instructor to Leave Polytechnic. Had Choice Offers in Five Other States. Has Helped in Bringing About Splendid Improvement in Texas Athletics," *Fort Worth Telegram,* April 26, 1908, p. 11. One of Joe Mills's contributions to Texas athletics was the implementation of a new set of rules for football which went into effect on an experimental basis during the 1906 season. As Mills explained them in an article he wrote for the *Fort Worth Telegram,* these rules, which allowed the forward pass for the first time, were designed to encourage skill and ability as opposed to brute strength and to prevent "rowdy and old-style methods which were the cause of most of the injuries occurring in the game." Enoch Mills, "Foot Ball Rules Are Successful," *Fort Worth Telegram,* December 2, 1906, p. 9.

12. *The Lariat,* vol. 11, March 18, 1911, p. 2. According to the news story, Mills said, "'This coaching business is all right for a while, but sooner or later a fellow must get out. I have enjoyed my work in Baylor, but as large a school as this took all my time and I could not indulge in anything which would help my finances out.' By this last clause Mills meant his writing for magazines and newspapers, for which he has quite a reputation."

13. The date of Joe Mills's first visit to Estes Park remains unclear. The summer of 1899 makes sense because he first enrolled at Colorado Agricultural College that year. This date is supported by a news item in the July 27, 1934, edition of the *Estes Park Trail* (vol. 14, p. 9) reporting the details of Joe Mills's fifty-fourth birthday dinner at the Crags. The same article, however, links his arrival with the Bear Lake Fire ["Mr. Mills arrived in Estes Park on a bicycle in 1899 (in time to see the Bear Lake fire) . . . ."], an event that did not occur, however, until 1900. It is logical that the two events would remain linked in Mills's memory, for the fire, which for several weeks raged unchecked and ravaged not only Bear Lake but the slopes of Flattop Mountain, Bierstadt Moraine, and Longs Peak, was a spectacular one. See Flora H. Eaton, "The Flattop Forest Fire," *Estes Park Trail,* vol. 2, April 14, 1922, p. 8. The scars of the fire were visible for years. Charles Hewes recalled that in 1908 "we walked for miles and miles thru the dead and fallen ranks

of what was once a glorious woodland." "The Autobiography of Charles Edwin Hewes," p. 233. Charles Edwin Hewes (1870–1947) came to Estes Park in 1907 and for the next forty years was the proprietor of Hewes-Kirkwood Inn, located near Enos Mills's Longs Peak Inn. The typewritten manuscript of Hewes's autobiography, which records his life through the year 1912, and his remarkable typewritten 1,116-page manuscript journal, which he faithfully kept from 1913 until 1944, were discovered in an Estes Park bank vault following his death. Both are now in the Estes Park Area Historical Museum. Hereafter cited, respectively, as Hewes "Autobiography" and "Hewes Journal."

14. Detailed accounts of the growth of Estes Park during the period can be found in June E. Carothers, *Estes Park, Past and Present* (Denver: University of Denver Press, 1951), pp. 74–82; F. Ross Holland, Jr., *Rocky Mountain National Park: Historical Background Data* (San Francisco: U.S. Office of History and Historic Architecture, Western Service Center, 1971), pp. 38–50; C. W. Buchholtz, *Rocky Mountain National Park: A History* (Boulder: Colorado Associated University Press, 1983), pp. 117–22; and Enos A. Mills, *The Story of Estes Park* (Longs Peak, Estes Park, Co., 1917), pp. 90–101.

15. During the summers of 1907 and 1908, Charles Hewes worked at Longs Peak Inn under Joe Mills's direction. Hewes's major responsibility was to drive the Inn's stage—a three-seat, canopy-topped, light spring wagon equipped with a foot brake and drawn by horses known locally as "mountain rats"—to and from Estes Park village, picking up and delivering the Inn's guests. Hewes reminiscences of these years, and of Joe Mills, are contained in his "Autobiography," pp. 206–9, 213–14, 230–32.

16. From an undated and apparently unpublished essay by Enos Mills entitled "The Training of a Long's Peak [*sic*] Guide": "In training another guide to assist me in the summer I selected a brother, Enoch J. Mills, who holds the Chair of Athletics in Fort Worth, Texas University. I sent him through a long course in rock climbing. I had him poise upon pinnacles, leap chasms, stand and walk upon the edge of precipices and climb perpendicular walls so rough as to be barely climbable." Enos Mills Papers, Western History Department, Denver Public Library. This collection consists of manuscripts, correspondence, speeches, biographical data, and clippings and articles by and about Enos Mills presented to the library by his widow, Esther Mills. Hereafter referred to as the Enos Mills Papers.

17. Hewes "Autobiography," p. 227.

18. Mila Tupper, "A Colorado Mountain and Mountaineer," *Denver Times,* March 23, 1906, p. 4. This newspaper article is also included in the Enos Mills Papers.

19. Patricia Washburn, "The Thirties in Estes Park," Estes Park Oral History Project (August 12, 1979), transcript, Estes Park Public Library.

20. Charles Hewes noted in his journal on January 28, 1916: "Joe Mills and wife and daughter came up to the Levings today for the weekend [Charles Levings, a Chicago architect, for many years had a home at the base of Twin Sisters Mountain, not far from Longs Peak Inn], the first time they have been to the Vale since their trouble with Enos Mills nearly eight years ago." Hewes "Journal" (January 28, 1916), p. 291. The relationship between the brothers remained a highly tentative one. For example, Joe Mills was numbered among the speakers on the evening of February 3, 1915, when the citizens of Estes Park turned out for a reception in the Odd Fellows Hall to honor Enos Mills for his efforts in securing "the formation of Colorado's newest national playground—the Rocky Mountain National Park" (newspaper clipping, Enos Mills file, Rocky Mountain National Park Library). He was also one of the speakers at the park's dedication ceremonies in September of that same year. However, some seven years later in September 1922, he chose not to attend Enos's funeral service though invited to do so (Emerson E. Lynn, "The Scottage" [1959], p. 29. Typescript manuscript, Rocky Mountain National Park Library. Lynn was deputed by Mrs. Mills to carry out the funeral arrangements that Enos Mills himself had specified prior to his death).

21. Harold M. Dunning, *Over Hill and Vale,* vol. 2 (Boulder: Johnson Publishing Company, 1962), p. 26. The hotel was so named because it stood near the juncture of the North and South forks of the Big Thompson River. Drake itself was originally known as the Forks.

22. For example, when a group of Colorado hotel men visited Estes Park in June 1913 the final event of their stay was a dinner at the Forks hosted by E. J. Mills. *Estes Park Trail,* vol. 2, June 28, 1913, p. 5. The same issue of the *Trail* (p. 7) announced the arrival of another visitor: "Mrs. Mills, mother of Enos and Joseph Mills, has arrived from Kansas, to spend the summer. She is at present with Joseph Mills and wife at the Forks hotel." Ann Mills had presumably come to Estes Park, in part at least, to see the granddaughter named in her honor.

23. Charles Edwin Hewes, who had worked for Joe Mills for two seasons at Longs Peak Inn, wrote a twelve-line poem entitled "Eleanor Ann" to mark the occasion. The second stanza, from p. 42 of his "Journal," March 25, 1912, reads:

> Our Eleanor Ann's a September girl;
>   Born when the aspen were all aglow,
>   From the mountain crest to the depths below;
>   To bend in the gorge in the wind's soft blow.

Hewes was a poet of some local repute. This poem was not included, however, in the volume titled *Songs of the Rockies,* a collection celebrating the beauty of Longs Peak Valley and the Estes Park area, which Hewes published privately in 1914. Neither was it included in the expanded second edition of 1922.

24. *Estes Park Trail,* vol. 2, Sept. 13, 1913, p. 1.

25. Hewes "Journal" (April 8, 1914), p. 215.

26. *Estes Park Trail,* vol. 3, July 11, 1914, p. 5.

27. Ibid., p. 18.

28. *Estes Park Trail,* vol. 3, Sept. 5, 1914, p. 6.

29. *Estes Park Trail,* vol. 3, Aug. 29, 1914, p. 16.

30. According to the *Estes Park Trail,* vol. 2, April 6, 1923, p. 12: "The dining room and lobby will be enlarged to accommodate three hundred or more guests, and probably about fifty new guest rooms will be added. A number of cottages will also be built. The total cost of the improvements to be made at the Crags this year will exceed $50,000.00." See also Hewes "Journal," April 5, 1918, p. 362; *Estes Park Trail,* vol. 3, March 21, 1924, p. 12.

31. During their first years in Estes Park, 1914–18, the Millses made the Crags their home all year round. When the hotel closed for the season, the family retreated to the hotel basement where the kitchen was located because its cookstove offered the only heat in the building. After Joe accepted the athletic directorship at Colorado in 1918, the Millses bought a house in Boulder that they continued to occupy during the winter months after his resignation from the University in 1924. Washburn, "The Thirties in Estes Park," p. 3.

32. "A Tribute to Mills," *Silver and Gold,* January 20, 1920, p. 2.

33. *Rocky Mountain News,* June 1, 1924, p. 13. Other reports, citing the same reason, were carried in the *Denver Post* and the *Estes Park Trail* on June 1, 1924, and June 6, 1924, respectively.

34. See n. 12, above.

35. Joe Mills, "Early Range Days," *Colorado: Short Studies of Its Past and Present* (Boulder: University of Colorado, 1927), pp. 91–100. The volume was republished in facsimile by the AMS Press, New York, in 1969.

36. In addition to the chapters of *A Mountain Boyhood* published serially in *Boys' Life* cited in note 1 above, these publications are as fol-

lows: "Off the Trail," *Country Life in America* (August 15, 1912): 20–22; "My Friends the Grizzlies," *St. Nicholas,* 41, (February 1914): 294–97; "The Black Hero of the Ranges," *St. Nicholas,* 42 (November 1914): 16–24; "Off the Trail," *Outing,* 66 (October 1915): 7–14; "Forest Canyon," *Trail and Timberline,* no. 32 (May 1921): 2–5; "Two Longs and Three Short," *Blue Book Magazine* (September 1922): pp. unknown; "Rocky Mountain National Park," *Estes Park Trail,* vol. 4, June 20, 1924, pp. 7, 10; "The Voice," *Blue Book* (July 1923): pp. unknown; "Our Friendly Wild Folk," *Trail and Timberline,* no. 109 (November 1927): 11–12; "Timberline Temperatures," *Saturday Evening Post,* 204 (April 16, 1932): 40, 44; and "Photographing Wild Animals," *Nature Notes from Rocky Mountain National Park,* 6 (May 1933), pp. 50–54. *The Comeback* (1926) was apparently also serialized in *Blue Book* beginning in April 1926.

37. John Burroughs, who was a firm friend of Theodore Roosevelt and other prominent nature advocates, wrote the classic indictment of nature-fakers for the March 1903 issue of the *Atlantic Monthly.* See "Real and Sham Natural History," *Atlantic Monthly,* 91 (March 1903): 298–309. Interestingly enough, Burroughs's initial indictment included Seton, though he later changed his mind and the two naturalist-authors became good friends.

38. *The Comeback* also owes something to Jack London's enormously popular novel *The Call of the Wild* (1903), to which Mills refers in *A Mountain Boyhood.* In London's story a half St. Bernard–half Scotch shepherd dog named Buck learns to adapt to the hostile environment of the Klondike, after which he escapes, throws off his domesticated habits to become "the dominant primordial beast," and assumes leadership of a wolf pack.

39. Joe Mills, *The Comeback: The Story of the Heart of a Dog* (New York: J. H. Sears and Co., 1926), p. 18.

40. The relationship between the American frontier experience and the development of American institutions and values found its purest, and most famous, articulation in Frederick Jackson Turner's essay of 1893, "The Significance of the Frontier in American History." Turner's thesis, however, was by no means an altogether new idea. That the wilderness frontier was a unique and potent force in American development had been suggested by many individuals, including Benjamin Franklin, Thomas Jefferson, Francis Parkman, Alexis de Tocqueville, Washington Irving, James Fenimore Cooper, and Henry David Thoreau, to name just a few.

41. Roderick Nash, *Wilderness and the American Mind* (New Haven: Yale University Press, 1967), p. 147.

42. A son, Mark Muir Mills, was born on August 8, 1917. He attended grade school and the first two years of high school in Estes Park but graduated from East Denver High School and then enrolled in the California Institute of Technology, where he earned a degree in physics in 1939. Following World War II, when he served with Army intelligence, Mills returned to Cal Tech in Pasadena for his doctorate in physics. Mark Mills went on to become one of the leading nuclear scientists of his time. On April 6, 1958, while serving as deputy director of the University of California's radiation laboratory, Mills was killed in a helicopter crash at the Eniwetok atomic proving grounds in the South Pacific, where he had gone in connection with an upcoming round of nuclear tests. He left a wife, Pauline Riedeburg Mills, whom he had married on January 31, 1941, and two children, Mark John Mills and Ann Mills. Harold M. Dunning, *Over Hill and Dale: In the Evening Shadows of Colorado's Longs Peak,* vol. 2 (Boulder: Johnson Publishing Company, 1962), p. 222; *Estes Park Trail,* vol. 21, Feb. 13, 1942, p. 6; *Estes Park Trail,* vol. 38, April 11, 1958, p. 13.

43. Like his brother Enos, who was famous for his bear stories, Joe Mills enjoyed a reputation as something of a raconteur. He entertained the annual wilderness outing of the Colorado Mountain Club on more than one occasion ("Joe Mills charmed us with his yarns of the wilds even while taxing our credulity"), and for several years offered illustrated lectures on such topics as "Wild Life in the Wild Country" to summer students attending the University of Colorado. On at least one occasion, in 1924, under the sponsorship of the Burlington Railroad, Mills traveled east to Omaha where he gave a talk over radio station WOW on "some of the attractions of the Colorado Rockies and Rocky Mountain National Park as a place to spend a real vacation." Three years later, during the spring and summer of 1927, he arranged with the Denver Tourist Bureau and the Union Pacific Railroad to offer slide lectures on Colorado to train passengers entering the state from Salt Lake City. *Trail and Timberline,* 16 (October 1919), p. 4; *Estes Park Trail,* vol. 10, July 18, 1930, p. 13; *Estes Park Trail,* vol. 4, June 13, 1924, p. 16; *Estes Park Trail,* vol. 6, March 4, 1927, p. 4.

44. Enos Mills married Esther Burnell Mills, his former secretary and protégé, on August 12, 1918. Mills had personally certified her and her sister as the first women interpretive nature guides in the region. Their only child, Enda Mills, was born on April 27, 1919. Esther Burnell, who, like Enos, was born in Kansas, was the daughter of the Reverend Arthur Tappan Burnell. While working as a consulting decorator for a large business firm, she suffered a nervous breakdown. It was her search for health that brought her to Colorado for the first time in 1916. Like so

many others, she stayed and took up a homestead, off Fall River Road near Castle Mountain just west of the village of Estes Park.

45. An account of both controversies is contained in Lloyd K. Musselman, *Rocky Mountain National Park: Administrative History, 1915–1965* (Washington, D.C.: Office of History and Historic Architecture, National Park Service, 1971), pp. 29–76. The purely legal aspects of the cede jurisdiction dispute are found in William Sherman Bell, "The Legal Phases of Cession of Rocky Mountain National Park," *Rocky Mountain Law Review,* 1 (1928): 35–46. Two scrapbooks containing newspaper clippings on the cede jurisdiction bill and its surrounding controversy are part of the permanent collection of the Rocky Mountain National Park Library. Hereafter cited as Cede Jurisdiction Scrapbooks.

46. Buchholtz, *Rocky Mountain National Park,* p. 151.

47. The controversy from Enos Mills's point of view is recounted in the appreciative biography of her husband that Esther Mills collaborated on in 1935. See Hildegarde Hawthorne and Esther Burnell Mills, *Enos Mills of the Rockies* (New York: Junior Literary Guild and Houghton Mifflin, 1935), pp. 223–51.

48. Memorandum by L. C. Way, October 29, 1919, Mills vs. Way correspondence, Rocky Mountain National Park Library. Joe Mills was a firm supporter of the Park Administration's transportation concessions policy, and he argued in its support on a number of public occasions. For example, he defended the policy before the Boulder Chamber of Commerce on February 10, 1927, on the grounds that "the concern operating in the Park must undergo government inspection, both as to the condition of their machines and the ability of their drivers; that the company must operate on a schedule set by the government and not by the company; [and] that 4 percent of the proceeds go to the Park after the company's books have been audited by a government man." *Boulder News-Herald,* February 11, 1927, p. 1.

49. *Boulder News-Herald,* February 23, 1927, Cede Jurisdiction Scrapbooks. The two met face to face on opposite sides of the issue on January 30, 1929, in a hearing before the Federal Relations Committee of the Colorado House of Representatives. According to the *News-Herald* (January 31, 1929), Esther Mills was the only one to speak against the pending bill. Cede Jurisdiction Scrapbooks.

50. Hewes "Journal," December 31, 1928, p. 775.

51. *Estes Park Trail,* vol. 14, March 22, 1935, p. 4.

52. Dorr G. Yeager (b. 1902) was born in Gilman, Iowa, and educated at Grinnell College and the University of Washington. Yeager began his Park Service career as a ranger at Yellowstone and was transferred to Rocky Mountain National Park in June 1931 as Associate Ranger

Naturalist. According to Park historian Lloyd Musselman, Yeager "brought new vigor to the [Park's] educational program. He organized lectures, field trips, auto caravans, and self-guiding nature walks and utilized a new Park museum [which opened early in 1935 in what had once been the recreation hall of the Moraine Park Lodge]." Yeager remained in Estes Park until December 1935, when he accepted a position with the Western Museum Laboratories in Berkeley, working primarily on dioramas. Among his responsibilities in Estes Park was visiting local hotels to present interpretive lectures to tourists, and it was while at the Crags that Yeager met and began to court Eleanor Ann Mills. Though she vowed she would never marry one of "them"—by which she meant one of the conservationists—the two were married in Denver on May 18, 1935. Yeager later served as assistant superintendent at Zion, Bryce, and Grand Canyon national parks and as regional chief of interpretation in San Francisco. Yeager was a prolific author in his own right. His publications include the series of Bob Flame novels, a successful attempt to publicize the daily life, albeit in a somewhat heightened and romanticized way, of members of the Park Service: *Bob Flame, Ranger* (1934), *Bob Flame, Rocky Mountain Ranger* (1935), which is set in Rocky Mountain National Park, *Bob Flame in Death Valley* (1937), and *Bob Flame among the Navajo* (1946). In addition, Yeager wrote a series of animal novels—among them *Scarface: The Story of a Grizzly* (1935), *Chita* (1939), and *Grey Dawn, the Wolf Dog* (1942)—as well as *National Parks of California* (1939) and *Your Western Parks: A Guide* (1947). Patricia Washburn, "Dorr Yeager,'" Estes Park Oral History Project (October 1972), transcript, Estes Park Public Library; Washburn, "The Thirties in Estes Park," p. 3; Musselman, *Rocky Mountain National Park,* pp. 153–55; *Estes Park Trail,* vol. 15, May 24, 1935, p. 7.

53. *Estes Park Trail,* vol. 14, July 27, 1934, p. 9.

54. *Estes Park Trail,* vol. 15, Oct. 4, 1935, p. 1. The news of Joe Mills's accident, hospitalization, and death was widely reported in the Denver press. See, for example, *Rocky Mountain News,* September 28, 1935, p. 1 ("Joe Mills Hurt in Auto Crash"); October 4, 1935, p. 8.

55. Hewes "Journal," October 5, 1937, p. 967.

56. *Estes Park Trail,* vol. 15, Oct. 4, 1935, p. 4.

57. *Estes Park Trail,* vol. 24, April 6, 1945, p. 1; vol. 27, May 2, 1947, p. 2.

58. Memorandum to the Director, Board of Geographic Names, National Park Service, December 8, 1948. Files, Division of Geography, National Park Service, Washington, D.C. See also *Estes Park Trail,* vol. 28, Feb. 25, 1949, p. 6.

CONTENTS

LIST OF ILLUSTRATIONS

A MOUNTAIN BOYHOOD

CHAPTER ONE

GOING WEST

FATHER and mother settled on the Kansas prairie in the early fifties. At that time Kansas was the frontier. Near neighbors were twenty miles or more apart. There was no railroad; no stages supplied the vast unsettled region. A few supplies were freighted by wagon. However, little was needed from civilized sources, for the frontier teemed with game. Myriads of prairie chickens were almost as tame as domestic fowls. Deer stared in wide-eyed amazement at the early settlers. Bands of buffalo snorted in surprise as the first dark lines of sod were broken up. Droves of wild turkey skirted the fringes of timber. Indians roamed freely; halting in wonder at the first log cabins of the pioneers.

In my father's old diary I found the following:

June, 1854.

Drove through from Iowa to Kansas by ox team. Located four days' drive south of Portsmouth.* Not much timber here.

* Later Kansas City.

1

October, 1854.

Just returned from visit to our nearest neighbor, John Seeright, a day's drive away. Took the chickens and cow along and stayed several days.

Father told me that the early settlers did not like a region after it got "settled up." He laughed heartily when he said this. It is quite true nevertheless; as soon as a region became "settled up," the pioneers were ready to push on again into the unknown. They loved the frontier—it held adventure, hazard always, mystery, ofttimes, romance, life. They moved ahead of and beyond civilization—even the long arm of the law did not penetrate their wilderness fastnesses. Their experience—so numerous books cannot hold them all—have become history.

It is not strange that my parents welcomed the gold rush of '59. It called them once more into the farther wilderness, the vaster unknown. When news of the finding of gold in the Rockies came across the plains, legions of adventurers trailed westward. The few roads that led across the rolling prairies to the Rockies were soon deep-cut. Wagons trains strung out across the treeless land like huge, creeping serpents moving lazily in the sun. Joyfully the adventurers went —happy, courageous. They were the vanguards of civilization, pushing ever to the West.

To my lifelong regret, my boyhood came after

the gold rushes were over; the buffalo bands had passed for the last time; the Indian fighting ended. However, these exciting events were still fresh in the memory of my parents. When neighbors came to visit us, long hours were spent in talking over and comparing experiences. I thrilled as my father told of climbing Long's Peak, the eastern sentinel of the Rockies—of Estes Park, teeming with trout and game. I thought then that I had been born too late—that all the big things in the world were past history. I feared then that even the Rockies would lose their wildness before I could explore them.

Within sight and sound of the farm where I was born, a number of Civil War skirmishes took place. The eastern Kansas border during the trying time of the early sixties was perhaps the worst place in all the world to live. Raiding parties plundered on both sides of the Kansas-Missouri line. My mother watched the battle of Mine Creek from the dooryard; saw the soldiers streaming by, and prayed fervently as the tide of battle swayed back and forth. My father was fighting in that battle. These frontier conflicts were still the favorite topics of conversation at neighborhood gatherings when I was a little boy. I listened breathlessly to them and lived them over in my imagination. Of all the tales recounted around our fire, I loved that of the gold rush of '59 best—my father and mother had participated in it—and I'm sure that story moved me most of all to obey Horace Greeley's injunction.

The wagons, in the beginning of the journey, formed a train, keeping close together for mutual protection. As they neared the Rockies, they scattered, each party following its individual route. Late in the summer, high up in the mountains near Breckenridge, Colorado, my father fell ill of "mountain fever." My mother, who weighed less than one hundred pounds, alone drove the pony team back across the plains to eastern Kansas. Many weeks were spent en route. Sometimes they camped for a night with westward-bound wagons; then resumed the eastward journey alone. Buffalo, migrating southward, literally covered the prairie—at times, so dense were their ranks, my mother had to stop the team to let the herds go by.

One experience of this trying trip, often related by my father, filled me with lasting admiration for my plucky mother.

"We were camped one night beneath some cottonwoods beside a wide, shallow stream," father would say, "and I was unable to move from my bed in the wagon. Your mother cared for the team, started a fire, and got supper. Shortly after dark, and before supper was ready, a dozen Indians filed solemnly into our camp and sat down facing the fire. They said nothing, but followed your mother's every movement with watchful eyes. If your mother tasted the brew in the brass kettle, every Indian eye followed her hand, and every Indian licked his lips eagerly. The brass kettle was about the only cooking utensil we possessed, and your mother guarded it carefully.

"This night the kettle held a savory stew of buffalo meat. When the stew was done, your mother set it off the fire to cool. During a few seconds—while her back was turned—the kettle vanished. From the shelter of the wagon I saw an Indian reach out stealthily and slip it beneath his blanket. The next moment your mother was facing the silent circle with blazing eyes. And there, hundreds of miles from a settlement, with no help at hand, she defied a dozen Indians. In spite of the fact that she weighed just ninety-two pounds, she swept around the circle slapping the surprised braves, pulling their hair and demanding the kettle. She noticed that the chief was sheltering something beneath his blanket. At once she gave his blanket a jerk. The hot brew spilled over the surprised redskin's legs. There was a yell that rent the stillness. The fellow leaped high into the air, and vanished into the night, leaving the brass kettle behind him."

Little did my parents realize that their recounted experiences would eventually lead me, still a boy, to venture into new regions.

At ten years of age I hazarded the statement that I was old enough to shift for myself; that I was going West to live the rest of my life in the Rocky Mountains. But my parents, in order to frighten me out of my plans, told me that Indians still infested the wilds; that terrible bull buffaloes and horrible grizzly bears roamed the wilderness.

These attempts to frighten me only strengthened my desire for adventure and my determination to seek it. When all else failed I was told that I was too young to strike out for myself. At last father put his foot down firmly, a sign that his patience was at an end—so I postponed my adventure.

The day finally came when I was aboard a train, heading westward, toward the mountains of my dreams. I possessed twenty dollars, my entire savings. During the journey I hardly slept, but kept watch out the window for the first glimpse of the Rockies. I have no recollection that there were sleeping cars at that time; anyhow, my thin little purse afforded no such gross extravagance if I had known. I recall that the individual seat of the chair-car gave me much concern. I had considerable trouble adjusting it—putting it up and laying it down.

Beside me in the companion seat rode a man of middle age, bearded, roughly dressed, who took keen interest in my destination. He was located, I learned, over the Continental Divide in that vast region beyond Grand Lake. He talked of the forests of uncut timber near his homestead, of the fertile valleys and grassy parks that would eventually support cattle herds. "Some day," he predicted, "there'll be a railroad built between Denver and Salt Lake City; and when it comes its bound to pass close to my claim."

At dawn I caught my first sight of the great snow-covered peaks, a hundred miles away, rearing rose-red in the early morning light. At first I mistook those misty ranges for cloud banks, lighted by the rising sun. Then, as we drew nearer and day wore on, I made them out.

Toward noon I reached Fort Collins, Colorado, fifty miles from Long's Peak, where there was no stage connection with Estes Park, but Loveland, a town fifteen miles south, had a horse stage that made three trips a week. The fare, I learned, was quite prohibitive, three dollars for something more than thirty miles. The walk would be interesting, I decided. But the old canvas bag, containing all my worldly possessions, was too bulky and awkward to be carried. After some hours of dickering, I paid eight dollars for a second-hand bicycle, tied the bag on the handle bars and started for the Mecca of my dreams.

That first journey to the mountains was filled

with thrills. The old stage road shot up successive mountain ranges, and plunged abruptly down into the valleys between. There was no Big Thompson route then; instead, the road ascended Bald Mountain, climbed the foothill range, crossed the top, then dropped into Rattlesnake Park. It squirmed up Pole Hill, a grade so steep that I could scarcely push up my wheel. Up and down, up and down, it seesawed endlessly. The afternoon wore on; each successive slope grew harder, for my legs were weary. Twice, braking with one foot on the front crotch and sliding the wheel, I had pitched headlong over the handle bars. Upon two descents that were too precipitous to venture unballasted, I tied fair-sized pine trees to the rear of my craft to act as drag-anchors.

As darkness came on I coasted down a sharp pitch to a little brook. In the aspens that bordered the road was a range cow standing guard beside a newborn calf. Across the road, like grisly shadows among the trees, skulked several coyotes. The calf half rose, wabbled, and went down. Three times it attempted to rise, grew weaker, and at last gave up the struggle. With the waiting coyotes in mind, I leaned my wheel against a bowlder and went to its rescue. Several things happened at once. The half-wild range cow misunderstood my good intentions. She was accustomed to seeing men on horseback; and one afoot was strange. She charged headlong. I dodged quickly aside but not in time to escape entirely. She raked me with her sharp horns. There was a wild race through the aspens; I leading, but the cow a close second, her horns menacing me at every leap, while I doubled and backtracked sharply about among the trees. I had no chance to "tree"; though no mountain lion was ever more willing, for Mrs. Cow was too near. Only Providence and my agility saved me from an untimely end. At last the cow halted, for she was getting too far from her calf. She shook her horns after me menacingly, turned and hurried back toward where her offspring lay.

Each mile I covered impressed upon me more and more that there is not even a distant relationship between mountain miles and my Kansas prairie miles. The latter are ironed out flat, the former stand on end, cease to be miles and become trials. Slowly the shadows filled the cañons, and came creeping up the slopes. I gazed in awesome wonder at the beauty of my land of dreams. My legs, cramped almost past pedaling, still kept on—for my goal, my mountians, were at hand. Exaltation of spirit overcame exhaustion of body.

At no time had I given any particular thought to what would happen when I arrived; so far my whole attention had been centered on reaching the Rockies. Such trivialities as no job, no relatives, practically no money, made little impression upon my Rocky-bound mind.

Long after nightfall I reached the crest of Park Hill, the last barrier to Estes Park. The moon shone full upon the valley below, and upon the snow-capped mountains beyond. The river murmured softly as its shining folds curled back and forth across the dark green meadow, suddenly vanishing between dark cañon walls. Coyotes raised their eerie voices; across the cañon, from the cliffs of Mount Olympus, an owl hooted gloomily. Before me loomed the Rockies, strangely unreal in the moonlight and yet very like the mountains of my imagination. I gazed, spellbound. My dream was realized.

It was midnight when, completely exhausted, I stopped before an old log cabin. Dogs charged out, barking furiously at the strange thing I rode and nipping at my legs; but I was too weary to remember distinctly even now what happened. I must have tumbled off my wheel for I learned afterward that I was picked up and put to bed; but for hours I tossed about, my body racked with pain, my thoughts jumbled. But boys must sleep, and I slept at last.

Next morning, pushing the wheel slowly, I headed for the most remote ranch in the region, that lay at the foot of Long's Peak. Progress was slow and painful for my body was stiff and sore; the road I followed wound upward, climbing steadily to higher altitude. Frequently I halted to rest, and spent my time of respite searching the mountains with eager, appraising eyes, planning explorations among them. Toward noon I came to the ranch I sought, located nine miles from the nearest neighbor, at nine thousand feet altitude, and surrounded by rugged mountains. Above it rose Long's Peak, up and up into the clouds, to more than fourteen thousand feet. The rancher was the Reverend E. J. Lamb, one of the early settlers of Estes Park. The Parson, as he was known, was more than six feet tall, straight as a lodge-pole pine physically—and even more so spiritually. He wore a long, flowing beard, rose habitually and unprotestingly at four in the morning—a man of diverse talents and eccentricities.

CHAPTER TWO

PARSON LAMB'S ranch consisted of a fenced garden tract surrounded on every side for miles by high mountains that shut it in. There was heavy forest on the slopes above the ranch; and out of these came many lively little streams that were almost as cold as their parent snowbanks.

I hoarded my few remaining dollars. The Parson gave me room and board, in return for which I helped about the place, doing various chores, such as wood-splitting and clearing land for more garden, and occasionally going the nine miles to the village for the mail. My work took only a small part of my time, leaving me free to explore the near-by region, with its deep, evergreen forests, and the wild animals which lived in them.

Many were the tales the tall, rawboned Parson told of his early pioneer days (for he had lived there since the early seventies, and was a loquacious old fellow), as he and his wife, Jane, and I sat beside the granite fireplace, when the coals

13

glowed low and the shadows scurried here and there over the rough logs of the cabin walls. He had been shot and nearly killed by a bandit, gored by a bull, dragged by a frightened horse, and bitten by a bear. Upon one lonely excursion far from any settlement, he had been followed by a huge, stealthy, mountain lion.

Harrowing as were these tales, the one that made me shiver despite the radiant pitch knots, was that of his perilous descent of the precipice on Long's Peak. Time has not changed the character of that face—it is sheer and smooth and icy now, as then. He was probably the first man to attempt its descent, and I was always weak and spent when he ended his story of it, so vividly did he portray its dangers. I sat tense, digging my nails deep into my palms, living through every squirm and twist with him, from the moment he slid down from the comparatively safe "Narrows" to the first niche in the glassy, precipitous wall, till, after many nearly-the-last experiences, he landed safely at its foot. That adventure had almost cost him his life, for he had once missed his foothold, slipped and slid and had hung suspended by one hand for a long, terrible moment.

Always I sat with eyes glued upon the story-teller, thrilling as he talked, planning secretly to emulate his example, proving some of his statements by daily short excursions. However, the

Parson was not always away on trips. Sometimes he guided visitors to the top of the Peak or worked on the trail to its summit. He chopped wood, worked in the garden, hunted stray cattle or horses. Frequently he rode off with his Bible under his arm, for he was a circuit rider, carrying the gospel into the wilderness. He gave good, if free, advice, officiated at weddings and funerals, at barn-raisings and log-rollings. He preached or worked as the notion moved him; lingered in one place or rode long trails to fulfill his mission. His own ranch was thirty miles from the railroad, but many of his calls were made on settlers even more remote.

Gradually I extended the scope of my explorations, frequently spending the night abroad, carrying a pair of worn and faded blankets and a little food. A number of times I climbed Long's Peak alone. On these trips to high country I scouted the high-flung crest of Battle Mountain, Lady Washington, Storm Peak, and Mount Meeker; explored Glacier Gorge, investigated Chasm Lake, and from the top of Peak and Meeker looked down into Wild Basin to the south.

I sketched a rude map of the great basin in my notebook and named it "Land of Many Waters," because of the scores of small streams that trickled down its inclosing mountain sides. The oval bowl I estimated to be fifteen miles

long by about half as wide, its sides formed of
mountain slopes densely wooded up to bleak
timberline. Save the murmur of falling water,
or the wind upon the heights, it was a land of
silence. Small streams converged, dropped into
deep cañons and reached the river that rumbled
far below. There were vivid, emerald lakes
everywhere—some lost in the woods near the
river, others pocketed behind the ridges, while
still more could be seen up above naked timberline.

I returned, thrilled with the thought of
exploring Wild Basin, sought the Parson and
told him my ambition. At first he was much
amused, but when he found I was serious he
grew grave.

"There's no neighbors over that way," he objected. "If anything happens, you'll be beyond
help." Even though he was older and much
more experienced, I thought him hardly quali-
fied, after his own foolhardy adventures, to dis-
courage me; but I decided to wait until fall before setting out. This delay would enable me to
know more about the mountains, to add to my
experience, and better fit me to cope with the
emergencies of that inviting, great unknown—
Wild Basin.

Everywhere I found strange birds and animals, and began to get acquainted with them.
The handsome, black and white, long-tailed mag-

pies were much like the crows I had known in Kansas, so far as wariness was concerned. The Rocky Mountain long-crested jays, quite unlike our prairie jays, much more brilliant in coloring, their gorgeous coats of turquoise blue and black flashing in the sunshine, were continually bickering, and following me through the woods to see what I was about. Chickadees and nuthatches were always inspecting the trees for food, running up and down, paying no attention to me and going about their business with cheerful little chirrups that expressed their contentment. Occasionally a crow flew up the valley with raucous calls; and sometimes a raven pursued his way toward the deeper woods. Meadow larks and robins were everywhere.

Woodpeckers and flickers did their bit to keep vermin off the trees, and performed daily operations on trunk and limb, removing borers and beetles that had penetrated beneath the bark, thus saving the lives of many evergreen monarchs. Around ten and eleven thousand feet there were campbirds, Canada jays, friendly and inquisitive; on first acquaintance they often took food from my hands, and helped themselves freely of any food accessible in camp. They were unruffled, flitting softly from tree to tree, with little flapping, calling low, and in a sweetly confidential tone.

However friendly I found the birds, the big

game animals were extremely wary. I mentioned the fact to the Parson.

"They've been shot at," was his explanation. "Every time they've come in contact with men they've suffered. They know men are dangerous, always have guns."

In spite of the Parson's observations we always had wild game hanging in the log meat house; there was never any question about securing whatever we wanted in that line. Except during the winter months, deer could be had with little effort. But the elk had practically vanished; occasionally a lone survivor strayed into the ranch valley. There were bears, of course, shy and fearful, in the rough, unsettled country. We had great variety of meat, venison, Bighorn sheep, grouse, ptarmigan, wild pigeon, sometimes squirrel and, rarely, bear steaks.

Wherever I went, even in the far-away places where few men had ever been, the deer and elk and bear were very wild, and I found it impossible to approach them unless the wind was from them to me, and I moved forward carefully hidden. I spent many eventful days, walking, climbing, sitting motionless to watch the scampering chipmunks, or to invite the birds up close. Thus, a little at a time, I came to know the habits of the wild folks I met; learned their likes and dislikes—the things that excited their curiosity, and that frightened them away in panic.

Upon my first climb to the top of Long's Peak alone, I halted above timberline and stared about in amazement at the wide stretches of rock-strewn slopes. From a distance these had appeared no larger than a back yard, but a close-up revealed they were miles across; and instead of being barren, were a series of hanging gardens, one above another, each of different shape and size, and all green with grass and with a hundred different kinds of wild flowers waving in the sunshine. I counted more than fifty varieties, none of which I knew, and still they seemed endless.

Usually I wandered off the trail to follow birds or animals. In the arctic-like zone above were birds entirely strange to me, and animals that never came down to the valley of the ranch. It was not long before I discovered that nearly all birds and animals live at a certain zone of altitude, rarely straying above or below it.

Occasionally I heard a queer "squee-ek." It sounded close, yet its maker was invisible. Many times I looked up, searching the air overhead for the elusive "squee-eker." At last I came upon a bunch of grass, no larger than a water pail, and stopped to examine it. Grass and flowers had been piled loosely in an irregular heap, resembling a miniature haystack.

"Something making a nest," I observed aloud.

"Squee-ek," denied a shrill voice almost at my elbow.

Ten feet away upon a bowlder that rose above the rest of the rocks, sat a small animal which at first I mistook for a young rabbit. In shape and size he closely resembled a quarter-grown cottontail, but his ears were different from any rabbit's, being short and round. His eyes were beady; somehow he made me think of a rat. He ran down the rock and climbed to another perch. Not even so much tail as a bunny—none at all. In some respects he resembled a rabbit, a squirrel and a prairie dog. His actions reminded me of all of them. In fact, he is sometimes called "Rock Rabbit" and "Little Chief Hare." He may have other names besides.

I watched the interesting little fellow for some time and later found his actions characteristic of his tribe. He literally makes hay while the summer shines. He is the only harvester I ever saw who works on the run. He dashed at top speed, without stopping for breath, bit off a mouthful of grass and again ran pell-mell for his growing stack. He scampered down its side, then leaped from an adjacent rock to its top, laden with his bundle of hay. Evidently he found the alpine summer short and felt it necessary to step lively. Altitude, that convenient scapegoat of tenderfeet, did not seem to affect his wind or his endurance. He stacked his harvest in one corner of the field from which he cut it. He cut flowers along with the grass.

Perhaps he used them for flavor as grandmother put rose-geranium leaves in her crab-apple jelly. The haycock he built was about the size of a bucket—I have since seen them as large as bushel baskets. His tiny fields lay between bowlders; some of them were but a few inches square, others a foot, several a yard, perhaps.

I was interested to learn if the little haycocks were blown away by the timberline gales, so returned later, not really expecting to find them. Nor were they in the same location, but their owners, not the wind, had moved them. Evidently, as soon as the hay was cured, it was stored for safe-keeping, usually beneath the overhang of a rock, away from the wind.

I was then curious to see how the cony would transport his hay in winter. Many of his under-rock passages would, at that season, be filled with snow, forcing him to appear on the surface where the wind was often strong enough to blow me over, to say nothing of what it would do to the little midget in fur with a load of hay attached. He met the storm situation easily. Whenever he exhausted one hayloft, he moved his home to another. Thus he solved the transportation question and gained a new home at the same time. Several times, upon digging beneath the slide rock, I discovered cony dens, merely openings far down between the jumbled rocks, beyond the reach of wind and weather. They were of great variety, large, small, wide, narrow; all ready to move into. They were the conies' castles, ready refuges from enemies, their devious passages as effective as drawbridge or portcullis.

The cony is something like the beaver far down on the flats below; working at top speed when he does work, and then resting for many months. Outside the brief harvest period I have found him sitting idly atop a rock, napping in the sun, dreaming apparently; thus for days and months he is idle, always harmless—a condition that does not apply to human beings under similar circumstances. He is energetic, ambitious, courageous, and acrobatic. He is the scout of the mountain top, always alert and friendly.

The altitude zone of the cony I found to be between eleven and thirteen thousand feet. He and the Bighorn, ptarmigan, weasels and foxes are mountain-top dwellers throughout the year. Marmots hibernate during the long alpine winters. But the cony I have seen on sunny days in January; his welcome "squee-ek," piercing the roar of the wind, has greeted me on the lonely storm-swept heights when not another living thing was in sight.

But in spite of his living in the out-of-the-way world the cony has enemies for whom he is always watching. In summer there are hawks and eagles, foxes and coyotes. In winter his feathered foes depart, but the foxes remain, as do the

weasels. Sitting motionless in the midst of
jumbled rocks I have faded into the bowlder
fields, and thus have been able to watch the cony
and his enemies. Usually his "squee-ek" announced the appearance of a foe before I discovered it. Then, if the enemy was a bird or a
beast, he merely hugged the rock, watching
alertly until he was discovered, then flipped out
of sight to the safety of rocky retreat, giving a
defiant "squee-ek" as he went. But if a weasel
appeared . . .

I sat watching a cony one day in early fall as
he lay in the sunshine upon a bowlder. From
somewhere below us came the distant "squee-ek"
of a relative, followed shortly by the shrill
whistle of a marmot. The cony sat up suddenly,
awake and alertly watching. The signals were
repeated. Instantly the little fellow departed
from his outpost and hurried away, circling the
bowlder, leaping to another, disappearing in the
rocks and reappearing again. His actions were
so unusual that I wondered what message the
signals had carried; to me they were no different
than they were when they announced my coming
—yet the difference must have been plain to the
wee furry ears, judging from their owner's ap-
prehensive actions. Indeed, a weasel was abroad
seeking his quarry. When his presence was announced, neither the cony nor I could see him
because of an intervening upthrust of rock.

Soon the weasel appeared, circling the rock where the cony had been sunning himself, searching beneath it, hurrying along the tunnels through which the cony had fled. Emerging upon the bowlder, he paused for a few seconds as he looked in all directions. The weasel was brownish-yellow in color. I was to learn later that he changed to pure white in winter.

I sprang to my feet and pursued him, shouting as I ran, throwing rocks and attempting to scare him off. Losing track of both pursurer and pursued, I stopped for breath. Suddenly, from almost beneath my feet, the agile villain reappeared, staring at me with bright, bold eyes, advancing toward me as though to attack. He was no coward; with amazing agility he dodged a rock I threw at him, turning a back-spring and landing at my feet. For a moment we glared at each other, then he made off as though utterly unconscious of my presence.

I watched the long slender body disappear among the rocks in the opposite direction to that taken by the cony, standing for a moment to regain my breath and recover from my surprise.

Suddenly there was a shrill whistle behind me. I jumped and whirled about. Twenty feet away a marmot stood erect atop a rock, eying me inquiringly, watching every movement. He had whistled his signal about me, whether good or bad news I could not detect, but from the distance came other whistles in reply. He was the cony's ally, broadcasting information about the skirmish taking place before his eyes; but whether he was attempting to interfere and divert my attention, I could not make out. Certainly, though, he was giving information, signaling my presence to all within hearing. My intrusion upon the heights in summer has ever been announced by the conies and the marmots.

From another direction came a second whistle; apparently I was surrounded. Then, as I moved, the second marmot hurried away from his observation post. He was short-legged, reddish-yellow in color, with a bushy tail, and he ran with great effort but with very little speed, like a fat boy in a foot race.

Down in the valley near the ranch were numerous grouse, old and young, so tame that it was like knocking over pet chickens to kill them. But there was a strange bird above timberline, the ptarmigan, the arctic quail of the north—fool hens, the Parson told me. These birds were mottled in color, matching the rocks among which they lived, and so closely did their color blend with their environment it was impossible to distinguish bird from rock so long as the fowl remained still. It was because they depended so utterly upon their protective coloration, making no effort to get out of the way but acting with

utmost stupidity, that they came to be called
"fool hens."

The days I spent above timberline were the
most wonderful of all. From high above the
world I could see tier upon tier of distant, snow-
capped mountains—ghost ranges—and southward, at the horizon, loomed Pike's Peak a
hundred airline miles away, a giant pyramid
above the foothills, standing sentinel over the
vast, flat plains that reached to its foot.

As weeks passed and my interest in the wild
things increased, I began to wish for a cabin of
my own, a home or a den to which I could retreat
and spend the time as I desired. Wherever I
rambled I was alert for a location for my little
house. I was not yet old enough to take up a
homestead and claim land for myself.

Climbing to the summits of various promontories I planned the sort of cabin I would like to
build there; I'd have a dog, and a horse too, and
a camera—I began to doubt whether I'd want my
rifle for as I developed my acquaintance with
the animals I found myself less eager to shoot
them.

Hunting and trapping was the habit of everyone I knew; even back in Kansas the boys and
men had gone shooting at every opportunity;
and the few men I encountered upon the trails
in the Rockies were for the most part real trappers and hunters, following the trade for a living.

They gave no thought to the cruelty of their traps or the suffering their operations occasioned. It is not strange, then, that such men saw no harm in their actions, for they considered all game fair prey.

Occasionally I left my gun at home and found that I rambled the heights above timberline in a changed mood from when I carried it. The animals were more friendly, perhaps my actions were more open and aboveboard. My rifle naturally inspired a desire to shoot something; a mountain sheep, a bear, even the fat marmots did not escape my deadly fire.

But, without a gun—there was interest everywhere. Many times I laughed at the antics of the animals, especially at the awkward, lumbering haste of the marmots. These animals, while very curious, were quick to take alarm. They would climb to a lookout post at the top of a rock, watching me eagerly and whistling mild gossip for the delectation of their neighbors who could not see me. One day, far skyward, I came upon an exceedingly fat marmot busily eating grass in a narrow little hayland between bowlders. He must have weighed more than twenty pounds, but this fact did not deter him from adding additional weight for the long, winter sleep. At best his active period was short, his hibernation long, so he ate and slept and ate again through all the hours of daylight. At my approach he reluctantly left off eating, crept up a rock and whistled mildly as though merely curious. For a time I amused him by advancing, retreating, and circling his rock.

Suddenly I dropped out of sight behind a bowlder. Instantly his whistle carried a note of warning. So long as I remained in sight I was merely a curiosity, but the instant I dropped from sight, I became a suspicious character. Again he broadcasted sharp warning to all within hearing. From near and far came answering marmot shrillings, and from near by a cony "squee-eked" his quick alarm.

My reappearance reassured the marmot. He whistled again, and I thought I distinguished a note of disgust or of disappointment.

This marmot lived on the south slope of the big moraine that shoulders against Lady Washington, neighboring peak to the giant mountain, Long's Peak. Sometimes I found the roly-poly fellow saving hay by eating it, or asleep in the sun on an exposed rock. Often he ventured down into the cañon at the foot of the moraine to investigate the grass that grew down there.

One day as I sat atop the big moraine, I heard his shrill whistle from the edge of the trees in the cañon below. It was somehow different from any signal I had heard him give before, but just how it was different I could not make out. The notes were the same, but the tone was different—

that was it, the tone had changed. Then the reason for the difference came out of the scattered trees—a grizzly bear stalked deliberately into the open and sat down facing the huge bowlder upon which the marmot sat.

The marmot stood erect on his hind legs, eying the bear warily, prepared to dash for his den beneath the rock the instant the visitor made an unfriendly move. But the bear was a very stupid fellow; he took no note of the marmot. Instead, he looked off across the cañon, swung his head slowly to and fro as though thinking deeply of something a hundred miles away. He was a young bear with a shiny new coat of summer fur. He had just had a bath in the stream where ice water gushed from beneath a snow-bank.

The marmot gave a second whistle, carrying less fear. Apparently the slow-moving, sleepy bear meant no harm. For half an hour the marmot watched alertly, then slid down beneath the bowlders and started eating. From time to time he sat stiffly erect, peering suspiciously at the intruder. But since the bear made no overt move, he continued his feeding as though he were too hungry to wait until his uninvited guest departed.

At length the bear rolled over on his back with all four feet in the air. The marmot surveyed the performance for a few seconds, then went on feeding, gradually grazing out beyond the shelter of the rock beneath which he had his den. The bear "paid him no mind," apparently asleep in the sunshine. Slowly the marmot fed away from the rock, the farther he ventured the more luxuriant his feast, for the grass was eaten off short around his dooryard. For an hour I watched every move of that silent drama, trying to guess the outcome, wondering if the bear were really asleep. All at once the little gourmand whistled reassuringly: "All right, it's a friend."

The marmot was not more surprised than myself at what happened next. The bear lay perhaps a hundred feet from the marmot's home, and the marmot had fed perhaps forty feet from it—a distance he could quickly cover if the visitor showed unfriendly symptoms.

But there were no symptoms. It was all over so quickly that I was left dazed and breathless. There was a small bowlder about four feet high in the midst of a tiny hayfield where the marmot fed. The unsuspecting whistler fed into the little field, passed behind the rock, and was out of sight for just a second. At that instant the bear came to life, leaped to his feet and dashed toward the den beneath the rock, cutting off the marmot's retreat.

Too late the quarry saw the bear. It made a frantic dash for home and shelter, its fat body working desperately, its short legs flying. Ten feet from the den the bear flattened the marmot with a single quick slap of his paw. Then he sat down to eat his dinner. His acting had been perfect; he had fooled me as well as the marmot.

CHAPTER THREE

FIRST CAMP ALONE—EXPLORING

MY short trips into the wilds tempted me to go beyond the trails. So far my rambles had taken me only to the threshold of the wilderness, I wondered what lay beyond; I wanted to follow the game trails and see where they led. Above all I was eager to pit my scant skill against primitive nature and learn if my resourcefulness was equal to the emergencies of the unknown. Somehow I never doubted my courage—I simply didn't fear.

As the short high-altitude summer began to wane, I grew restless. September advanced; the aspen trees near timberline turned to gold; from day to day those lower down turned also until a vast richly colored rug covered the mountain sides. Ripe leaves fluttered down, rustling crisply underfoot. Frost cut down the rank grass, humbled the weeds and harvested the flowers. Forests of spruce and lodgepole were dark with shadow. A beaver colony returned to its former haunts at the foot of Long's Peak and was working night and day. Its pond of still water was glazing over with clear ice.

October came. The nights grew colder. The snow of early winter came to the high peaks, dusting their bare, bald crowns.

"Fur ought to be getting prime now," the Parson said one day. "It'll be better still, higher up."

This was the message I had been waiting for. It set me packing at once, for I was going into Wild Basin, alone, to hunt, trap and explore.

On a morning near the middle of October, much excited, I set out for the land of mystery. Ahead lay the unknown, uncharted wilds. I could go where I chose and stay as long as I wished. Bold Columbus, looking westward, could not have been more thrilled. Mountain maple beckoned with ripe, red banners. The mountains peeked through the autumn haze, divulging nothing, promising everything!

My outfit consisted of an old, ragged tent, a little food, a camera that had been through a fire and leaked light badly, a knife, an ax, a six-shooter, and an old rifle that had been traded about among the early settlers and had known many owners. In addition I had bought six double-spring steel traps sufficiently large to hold beaver, coyotes or wolves. The pair of ragged blankets that had served me on my short trips about the region had been reinforced with an old quilt, faded and patched, but sweet and clean.

All this duffle I packed upon a "return" horse,

lent me by the Parson, one that would return home as soon as it was let loose.

The Parson chuckled at the appearance of my pack, even the horse turned his head inquiringly, but I was too excited to mind their insinuations. As the sun topped the mountains, I led the horse slowly down the old tollroad toward a game trail, and swung up in the direction of Wild Basin.

Deer tracks showed in the old road and in the game trails; I also recognized coyote tracks, and puzzled over strange tracks which I could not make out. The small streams I crossed had many deep pools where trout were collecting for the winter. I tossed stones into them and the fish, like rainbow darts, dashed for shelter beneath the rocks. Hourly my excitement grew— a million plans ran through my head. I would become a mighty hunter and make a fortune trapping; I would turn prospector and locate a mine: Father and Mother would yet have the gold of which they were thwarted.

The second evening brought me into such rough country that going farther with the horse was next to impossible. With excited hands I unpacked, bade the beast good-by, and started him toward home on the back trail. He trotted off, neighing eagerly.

Save for the rumble of the river deep down in its cañon, the great basin was voiceless. The forest showed no signs of man. Above and be-

yond rose a circle of snow-capped peaks. I
paused in awe; the world was bigger than I had
dreamed. I was a boy without a woodsman's
skill—a boy alone in the heart of an overwhelming silence. I turned, with a pang of homesick-
ness, just in time to see the return horse
disappear. Whistling loudly, I set about making
camp. It should be my headquarters, from which
I could explore in all directions, returning as
often as necessary for supplies.

A lake with sandy shores lapped in and out
among immense bowlders. On the west side a
cliff rose straight from the water. At the upper
edge a small cataract came leaping down the
ledges and plunged noisily into the pool that overflowed into the lake. Above the water was a
grove of Engelmann spruces, giant trees that
rose straight for more than a hundred feet. I
pitched my tent in a small open glade, but had
trouble getting down the stakes, for everywhere
was granite. The first test of my resourcefulness
had come—I met it by piling stones around the
tent stakes, bracing them taut for the ropes.

The call of the wild was too loud to ignore—
I hastened my camp making. The sun was going
down on a world of splendor. Overhead were
brilliantly colored clouds, while deep in the cañon
below the early darkness was thickening. From
somewhere in the distance came the cry of an
animal. Camp was left unfinished; I climbed

to a jutting shoulder that overlooked the cañon. From far below came the noise of the river as it chugged and sobbed and roared endlessly between its towering walls. I promised myself I would go down and explore that dark cañon at an early date.

Of a sudden there came an indescribable, unearthly sound that echoed and reëchoed among the cliffs. I could not tell the direction from which it came; a sudden chill crept along my spine, my hair prickled and lifted. Then the echoes ceased, the silence that followed was equally terrifying. I bethought me of my unfinished camp. Later I learned that alarming sound was the bugling of a bull elk. It was the mating season.

As darkness came on I ate beans and bread by the light of the campfire. The beans came out of a can, so were well cooked; but the bread was my first campfire, culinary concoction. It was a flour and water mixture, plus salt and baking powder, cooked against a hot rock. It was smoked black and cooked so hard it nearly broke my teeth, besides, it had a granite finish from association with the rock oven. But I ate it with boyish relish in spite of its flaws. My imagination expanded as I watched ghostly shadow-figures dance upon the face of the cliff. The shifting flame, the wood smoke, the silent, starry night swelled my heart to pride in my great adventure. I ignored the incident of the animal cry that had sent me scurrying to camp. This first camp was just below timberline, at an altitude of eleven thousand feet or more.

I had much to learn about altitude, as well as of winds and weather, woods and mountains. In the mountains the higher one goes the harder the wind blows. In the Rockies, around timberline, gales often reach a velocity of a hundred miles, or more, an hour. Here during the long alpine winters, the wind booms and crashes among the peaks, roars through the passes, and rips through the shattered trees. That first night I lay in camp and listened to its unceasing roar, as it tore along the ridge tops. Occasionally, a gust would scatter my fire. It raged through the spruces like a hurricane, causing me much uneasiness lest one of the trees should come crashing down upon my frail shelter. At last, after dozing before the dying fire, I went inside the tent, crept between my blankets and fell asleep.

I was aiming at a charging grizzly, when there came a swishing, banging crash! I sat up, half awake. The tent flapped wildly, lifting clear of the ground. My stone cairns had been jerked down by the repeated yanks of the stake ropes. A stronger gust, the tent went down, or rather up, and vanished into the night. The spruce tree, which was my tent pole, struck me on the head.

I sat dazed. Gradually it came to me that my clothes, as well as my tent, were gone. I realized, too, that I had pitched camp on the wrong side of the little stream, for the mischievous gusts, saturated with water from the falls, spat upon me and soaked my blankets. I managed to strike a match, but the wind snuffed it out instantly. I tried again and again to make a light—with no success. I crawled dazedly about—I struggled upright—my toe caught beneath a rock, and I pitched headlong. That hour of darkness taught me never to venture about blindly.

The night was unbelievably cold. During the day, while the sun had shone brightly, the temperature had been very comfortable, even warm. But now, with wind blasts from the snow-fields and glaciers and waterfall, I was chilled through and through. As I felt about for my vanished clothes, my teeth chattered. Soon I gave up the search and sought shelter in the spruces; I found a leaning slab of rock and crept beneath it as a wild animal would have done. Through the remaining hours of the night I shivered and shook there; my imagination dulled, my ambition dampened. I decided to break camp as soon as it was light.

But it is marvelous what sunshine will do. When at last the tardy sun came up, and the wind died down and I had recovered my clothes and warmed myself at a leaping fire, my heart too leaped up with renewed courage. All was serene. It seemed impossible that I could have been so miserable in the night.

As soon as I had eaten I dragged the tent back among the spruces where I set it up and anchored it securely. Lesson Number One had sunk in. It would not need repeating.

When camp was at last secure, I climbed slowly to the ridge top above. Its crest was above timberline. On all sides rose lofty mountains, many of them patched with snowbanks. Deep cañons cut sharply between the ridges and shoulders. Ice fields indicated possible glaciers. I wanted to explore everything at once; wanted to climb the peaks, and delve into the cañons; hunt out the game and explore the glaciers.

At timberline I stopped in silent wonder. Broken trees were scattered about upon the ground like soldiers after a battle. I didn't quite comprehend its significance, but Parson Lamb had described it to me. I had seen other timberlines in my rambles, but none so impressive as this. Here was the forest frontier. How dauntless, how gallant, these pioneers were! How they strove to hold the advantage gained during the brief summer respite! Here a canny stripling grew behind a sheltering bowlder, but whenever it tried to peep above its breastworks, the wind, with its shell-shot of sand and gravel and ice bullets, cut off its protruding limbs as neatly as

a gardner might have done.   Consequently its
top was as flat as a table.

In the open, other trees trailed along the
ground like creeping vines, their tops pointing
away from the wind.   It seemed as if they banded
together for mutual protection, for they formed
a dense hedge or "bush."   Here was the deadline
established by altitude.   The forests were commanded to halt; this line of last defense was not
unlike the sweeping shoreline of the sea.   Here
and there were lone scout trees in advance of the
ranks.   They were twisted and dwarfed, mis-
shapen, grotesque.

There were wide, naked stretches bare of snow.
Great drifts lay in the woods; the deep, narrow
cañons were piled full of it.   Many of these drifts
would last far into the following summer; a few
would be perpetual.   At the approach of summer,
such drifts turn to ice through frequent thawing
and freezing, since the surface snow, melting under the glare of the summer sun, seeps down
through the mass beneath in daytime, and freezes
again at night.   From such drifts flow icy streams
for the leaping trout.   Countless sparkling
springs gurgled forth at the foot of the slopes.

Here I had my first lessons in conservation
and learned that it is indeed an ill wind that does
no good.   Here nature hoards her savings in
snowbanks.   To these savings she adds constantly
throughout the winter.   Long I sat upon a prom-

ontory and marveled. Dimly, only, did I grasp
the significance of what lay before me! The
ranks of primeval forest waiting to aid civilization; snow, that white magic eventually destined
to water crops on the distant plains; and, above
all, woods, the final refuge of the big game; the
sanctuary of the birds.

Everywhere were scattered unnamed lakes.
These edged out and around the rock penin-
sulas, folded back into dark coves and swung
out of sight behind the timbered bends. Some
were almost pinched in half by the crowding
cliffs till they formed giant hour-glasses; again
they bulged and overflowed like streams at high
water. I began to name them according to their
shape. "Hourglass," of course; the one that
bulged out at one end was surely a plump "Pear"
—yes, and "Dog-with-three-legs"! My imagination was recovering.

For miles I followed the strange, fantastic
timberline. Occasionally I found stunted little
trees scarcely knee high, peeping through the
crushing weight of snow that had smothered
them, even throughout the summer. I cut several trees to count the rings of growth. I found
trees growing close together and about the same
size, with centuries of variation in age. One,
that had been broken off by a rock slide, had two
hundred and ninety-six annual rings. It had
grown in a sheltered nook. Ten yards away an-

other, much smaller, but growing upon an exposed, rocky point, was no higher than my head, yet I counted five hundred and seven rings; for half a thousand years it had stood at its post. I found the counting of these annual rings extremely difficult, as they were so dense that it was hard to distinguish them and they averaged from fifty to a hundred rings to an inch of thickness, but the small magnifying glass I carried made it possible.

The most striking thing I discovered about the timberline trees was their irregularity. There was no similarity of form, as prevails among trees of the deep forest. Each tree took on a physical appearance according to its location and its opportunities. One resemblance only did they have in common: none had limbs on the west side. All their leafy banners pointed toward the rising sun. Thus I learned the direction of the prevailing winter winds. The west side of the trees were polished smooth, many cut halfway through. Trees that had reached maturity, or had died, were stripped almost bare of limbs, which had been cut away by the constant scouring.

There were abundant tracks of deer, and some of elk, but I saw not a single animal. Near the spot from which had risen the terrifying sounds of that first night, a deep-worn game trail led down into the heavy forests. Sharp hoofs had cut into it recently, yet neither hide nor hair of an animal did I glimpse. There were no traces of beaver nor any coyote tracks. There were bear tracks, but the small traps I had brought would not hold bear, so I did not set them. I was running low on provisions, for I had counted on the game for meat: I had meant to have venison steak as soon as I had got settled in my permanent camp.

Here was mystery! My curiosity was challenged; I determined to fathom it!

How I studied those tracks! Those of the sheep could be distinguished by the rounded toe marks of their hoofs, worn blunt by the granite rocks they lived on. This was especially true of the forefeet. They were also wide apart, while the deer tracks were sharply pointed, with the hoofs close together. Days passed and the tracks in the trails grew dim, but not before I had read their story. I followed the sheep's up above timberline—they grew plainer and more numerous. So that was it! The sheep climbed where the wind would keep their tables, spread with sweet cured grass, swept free of snow, and had placed the barrier of timberline drifts between them and their enemies!

The other tracks all led down to the valleys. There in the foothills winter would be less rigorous, and the grass would not be buried for months beneath the snow. Winter was at hand in the high country and all but the Bighorn had deserted it. What with them above me, and the rest below, I found myself in a no-game zone.

There was no repetition of the frightful sound that had sent me scurrying for camp. I suspected a bull elk had made it, though I recognized no resemblance between that hair-raising sound and a bugle.

My thoughts turned to other game. I must have meat—how about a bear? If I couldn't trap one, perhaps I could shoot one. I got out my battered old rifle, so like the timberline trees, and boldly set out for "b'ar." In and out of the dense forest I blundered; crashed through the tangle at timberline; toiled up the rocky ridges. Up and up I climbed, paying no heed to the direction of the wind. I found bear tracks, both large and small, but no sight of Bruin himself.

Discouraged, I lay down to rest and had a nap in the sun. Later, with the wind in my face, I peeped over a rocky upthrust near a large snow-bank. My eyes bulged, my mouth opened. There was a bear just ahead. Surely it was mad—crazy—for no animal in its right mind would do what it was doing.

First it would lumber along a few feet from the edge of the snow, stopping, sniffing, striking out suddenly with its forepaws; it repeated this performance again and again. I watched, hypnotized, unaware of the gun gripped tightly in my hands. Anyhow, who'd want to eat a mad bear?

A slight sound caused me to turn my head. Twenty feet away another bear stood regarding me curiously.

Not being absent-minded, I have never been able to understand why I left my rifle on the mountainside after lugging it up there for an avowed purpose. At any rate I made record time back to camp, glancing rearward frequently, to see if the "flock" of bears was pursuing me.

The next day, after surveying the mountainside to make sure that no bears were lurking there, I went back up and recovered the rifle. The sand beneath the shelving rock where I had seen the second bear was disturbed. Claws had rasped it sharply. It appeared as though this bear had been startled suddenly; had wheeled about and fled for its life in the opposite direction to that I had taken. The tracks were small, too, apparently those of a cub. This was my first bear experience. I had yet to learn that bear are as harmless as deer or mountain sheep; they attend strictly to their own business, and they never come near man except through accident. At that time, though, I was willing to give all bears the benefit of the doubt—and the right of way.

While further exploring the ridge above the camp I came upon an old abandoned tunnel with its dump concealed among the trees below timberline. The entrance to the tunnel had been timbered to prevent its caving. There was nothing in its appearance to tell how long it had been abandoned. Beside the dump was a small selected pile of ore. This I gloated over happily, mistaking mingled stains and colors for pure gold. But if it was a gold mine, why had the owners departed—and why had they left rich ore? These and other questions unanswered, left me with an uneasy feeling. I wondered if a tragedy had happened here, so many miles from civilization. With a torch of small twigs I ventured into the dark hole running straight back beneath the cliff. A short distance inside the tunnel I stopped uneasily. The silence was intense. The twig torch fluttered faintly and went out. The darkness was black beyond belief. Without delay I felt my way out into the sunshine, leaving further exploration for another day.

For weeks I roamed the forest, circled the scattered lakes, climbed to the jagged tops of high-flung peaks; and daily, almost, had new and strange experiences. Everything was intensely interesting, and all was fairyland. Many times I was torn between timidity and curiosity. Though I often carried the huge old rifle with deadly intent, I failed to bring down any big game. Invariably when I had a good chance, my gun would be at camp.

Before breakfast one morning I made an excursion to a promontory to watch the sunrise. Deep down in the cañons below, darkness still lingered. Slowly the world emerged from the shadows like a photographic plate developing and disclosing its images in the darkroom. Beyond the promontory a great spire lifted high above the cañon; I climbed to its top. Above the spire was a higher crag. Again I climbed up. Up and up I climbed until almost noon. Each new vantage point revealed new glory; every successive outpost lured me on.

At last the long ridge I followed shouldered against a sheer-topped peak of the Continental Divide. It was mid-afternoon and hunger urged me homeward. The way I had come was long and circuitous. There was a short cut back to camp, but this threatened difficulty, for there was a deep cañon to be crossed; and even though I reached its bottom there seemed to be no possible way up the precipitous farther wall.

I did, however, make the homeward side of the cañon very late. The clouds had shut down over the peaks, leveling their tops to timberline. All day I had carried the heavy camera with a supply of glass plates. Besides I carried my six-shooter, with belt and cartridges, buckled around my waist. Several times I saw grouse and fired at them, but not once did I get a close-up shot.

As I toiled upward to cross the ridge that overlooked camp, I entered the lower cloud stratum. The air was biting cold. It was impossible to see more than a few feet ahead. I regretted that I had brought no food. Snow began to fall; and the higher I plodded the thicker it fell. Darkness came rapidly; footing became precarious. The snow plastered the rocks; the light was ghostly and unreal. I began to stumble; I slipped and slid, lost my balance, and fell.

Then, as the snow deepened and the darkness increased, I realized that to attempt the descent of the slope above camp would be folly, for it was as steep as a house roof, and covered with loose bowlders. Besides it had many abrupt cliffs fifty to a hundred feet high. There was only one thing to do—camp here, for the night. But I was on an exposed shoulder of the mountain, above timberline, and it would be impossible to live through the night without shelter and fire.

I headed downhill without regard for direction. I was becoming numb, but in half an hour I safely reached the dwarf trees at timberline and plunged through them to a dense grove of spruce. Occasionally there was a dead tree, and nearly all trees had dead limbs low down. With such limbs or small trunks as I could find I constructed a rude lean-to, with closed ends. With my pocket knife I cut green boughs, covered the lean-to and plastered the boughs with a coating of wet snow. The green branches, together with the snow that was streaming down like a water-fall, soon rendered the shelter windproof.

With a glowing fire in front to light my way, I ranged in ever-widening circles for fuel to last through the long night ahead. Within an hour I had collected a fair-sized pile of wood, but I thought I'd better have even more. My quest took me farther among the trees. Of a sudden there came a whirr of wings that made me jump and drop my load, as a number of grouse flew in all directions, their booming wings fairly exploding with energy.

One of the grouse alighted in a tree overhead and I snatched out the six-shooter, aimed carefully and fired. It was a new experience for the grouse; it stretched its head out, and, twisting sidewise, stared down at me curiously. Once more I fired. The interest of the grouse increased. Again and again I fired, pausing confidently after each shot for the bird to tumble down. Three times I emptied the cylinder without a hit. Then in disgust I shoved the gun back into its holster and fumbled in the snow for a stone. The first throw was close, the second hit its mark, and the bird came fluttering down.

The clouds dropped lower, enveloping my camp. The night was inky black. I lay beneath my lean-to, watching the fire before which the plump grouse was slowly turning round and round as it roasted. The turning was accomplished by hooking a green twig into its neck and tying the other end of the twig with a string that wound and unwound as the bird alternated directions. I unloaded one of the revolver cartridges and used the salty powder for seasoning my feast. I saved some ammunition after all!

It was noon next day before I reached camp. Then the storm shut down again. Snow began to accumulate. In the woods it lay knee deep, while the high ridges above the timberline were swept bare by the howling wind.

Quite unexpectedly, in the dead of night, I had a visitor. He was uninvited, but was determined to make himself at home. Awakened by the rattle of tin, I sat up, listened and waited. I struck a match and caught a glimpse of a huge mountain rat disappearing in the darkness. I had scarcely fallen asleep again before he returned, and when I struck a light he stared at me with villainous, beady eyes. By the uncertain light of a match I took aim with the faithless six-shooter and fired. When I sprang up, expecting to find the mangled remains of the intruder, I discovered a gaping hole in my only frying pan.

After an hour the pest came again, satisfied, no doubt, that my marksmanship was not dangerous. This time I was prepared for his coming. I had a lighted pine torch to see to aim by. I tried another shot. The rat kept moving while in the open and only stopped when behind shelter, peeping out with one eye. At last he left the tent, and I followed him into the woods. Beneath the overhang of the cliff he stopped, his piercing eyes flashing in the darkness as I advanced with the torch. Patiently he waited beneath a leaning tree trunk. Ten feet from him I knelt upon the velvet needles of the forest, and with torch held aloft, steadied the six-shooter, aimed carefully, and fired.

At the shot the rat disappeared. I pressed forward confident that at last I had scored a hit. The torch had gone out. I was feeling among the dead needles for the rat's mangled body when my fingers touched something wooden. Instantly the pest was forgotten. By the light of a match I saw that I had uncovered the corner of a little box. It flashed upon me that I had stumbled upon the cache where the old prospectors had hidden their gold. They were gone; the gold was mine!

I tugged and tugged till I dragged it from its concealment beneath the rotting log. In trembling haste I tore off its cover. Then . . .

I staggered back with a cry of dismay! The box was filled with old, crystallized dynamite. An inch above the top layer of the deadly stuff was a fresh hole where my bullet had crashed through. A little lower and it would have hit the powder crystals!

The next morning snow lay deep about the tent. It was impossible to make my way through the woods. I was marooned far from civilization. The wind rose; crashing among the peaks, tearing along the ridges, roaring through the passes. Blinding clouds came sifting down from the wind-swept heights.

After days of patient waiting, I started the laborious climb upward, for it was impossible to make progress downward, where the soft snow lay. Now, like the sheep, I would take advantage of those wind-swept stretches above timberline.

Before dawn I was on my way. It required three hours to gain the first mile. Then, as I reached the cleared stretches, progress became easier. Though the wind came in angry squalls, that sometimes flung me headlong, and buffeted and drove me about, the going underfoot was good.

If I could keep my bearings and head northward, steer out around the heads of countless cañons, hold my given altitude above timberline, I would eventually reach a spot some miles above the valley where the home ranch lay. All day I plodded. The wind did not abate, but came in a gale from the west. At times it dropped to perhaps fifty miles an hour, and again it rose to more than a hundred miles; it shrieked, pounded at the cliffs, tore the battered timberline trees to bits, caught up frozen snow crust and crashed it among the trees like ripping shot. At such times I was forced to turn my back, or to feel my way blindly, head down. I moved with utmost caution lest I walk over a cliff.

The time came when I had to abandon the wind-swept heights and flounder through the soft snow of the cañons. Through narrow passes I had to crawl, so terrific was the wind that poured through the channel like a waterfall. Nothing short of a Kansas cyclone can match the velocity of a mountain-top gale. All day I stemmed its tide, which sapped my strength, bowled me over and cut my face.

As early darkness came on I reached a familiar cañon that dropped down toward the valley where the ranch lay hidden. Drunkenly I staggered homeward, too exhausted to care what happened. The last three miles required three hours of heroic work. I became extremely weary and wanted nothing so much as to sink down in the snow and go to sleep; but I knew what that would mean, so I kept slapping and beating myself to keep awake. In the end I reached the ranch, pounded upon the door and, when it was opened, pitched headlong across its threshold.

The Parson gazed down at me from his six feet of height.

"Well," he said at length, "guess you found a pretty big world."

CHAPTER FOUR

DANCING ACROSS THE DIVIDE

SO new was the life, so fascinating the animals and elements of the primitive world, so miraculous was it that my lifelong dreams were come true, that I never thought of home-sickness, nor missed the comrades left behind me, although the Parson and his quiet wife were rather elderly companions for a youngster. There were, too, the diversions of going for the mail, either horseback or in the old spring wagon behind the steady, little mountain ponies, the swapping of yarns while waiting for the generally belated stage to dash up, its four horses prancing, and steaming, no matter how cold the weather, from the precipitous ups and downs of the mountain roads they had traveled. The return journey in the dusk or by moonlight was never without incident: porcupine, deer, bear, Bighorn, mountain lion—some kind of game invariably crossed my trail.

And, as was true in all pioneer regions, the community abounded in interesting personalities. During the first half of the nineteenth century, the fame and fairness of the country had reached the centers of Eastern culture, and had lured the ambitious and the adventurous to try their skill in hunting and trapping and fishing in this Paradise, roamed over by big game, crossed by sparkling streams, alive with trout. Kit Carson was the first white man to look down upon its beautiful valleys. Others soon followed: Joel Estes, for whom the Park was eventually named; "Rocky Mountain Jim," a two-gun man, living alone with his dogs, looking like a bearded, unkempt pirate, taciturn, yet not without charm, as later events proved, unmolesting and unmolested, enveloped in a haze of respected mystery. There was also that noted lady globe-trotter, Miss Isabella Bird, an Englishwoman of undoubted refinement, highly educated—whose volume, "A Lady's Life in the Rocky Mountains," is one of the earliest and most picturesque accounts of that time—upon whom "Rocky Mountain Jim" exerted his blandishments. Some sort of romance existed between them, how serious no one knows, for the tragic shooting of Jim, by an irate pioneer father, cut short its development.

In the early sixties, an English nobleman and sportsman, the Earl of Dunraven, attracted by the wealth of game in the region, attempted to make it into a private hunting park or preserve. He took up all the acreage which he could legit-

imately acquire in his own name, then took up
fraudulent claims in the names of his tenants.
But the hardy pioneers, who were coming into
the country in ever-increasing numbers, rightly
doubting the validity of his own ownership of so
many thousands of acres, homesteaded land to
their liking and built their log cabins upon it.
Lord Dunraven tried to scare them off, but they
would not be bluffed, and in the contest which
followed, he lost out and departed from the
region. Although his coming to the Park contributed much to its romantic history, in his
"Memoirs"—two thick, heavy volumes, published a few years ago—he devotes only half a
page to his Estes Park experiences. Whether
this is because he considered them negligible or
unworthy, would be interesting to know.

The old Dunraven Lodge was the first hostelry
in the region, and about the great fireplace in
its spacious, trophy-hung lobby gathered many
of the political and artistic celebrities of that day.
The fame of the mountain beauty spot spread
—visitors came. The settlers added "spare
rooms" to their log cabins, and during the summer and early fall "took in boarders," thus
helping to eke out their living expenses and, what
was even more far-reaching perhaps, the outer
world was thus "fetched in" to them: they heard
of railroads annihilating the long oxen-traversed
distances of covered wagon days, of new gold

strikes, of national politics, rumblings of the
Civil War, slavery agitation, presidential elec-
tions, and those other momentous, history-mak-
ing events of their time.

The most important and regular social occasion of that day was the community dinner and
"literary." Imagine the picturesque company,
congregated from miles around, each contribut-
ing whatever he could muster of food and drink
—the old Earl of Dunraven, as well as others,
had a bar!—and seated at a long, single table.
What genuine, home-made fun! What pranks,
what wit—yes, what brilliance! Some one, usually Parson Lamb, sometimes gaunt old Scotch
John Cleave, the postmaster, rarely some noted
visitor, who either from choice or ill-health lingered on into the winter, made a speech. There
were declamations, debates, the interminable,
singsong ballads of the frontier, usually accompanied by French harp or fiddle. Families were
few, bachelors much in the majority; I remember that at one of the community affairs there
were eighteen bachelors out of a total attendance
of thirty persons! But as the region settled up,
the bachelor ranks dwindled. They, like the big
game, disappeared, as though in their case "open
season" prevailed likewise.

I had attended several of these pioneer festivities and had enjoyed them greatly, and was
much impressed with their importance, for under-

lying all the fun was an old-fashioned dignity
seldom found nowadays.   But Parson Lamb
told me these dinners were tame compared to a
real mountain dance.   "Just you wait till you
see a real shindig" he said.   "Then you'll have
something to talk about."   In January, there
was a letter in the mail from Jim Oss, my acquaintance of the train on which I came West.
We had been carrying on a desultory correspondence, but this message was momentous.

"I am giving a dance Monday," he wrote, "to
celebrate proving up on my homestead.   Come
ahead of time so you can see all the fun."   His
hundred and sixty acres lay on the western slope
of the Continental Divide—fifty-five miles away.
Snow lay deep over every one of those intervening, upstanding miles!   The Parson was concerned about my going alone.

"'Tain't safe to cross that old range alone any
time of year, let alone the dead of winter.   Hain't
no one else agoing from here?"

I inquired, but it seemed there was not.
Secretly I was well pleased to have it so.   I was
young enough to thrill at the chance of so
hazardous an experience.

Parson Lamb agreed that Friday morning
would be a good time to start.   We were not
superstitious, and it wasn't the thirteenth.   The
trip had to be made on snowshoes, with which
I was not very adept, but that only added to its

attractions. In order to cross the Divide, it was necessary to descend from my lofty nine thousand feet elevation to seven thousand five hundred, before starting to climb Flattop trail, which led over to Grand Lake, the last settlement before reaching Oss's place. By sundown I reached a deserted sawmill shack, the last shelter between me and Grand Lake. It was six miles below the top of the Divide, and twenty miles to the Lake. There I spent the night and at dawn was trailing upward, in the teeth of a sixty-mile gale!

The first two of those uprising six miles were fair going, and took only a little more than an hour. Thereafter the trail grew more precipitous. The third mile required one hour, and the fourth, two hours of exhausting work. The sun rose, but not the temperature; powdery snow swirled around the heads of the peaks; clouds swept above the ridges, flayed and torn; from above timberline came the roar of the wind.

Dark glasses protected my eyes from snow and wind; and I was warmly dressed. I left my bedding roll at the sawmill, to be picked up on the return trip, for shelter could be had at Grand Lake. The light pack I carried contained peanuts, chocolate, and a change of socks.

The higher I climbed the wilder became the wind. From timberline I surveyed the prospect ahead and hesitated. Clouds and snow whirled up in a solid mass, blinding and choking me. The cold penetrated my heavy clothing. I went on. In a few minutes I was in the midst of the turmoil, utterly lost, buffeted about. I tried to keep the wind in my face for compass, but it was so variable, eddying from all directions, that it was not reassuring. Near the top of the mountain a blast knocked me down, and half smothered me with flying snow. I arose groggily, uncertain which way to head; it was impossible to see even a step in front. The staff I carried served me well, with it I went tapping and feeling my way like a blind man. There I was on the top of the world, thirteen thousand feet above sea level—and overlooking nothing.

Flattop mountain is shaped like a loaf of bread, sloping off steeply at the ends, its sides guarded by sheer cliffs. It was these cliffs I feared and strove to avoid. I had heard startling tales of the effects of high altitude on one; how the atmosphere was very rare and light. Had it been any heavier that day, I could not have survived. Violent blasts of wind frequently bowled me over. After one of these falls, I arose uncertainly, drifted with the wind for a moment's respite, neglected to feel ahead with my staff—and walked out upon a snow cornice that overhung the top of the cliff. The cornice broke away! Amidst an explosion of snow I plunged downward, struggling frantically as I went!

I landed in a snowdrift featherbed which, while it broke my fall, almost buried me alive. The wind reached me only in occasional gusts, so I realized that I must be sheltered by the cliff wall. In the first brief lull I took my bearings. I had landed upon a narrow ledge a few feet wide. Below me yawned the gorge. It was a terrible half hour's work with a snowshoe as a shovel to extricate myself, but a few minutes later I was once more on top.

Again I struggled upward. I reached the pass and started down the western slope toward timber. My fingers and toes were frosted, I was numb with cold, and so battered by the gale I could only pant. My careful calculations had come to naught, as I was far behind the schedule I had planned. I decided to make up time by abandoning the trail and taking a shortcut to timber and shelter through an unknown cañon which I thought led to Grand Lake.

But the cañon was hard going. Thick, young evergreens, entangling willows and fallen logs impeded every step. I could make no headway and darkness was coming on. Disgusted, despairing, I took to the frozen stream, only to skid over icy bowlders and at last to break through the ice crust into the frigid water.

Long after dark I staggered down the single

I Plunged Downward, Struggling Frantically.

street of Grand Lake toward a dim patch of
light. It proved to be the window of a store.
Within was a glowing stove, surrounded by a
group of men.

The proprietor eyed me with suspicion.
"Where'd you drop from?"

I waved vaguely toward the Continental Divide.

"Must 'a' bin something urgent to make you
tackle the Flattop trail in winter."

He awaited my explanations curiously—but
I had slumped down near the stove and was
half asleep.

Next morning I looked back up the way I
had come—low clouds, tattered to shreds. Even
at that distance I could hear the roar of the wind
among the loft crags. I was thankful that I
had crossed the Divide the day before. It was
still thirty miles to the cabin of my friend, but
they were fairly easy miles compared with those
I had just traversed. Even so, so spent was
my strength, it was pitch dark when I dragged
wearily up the broken road to where that cabin
nestled in its grove of spruces.

The dance was not until Monday night, so I
took it for granted that I should be the first to
arrive, since I was a full day ahead of the func-
tion. But no! Many were already there!
They were eating supper and made room for
me at the long table before the open fire. They

were cordial and made me feel at home at once, marveling over my making the trip alone, and praising my pluck. I was much too weary and hungry to protest, even though I had been becomingly modest. Seeing this, they filled my plate and let me be, turning their nimble tongues on our host—What handsome whiskers—la! la! He'd better be careful with those hirsute adornments and a cabin with a plank floor! He couldn't hope to remain a bachelor long! So the banter ran.

Supper over and the dishes cleared away, the candles were snuffed out and the company (visitors were never called guests) sat around the flickering hearth and speculated over the possible coming of the Moffat railroad. What an assorted company it was! Young and grizzled —trappers, miners, invalids seeking health, adventurers, speculators, a few half-breeds; all men of little education, but of fascinating experience; a few women of quiet poise and resourcefulness. Their clothes were nondescript and betrayed the fact that they had come from the East, having been sent west by condoning relatives, no doubt after having lived in more fashionable circles. There were two little children who fell asleep early in the evening in their parents' arms.

The company was put to bed in Oss's one-room

house by the simple means of lying down upon the floor fully dressed, feet to the fire.

All were up early next morning, and each found some task to do. Some of the men cut wood and piled it outside the door; the women folks assisted Oss with breakfast which was cooked in the fireplace; for he had not yet reached the luxury of a cook stove, which would have to be "fetched in" over sixty miles of mountain roads and would cost a tidy sum besides.

Some artistic soul, with a memory of urban ways, made long ropes of evergreens and hung them in garlands from the rafters, a flag was draped above the fireplace, lanterns were hung ready to light.

Distant "neighbors" kept flocking in all day, each bringing a neighborly offering; fresh pork from the owner of an only shoat; choice venison steaks; bear meat from a hunter who explained that the bear had been killed months before and kept frozen in the meat house. Wild raspberry jam, with finer flavor than any I have ever tasted before or since, was brought by a bachelor who vied with the women folks when it came to cookery. The prize offering, however, were some mountain trout, speared through the ice of a frozen stream.

Dancing began early. The music was supplied by an old-time fiddler who jerked squeaky tunes from an ancient violin, singing and shouting the dance calls by turns. Voice, fiddle and feet, beating lusty time to his tunes, went incessantly. He had an endless repertoire, and a talent for fitting the names of the dancers to his ringing rimes.

Some of his offerings were:

> "Lady round lady and gents so low!
> First couple lead to right—
> Lady round lady and gents so low—
> Lady round gent and gent don't go—
> Four hands half and right and left."

The encores he would improvise:

> "Hit the lumber with your leather—
> Balance all, an' swing ter left."

All swayed rhythmically, beating time with their feet, clapping their hands, bowing, laughing. The men threw in their fancy steps, their choice parlor tricks. A few performed a double shuffle; one a pigeon's wing; a couple of trappers did an Indian dance, twisting their bodies into grotesque contortions and every so often letting out a yell that made one's hair stand cn end.

There was little rest between the dances, for the old fiddler had marvelous powers of endurance. He sawed away, perspired, shouted and

I SAT DOWN BY THE FIDDLER AND DOZED.

sang as though his life depended on his performance. He was having as good, or better time,
than anyone. With scarcely a moment to
breathe he'd launch into another call—and not
once the whole night through did he repeat:

"Ole Buffler Bill—Buffler Bill!
Never missed an' never will."

Then as the dancers promenaded he'd switch
to a new improvisation, ending in a whirlwind
of wit and telling personalities, which sent the
company into hysterical laughter. I joined in
the dance, rather gawkily no doubt, for my
mother's father was a Quaker preacher and we
had never been allowed to dance at home. The
ladies regarded my clumsiness with motherly
forbearance, and self-sacrificingly tried to direct
my wayward feet. But either because I was not
recovered from my trip or because the strange-
ness and confusion wearied me, I could not get
the hang of the steps. Presently an understand-
ing matron let me slip out of the dance, and I
sat down by the fiddler and dozed. Clanking
spurs, brilliant chaps, fur-trimmed trappers'
jackets, thudding moccasins, gaudy Indian blankets and gay feathers, voluminous feminine
flounces swinging from demure, snug-fitting
basques—all whirled above me in a kaleidoscopic
blur!

A wild war whoop awakened me—nothing but a little harmless hilarity! It was two o'clock in the morning. I wished the dance would end so I could sleep undisturbed. I envied the two children asleep on the floor. But the dance went on. The fiddle whined, its player shouted, heavy shoes clumped tirelessly on the plank floor. There was still energetic swing and dash to the quadrilles, still gay voices were raised in joyous shouts. Those hearty pioneers were full of "wim, wigor and witality"!

Dawn broke redly over the Divide; still the dance continued. Daylight sifted over the white world, and yet the dancers did not pause. At last as the sun came up, the old fiddler reluctantly stood on his chair and played "Home Sweet Home."

All-night dances were at that time the custom of the mountain folk; the company assembled as far ahead of time as was convenient, and remained, sometimes, a day or two after the close of the festivities. There was no doubt as to one's welcome and there was no limit to the length of his stay. Isolation made opportunities for such social intercourse rare and therefore everyone got more "kick" out of these occasions than is possible in our swiftly moving, blasé age.

Weather conditions changed while we danced: the wind eased off and the mountain tops emerged from the clouds and drifting snow. I trailed up the cañon I had struggled through in the darkness; and except for the final stretch of the steep mountain above timberline the snow-shoeing was nothing except plain hard work. In some places the wind had packed the snow hard; again it was soft so that I sank knee deep at every step. In the soft snow, where there was a steep slope to negotiate, each snowshoe had to be lifted high, until my knee almost touched my chest. The webs accumulated snow, too, until each shoe weighed many additional pounds.

But the fairyland that I found on top of the Divide was worth all the effort required to reach it. It was the first time I had found the wind quiet; every peak stood out sharp and clear, many miles away seemed but a few minutes' walk. There were none of the usual objects that help estimate distance; no horses or cattle, no trees or trails, nothing but unbroken space. The glare of the sun was blinding; even my very dark snow glasses failed to protect my eyes.

The silence was tremendous. Always before there had been the wind shrieking and crashing. Now there was not a sound, not a breath of wind, not even a snow-swirl. I shouted, and my voice came back across the cañon without the usual blurring; each word was distinct. I whistled softly and other echoes came hurrying back. Never have I felt so alone, or so small.

As far as the eye could reach were mountains, one beyond the other. Near by loomed the jagged Never-summer range, while farther down the Divide Gray's and Torry's peaks stood out; then the Collegiate range—Harvard, Yale and Princeton.

In the midst of my reverie there came a creaking, groaning sound from almost beneath my feet. I had paused on the brink of the same precipice over which I had fallen on my way to Grand Lake. Before I could move, the snow-cornice broke away and several hundred feet of it crashed down the cliff. In places it appeared to be ten to forty feet thick. It must have weighed thousands of tons. It fell with a swishing roar, with occasional sharp reports, as loose rocks dropped to the clean-swept ledges of the cliff. It seemed to explode as it struck, to fly into powder which filled the gorge between Flat top and Hallett peaks.

The wind had drifted the snow over the edge of the precipice where some of it had clung. Farther and farther it had crept out, overhanging the abyss, its great weight slowly bending the cornice downward until it had at last given way.

I shuddered a little at the awfulness of it; felt smaller than ever, backed away from the rim of the cañon, and headed for home.

CHAPTER FIVE

GOLD and fur have ever been beckoning sirens, luring men into the unknown.
As I have said, the famous trapper, Kit Carson, was the first white man to look down upon the picturesque, mountain-guarded valley, later known as Estes Park. From the foothills, he had followed up one of the streams, seeking new fur-fields, until, after crossing the last barrier range, he looked down upon a broad, river spangled park set like a gem in the midst of the encricling peaks of the Divide, with that sheer, pyramidal face of Long's Peak dominating all.

We like to think that these early adventurers appreciated the beauty of the primitive lands they explored, but whether or not Carson thrilled at that exquisite alpine panorama, he noted keenly the profusion of tracks criss-crossing its green and white expanse, promising an abundance of game, for he moved down into the region and at the foot of Long's Peak built himself a rude log cabin. There he spent the winter trapping beaver, and the following spring bargained

with the Indians to help pack out his catch. The
walls, the hearth, and part of the stone chimney
still mark the site of that first cabin.

I selected the top of a high cliff overlooking
these storied ruins for the location of a cabin
which I planned to build as soon as I could
manage it. I, too, would be a trapper, and
though the beaver and other fur-bearing animals
were not nearly so numerous as they had been
that day, sixty years gone, when Carson first
beheld their mountain fastness, there still remained enough to make trapping interesting and
profitable. Game tracks still abounded, and not-
withstanding that I was a mere boy, inexperienced in woodcraft, I could distinguish that they
differed, even though I could classify only
a few of them: coyote tracks, I found, were
very like a dog's; sheep, elk and deer tracks were
similar, yet easily distinguished from one another; bear left a print like that of a baby's
chubby foot. Yes, there was still a chance for
me!

As soon as I returned from the dance at Jim
Oss's, I set about carrying out my plans. I
mushed over deep snow back into Wild Basin, to
recover the six traps I had abandoned there on
that memorable first camp alone, and found my
tent crushed under six feet of drifted snow and
the region still deserted by game. I set the
traps out in the vicinity of the home ranch.

Every few days I inspected them, only to find them empty. Indeed, over a period of long weeks I caught but one mink, two weasels and three coyotes. The Parson kindly said the country was trapped out; still, I suspected my lack of skill was responsible for my scanty catch.

One morning in following up my trap line, I found a trap missing. In the sand about the aspen tree to which it had been anchored were coyote tracks. Ignorantly fearless, I set out to track down the miscreant. The trail led down toward a forest, where dense thickets of new-growth lodge-pole pines livened the stark, fire-killed trees. As I neared the forest, the tracks were farther apart and dimmer, but here and there were scratches on fallen logs as though a trap had been dragged across them; moreover, there were occasional spots where the earth was greatly disturbed, showing that the animal had no doubt threshed about in his efforts to dislodge the trap, caught on the snags or bowlders.

No denying I thrilled from head to foot over the prospect of meeting Mr. Coyote face to face! If he showed fight I'd snatch my six-shooter from its holster (forgotten was its faithless perform-ance in Wild Basin!) and show him I was not to be trifled with. Of course, I'd aim to hit him where the shot would do least damage to his fur; it would be more valuable for marketing.

Just then I heard the clank of the trap chain.

Heart pounding, hands trembling, I shakily drew my gun, and cautiously advanced. Around the corner of a bowlder I came upon a large coyote, with a black stripe running along his back, squatting in an old game trail, apparently little concerned either at my presence or at his own dilemma. As I stumbled toward him, he faced about, and without taking his eyes off me, kept jerking the trap which was wedged between a root and a bowlder. Twenty feet away I stopped, and with what coolness I could command in my excitement, took aim and fired. The bullet only ruffled the heavy fur at his shoulder. Determined to finish him next shot, I edged nearer. My target refused to stand still—he sprang the full length of his chain again and again, striving to dislodge the trap. Finally it jerked free and he was off like a rabbit, despite his dragging burden, leaping logs or scuttling beneath them, zigzagging along the crooked trail, dodging bowlders, tree limbs and my frequent but ineffective fire. For I madly pursued him though hard put to keep up his pace.

Suddenly the trap caught again and jerked its victim to an abrupt stop. He whirled about and faced me defiantly, eyes blazing, fangs bared. I reloaded my revolver, aimed—fired, aimed—fired again and again, until the cylinder was empty, without once hitting him.

I began to think that, like old Tom, he led a

charmed life. Just then he jerked loose, and once more the chase was on. I reloaded my six-shooter and fired on the run, shouting excitedly. He ran on with tireless, automatic motion, apparently as unperturbed as he was impervious to bullets.

All at once I discovered my belt empty—I had exausted my cartridges! Disgusted, I shoved my gun back into its holster, and, picking up a stout club, ran after the coyote. Several times I was close enough to hit him, but he deftly dodged or else sprang forward beyond reach. Once when the trap caught and prisoned him an instant, I swung my club, sure of ending the race, but it collided on a limb overhead and went wide of the mark! Again I overtook the coyote as he struggled through hindering bush, and, reaching forward, swung my bludgeon with all my might and fell headlong upon him! I gave a terrified yell; my battered hat flew off; I dropped my club. The coyote was out of sight before I gained my feet!

Suddenly we popped out of the forest on the edge of a cañon; its sides were smooth and almost bare. On this open ground, my quarry gained on me by leaps and bounds. I spied a rock-slide below—great slabs that had slid down from the cliff above—between openings amply large to admit almost any animal. Once the coyote reached that slide, he would escape. Panting loudly, I sprinted forward to overtake him.

The trap chain wedged unexpectedly, the coyote changed ends, and came up facing me. I could not put on brakes quickly enough and skidded almost into him. He sprang at my throat. As he launched upward I glimpsed his flaming eyes and wide-open, fang-filled mouth. I do not know what saved me; whether my desperate effort to reverse succeeded, whether I dodged, or whether the restraining trap chain thwarted him. As it was, his teeth grazed my face, leaving deep, red scars across my chin. . . . His was the handsomest skin that adorned the walls of my cabin when that dream eventually became a reality. I did not sell the skin as purposed—not, however, because my bullets had ruined it for marketing!

In common with all small boys, I was the hero of my dreams, and in my fancy saw myself growing into a magnified composite of Nimrod, Robin Hood, Kit Carson, and Buffalo Bill, all molded into one mighty man who dwarfed the original individuals! I confess reality was retarding my growth considerably. It looked as though Kit Carson would go unrivaled by me as a trapper; certainly the shades of Nimrod and Robin Hood had no cause to be uneasy lest I win their laurels from them, and as for Buffalo Bill —both the Buffalo and the redskins, whose scalps had always dangled in fancy from my belt in

I Glimpsed His Flaming Eyes and Wide-open, Fang-
filled Mouth.

revenge for their plaguing my mother on her brave drive with my sick father across those long unsettled miles, were far beyond my puny vengeance.

The Parson told me that the Utes, a nomadic tribe, had once roamed the mountains and valleys around Estes, but that it was not generally believed that they had permanent settlements here. It was thought they made temporary or seasonal camp when hunting or fishing was at its height, and that they used the alpine valley as a vast council chamber when they met to discuss intertribal matters. Certain it is, I puzzled over curious, dim, ghostly circles, or rings, in the valleys, where neither grass nor any other vegetation had gained root even after all these years. The old-timers told me these had been made by the Indians banking dirt around their lodges. A few scattered tepee frames still stood, here and there, in sheltered groves along the river. Occasionally I picked up arrowheads—once upon a high-flung ledge I came upon a score or more. How my imagination soared! Here, no doubt, an Indian had stood, in eagle-feathered war bonnet and full regalia, guarding this pass; he had been wounded sore unto death, he fell! His bones, and all his trappings, the wooden shaft of his arrows, had disintegrated and disappeared. Only these bits of flint enmeshed in the clinging tendrils of Indian tobacco, or kinnikinic, were left to tell the tale of his heroism.

Of course, I didn't give up hunting or trapping or even my hope of finding a gold mine, altogether. I continued to exercise my six-shooter, though repeated failures to find my mark made it easy for me to depend more and more on my camera for "shots." I still inspected my trapline, with mental resolutions against trailing trap-maddened coyotes.

My trip over the Divide gave me a keener appreciation of winter upon the heights. When, from the window of our snug log cabin, I looked up toward Long's Peak, and saw the clouds of snow dust swirling about its head, I pictured just what was happening up there far more accurately than I could ever have done before I had that experience. I made frequent trips above timberline, sometimes to find arctic gales that filled the air with icy pellets which penetrated like shot, cutting my face; gales that drove the cold through the thickest, heaviest clothes I could put on; gales that blew the snow about until it enveloped me in a cloud-like veil, making vision impossible. On such days, retreat was the only possible, if not valorous, course. To have remained would have been foolhardy, for blinded and buffeted by the storm, I might easily have stepped off a precipice with less fortunate consquences than had attended my experience on my journey over the Divide.

But sometimes, the conditions on the heights were astonishing. Once I left our valley chill and gloomy, all shut in by lowering clouds, and climbed up toward the hidden summits of the peaks, to emerge above the clouds into bright, warm sunshine. Another day, at an altitude of twelve thousand feet, I found it only twelve below freezing, while, at the same time, as I learned later, it was twenty-four degrees below zero at Fort Collins, a town forty miles away on the plains. Strange freak of weather! The explanation lay in the difference between the winds that blew over the respective sections, a blizzardly north wind was sweeping over the low, exposed plains, while up on the peak-encircled heights a balmy "chinook" gently stirred from the west. Mountaineers know that as long as the west wind blows no severe storm is to be feared. It is the chill east wind that comes creeping up the cañons from the bleak plains and prairies of the lowlands, which bring the blizzards.

One rare, windless day upon the heights, my little hay-making friend, the cony, greeted me with an enthusiastic "squee-ek." He was sunning himself upon a rock and looked so sleek and plump I knew his harvest had been bountiful. He lay gazing off into space, apparently contemplating the Divide. But when, a few minutes later, a beady-eyed weasel challenged my right of way, I wondered whether little "Squee-ek's" thoughts were so remote as those distant peaks! In both storm and sunshine, I saw weasels abroad on the heights. They were bold, fearless little cutthroats, approaching within a few feet to stare at me wickedly. I saw them below timberline pursuing snowshoe rabbits many times their size.

Occasionally I came across fox tracks. These sly fellows seemed indifferent to cold or wind. They stalked the ptarmigan above timberline, and the grouse that had migrated up the slopes to winter, below it, and accounted for the death of many. One moonlit night, as I prowled upward, I heard an unearthly, uncanny squall. I couldn't help the shiver that ran down my spine. All the pent-up anguish and torment in the world broke forth in that sound. But perhaps it was only his foxy protest because his prey had out-foxed him.

But by far the most interesting mountain-top dwellers were the Bighorn sheep, which adopted those frigid regions as a winter resort. I had often wondered about those lofty-minded animals I had tracked over in the Wild Basin country. Were they still on those wind-blown heights? It seemed incredible that they could stand a whole winter of such bitter buffeting. Yet, on the days when I climbed above the timberline, no matter the weather, they were always there, contentedly feeding on the sweet, early-cured tufts of grass that the raging alpine gales kept uncovered. It was fascinating to watch them; neither wild winds nor blinding snow seemed to disconcert them; their thick wool coats were impervious to the keenest, most penetrating blasts. True, on terribly stormy days they sought the shelter of giant upthrusts of rock, towering cliffs or sky-piercing spires that faced eastward, away from the prevailing winds. There they probably stayed for days at a time, as long as the worst storms prevailed. Such days I did not dare venture upon the heights, but I often found signs of their bedding down among similar crags.

And such nerveless or nervy creatures as they were! From the top of a cliff, one day, I watched a band of them go down a nearly perpendicular wall. I could not follow, though I did go part way down to where the wall bulged outward. There the ledges had crumbled away, leaving sheer, smooth rock. It did not seem possible that anything could go down that smooth face. But half a dozen sheep in succession made the descent safely, as I watched, breathless, from above. They seemed to defy the laws of gravitation in walking over the rim rock; for, instead of tumbling headlong as I feared, they went skidding downward, bouncing, side-stepping, twisting and angling across the wall like coasters on snow; they could not stop their downward drop, but they controlled their descent by making brakes of their feet, and taking advantage of every small bump to retard their speed. By foot pressure they steered their course for a shelving rock below. One after another, in quick succession, they shot down, struck the shelf and leaped sidewise to a ledge a dozen feet beneath. In spite of their efforts to retard their speed, they had gained tremendous momentum before reaching the ledge and landed with all four feet bunched beneath them. It seemed that their legs would surely be thrust through their bodies. Their heads jerked downward, their noses threatened to be skinned on the rock! Yet that rough descent neither disabled nor unnerved them. They recovered their balance instantly and trotted away around a turn of the wall.

One young ram thought to escape by leaving the cliff and making his way across a steep, snowy slide to another crag. In places he struck soft snow and plunged heavily, breaking his way through. Midway between crags, however, he came to grief quite unexpectedly. An oozing spring had overflowed and covered the rocks with a coating of ice. Then snow had blown down from above and covered it. The ram struck this at top speed, and a moment afterward was turning somersaults down the slope. A hundred feet below he nimbly recovered his balance and proceeded on his way, carrying his head haughtily, as though indignant at my burst of laughter.

Part way down the cliff I found the tracks of the big ram leader of the band. I had long since named him "Big Eye," which an old trapper had told me was the Indians' expression for extraordinary eyesight. Not that "Big Eye" was exceptional in this respect, not at all! Every one of his band possessed miraculous eyesight. But he was always alert and wary. It was unbelievable that he could detect me such a long way off, around bowlders, through granite walls, in thick brush, but it seemed to me he did. No matter how carefully I concealed my approach, he always discovered me. This day he had left his band and had turned aside upon an extremely narrow shelf and made his way out of sight. I followed his tracks, curious to learn where he had gone. Many places he had negotiated without slacking his speed, whereas I was forced to make detours for better footing, to double back and forth, and generally to progress very slowly. Apparently he was not much frightened, for his tracks showed that he had frequently halted to look behind him.

So intent was I upon overtaking him, that I ran into a flock of ptarmigan and nearly stepped on one of the "fool hens" before it took wing and got out of the way, so utterly did it stake its safety on its winter camouflage. The whole flock had been sitting in plain sight but their snow-white coats made them hardly distinguishable from their background. They faded into the landscape like an elusive puzzle picture. In summer they had depended on their speckled plumage, so like the mottled patches of sand and snow and grass and granite whereon they lived, to protect them. They certainly put their trust in nature!

Around a turn, I came upon the old Patriarch. He was standing with his back to the wall, facing out and back, for here the ledge he had been following pinched out, and even he, champion acrobat of the cliffs, could neither climb up nor find a way down. For several minutes we faced each other, ten yards apart. I had heard that mountain sheep never attack men, and that even the big leaders never use their massive, battering ram heads to injure anyone. With this in mind I moved up to within ten feet when a movement of his haughty head stopped me. Somehow in his action was the suggestion that he might forget tradition. One bump of his huge head would knock me overboard. There was nothing but space for a hundred feet below, then sheer wall for several hundred feet more.

Arrogantly he faced me, unflinchingly; his eyes of black and gold never wavering; statuesque, his heroic body set solidly upon his sturdy legs, his regal head high, his lodestone feet secure

upon the sloping rock, he was a handsome figure.
He outweighed me about three pounds to one; so
the longer I looked at him, the less desire I had
to crowd. At length I mustered up courage to
try him out. Slowly, an inch at a time, I edged
forward, talking quietly—assuring him that my
intentions were good, and that I merely wanted
to learn how near a fellow might go without his
lordship's taking exceptions.

Suddenly he stiffened; half closed his eyes and
lowered his head. At the same instant he shifted
his feet as though to charge. As I backed carefully away, I recalled again that his kind had
never harmed anyone, but I gave him the benefit
of the doubt and left him in undisputed posses-
sion of the ledge.

On many a windy winter day thereafter, I
saw "Big Eye" and his band. Always I laughed
a bit at my experience upon the ledge. The ram
appeared so dignified, so quiet, so harmless!
Still, I had no fault to find with my retreat that
day.

One day there came a change over the world.
Signs of spring came creeping up the valley.
The pussy willows put on their silvery furs, the
birches and elders unfurled their catkin tassels.
Bands of deer and elk began to drift back into
the valley; the Bighorn eagerly forsook the
heights. The few coyotes that had remained
throughout the winter were joined by more of

their kin; fresh bobcat tracks appeared daily. The mountain lions that had trailed the deer and elk down to warmer climes, returned close on their heels as their red records testified. On my rambles I often came upon the scenes of their kills; deer, elk and even wary sheep were their victims.

The wet, clinging, spring snows lent themselves readily as recording tablets for the movements of all the woods folk. Not far from the proposed site of my dream cabin, the story of a lion's stalk was plainly told by tracks. He had climbed to the top of a rock that stood ten feet above the level floor of the valley, a huge bowlder that had rolled down from a crag above, torn its way through the ranks of the trees and come to rest at last in the grassy meadow. There he lay in wait for the slowly advancing, grazing deer.

As they approached the rock, the band had split; a section passing on either side of the bowlder. Out and down the lion had leaped—ten feet out and as far down. His momentum had overthrown his victim which had regained its feet and struggled desperately. The turf was torn up for thirty feet beyond the rock. I found only the tracks of the hind feet of the lion; it was not hard to imagine that, his front claws were fastened in the shoulders of his prey, and that his terrible teeth had reached an artery in his victim's

neck. Many such slaughters the soft snow revealed! Aroused by them, I determined to revenge the shy, innocent deer family. At every
opportunity, I have taken toll of the lion tribe.

As soon as the first new grass painted the
meadows pale green, the sheep flocked down
from their lofty winter resort: the sunshine in
the hemmed-in valley was hot; they still wore
their heavy winter coats, they grew lazy; hours
on end they lay dozing, or moving tranquilly
about, feasting on the succulent young shoots.
For six or seven months,—it was at least that
long ago since my discovery of their uprising
migration in Wild Basin—they had been living
on dried fare—unbaled hay—with no water to
wash it down, for there were no flowing springs
about their airy castles. Snow was the only
moisture to be had.

I was all eagerness to "shoot" them with my
camera! I had watched them so often I felt we
were at least acquainted. But out of respect for
their tremendous dignity, I decided to keep my
plans secret from them, to approach under cover,
to creep forward cautiously, soundlessly. To
my dismay, as soon as I got within a quarter of
a mile of them, some busybody of a sentinel would
see me, and if I continued advancing, no matter
how stealthily, the flock would move away. It
seemed offish, not to say unfriendly; time
and again I tried the same tactics, with the

same result. I was disappointed and puzzled.

I came to the conclusion that I had presumed too much on our previous friendship, that such regal creatures could not be expected to capitulate after a brief winter's acquaintance. I would visit them in their little valley, learn their peculiarities—who would do less to gain a friend worth while—and gain their confidence. Accordingly, every day I strolled casually in plain sight, over toward their feeding ground. They gradually lost their nervousness at my advances and eventually let me come within a hundred feet of them.

One morning, after several weeks of this chivalrous conduct, I set out with my camera, to spend the day with them. Not that they had extended an invitation, but they unconsciously invited me. There were thirty-two of them, including two huge old rams, grazing at the edge of the valley. I approached them from the windward side, so they would be doubly sure of my identity, for I knew that with their telescopic eyes they would recognize me while I was still a long way off.

I halted first while about a hundred yards distant. Pausing a few moments, I advanced again, until I cut the distance between us in half. I affected the utmost indifference—I lay down to rest, I got up and prowled about. They left off feeding, and bunched together, the wary old

rams on the far side of the flock. They gallantly
let the ladies and children be first to meet me!

For an hour the game went on. Little by
little I cut the distance to thirty feet. Some of
them even forget themselves so much as to lie
down and doze, others were discourteous enough
to resume feeding, but a canny few continued to
watch my every movement sharply. Several
times I tried to circle round them; each time they
edged away towards the mountain slopes. At
last they bunched together beside a jutting rock
and made such a beautiful picture, I could no
longer control my desire to photograph them.
Setting my camera at forty feet, I again slowly
advanced. At thirty feet, the sheep still being
quiet, I shortened the range. My greediness
threatened to be the end of me!

Below my subjects was a smooth rock slope.
Having set my camera for twenty-five feet, I
ventured across it. If I could only reach the
edge of that sloping rock before they took fright
what a wonderful picture I'd get! Slowly, inch
by inch I crept toward them. My eyes were
glued to the finder, my finger trembled at the
button, all at once, I stepped out, on nothing!
Boy and camera turned over in midair and
alighted, amid a shower of cones, in the top of a
young spruce tree.

After the first instant of astonishment, my
exasperation grew. I had lost my first chance

at getting a photograph of the sheep—most likely the best chance I'd ever have, too. Maybe ruined my camera, my clothes, and my hide! My disposition was past mending. My second surprise belittled my first. For when I looked about, expecting the sheep to have vanished, there they all were, crowding forward, and peering over the edge of the rock, in friendly solicitude! How often the unpremeditated exceeds our fondest plans! The picture I finally made far excelled the one I had first counted on!

After my fall, the game was taken up again. The sheep moved higher whenever I came too near them. Sometimes I dropped to all fours and gave an imitation of a playful pup; stopping to sniff loudly at a chipmunk's hole or to dig furiously with both hands. The sheep crowded forward appreciatively. Evidently they had a weakness for vaudeville. No acrobat, no contortionist, ever had a more flatteringly attentive audience. I laughed at my foolishness, but the sheep were courteously grave.

Toward noon the band set off for a steep cliff, where each day they took their siesta. The two old rams led the way. After making pictures of them silhouetted against the sky, I circled the cliff and hid at the end of a ledge. I counted on getting a good photograph when the old leaders surmounted the crag and marched forward at the head of their single-file column. To deceive them, I built a dummy at the spot where they turned aside upon the ledge. Coat and cap and camera case went into the sketchy figure, and after it had been propped in place to block the downward retreat, I hurried around the point and hid in some bushes behind a granite slab, first setting my camera, well camouflaged with stones, atop the rock, and focusing it toward the point where the sheep would pass in review. Minutes passed. Not a sheep rounded the point! More waiting. I sallied forth to reconnoiter. The sheep were feeding peacefully in the valley below. They had knocked down the dummy, trampled over it, and retreated along the ledge the way they had come!

The joke was on me, but it had been a glorious day for all that. I retrieved the remains of my down-trodden dummy and started home. I halted midway down to the valley to study some queer records in the sand. Surely a crazy man had made them! What would a stranger have thought if he had happened upon that grotesque trail? But a stranger *had* been there. On the heels of my crazy trail were the tracks of a mountain lion. He had been stalking me!

From my experience with these sheep I made some naïve deductions and wrote them in my notebook. From it, lying open before me now, I transcribe these boyish but none the less accurate observations:

"Mountain sheep have all-seeing eyes—therefore, one keeps in the open at all times and never attempts stalking them under cover. If you do, you are acting suspiciously, and they will treat you in the same manner."

"They will not permit you to approach from above them. They are lofty minded; so keep your place beneath them."

"If sheep are in the open, and on level ground, they will not permit a near approach."

"Keep in the open, below them, permit them to retreat to the rocks. If these rocks give way to sheer cliffs the sheep will feel at home. They will then permit you to approach quite near."

"Sheep are tremendously curious. Take advantage of this fact and offer them something in the way of entertainment. If you want to get on with sheep, make a fool of yourself."

As spring advanced, the ewes left the flock and sought safety among the cliffs where they raised their young in partial concealment. While their lambs were yet mere infants, a week old or so, they hid them among the rocks. Instinctively the youngsters lay low, remaining immovable until their mothers returned from feeding near by, to claim them. Eagles hovered high overhead, waiting to drop like plummets upon the helpless babies. These great birds accounted for many a bleating little lamb's passing. Lions, likewise, visited the heights and took

SHEEP AND ROCK DROPPED STRAIGHT TOWARD ME

toll of mothers as well as of offspring; even bobcats pounced upon them. Sometimes coyotes or wolves surprised partly grown sheep, that had brashly ventured too far from sheltering rocks.

While returning home one day I stumbled upon a very young sheep. The youngster lay low, like a wounded duck. Several times I walked within a few feet of him, coming closer each time until at length he sprang up and fled in terror. He took refuge by climbing an almost perpendicular cliff wall. Camera in hand, I followed as best I could. Fifty feet up, he came to a point where even his nimble feet could find no adequate footing. His retreat ended. He scrambled to a little jutting point not much larger than a hand's breadth, and took refuge there with all four feet bunched together.

Carefully I worked up toward him. Several times he bleated for his mother and shifted his position. Every moment I feared he would lose his footing and plunge down the rock face. Twenty feet below I stopped because I could climb no higher. Carefully I turned about and faced the wall, hugging it as closely as possible. Holding the camera at arm's length, and pointing it straight up, I sprung the shutter. The click, slight as it was, startled the lamb. He leaped several feet to another nub of rock, teetered precariously several seconds, then suddenly his pedestal broke off. Sheep and rock dropped

straight toward me. To avoid the rock, I sprang
sideways. The sheep plunged down upon me as
the rock hurtled past. Together we revolved,
that sheep and I, the camera being abandoned
in midair to shift for itself. Together the struggling youngster and I struck the rock, slid and
bounded outward, turning over as we fell, first
one on top, then the other, until at length I
clutched a bush growing out of a crevice in the
slide and stopped myself; but the lamb continued
his bouncing fall down the mountain. In all,
he must have rolled three hundred feet before
he stopped, his feet sticking up out of the brush
like the legs of an overturned bench.

It was some time before I was able to walk.
But as quickly as possible I went to the rescue
of that sheep because I had caused his downfall.
He was still breathing, but unable to stand.
With great effort, for he was heavy and I was
shaking from my fall, I carried him down to the
stream and soused him in its icy water. He
revived at once. The camera had smashed to
pieces before it finished its bouncing flight down
the mountain.

After all, it was a great experience, and though
it cost me my camera, some of my hide and most
of my clothes, I wouldn't have missed it for all
Kit Carson's priceless furs!

CHAPTER SIX

A T last, that long-anticipated day dawned, when my dream cabin became a reality. High upon a shoulder of Twin Sisters Mountain, a thousand feet above the floor of the valley, where Parson Lamb's ranch stood, overlooking the ruins of Kit Carson's own cabin, I built it. Across the valley, towered Long's Peak and its lofty neighbors. Forty miles of snowcapped peaks were at my dooryard, and beyond, toward the rising sun, hazy plains stretched away to the illimitable horizon. Between its craggy shoulder and the main body of the mountain, lay an unsuspected, wedge-shaped valley, down which a little brook went gurgling. There ancient spruce and yellow pine and quaking aspens grew in sheltered luxuriance.

"Silent valley," I named it, though "Peaceful," or Hidden," or "Happy" might have fitted it as well. About eighty years previously, as I calculated by the age of the new trees since sprung up, fire had burned over Silent Valley. Many of the fire-killed trees were still standing, sound to the heart. These solid, seasoned trunks, I cut for the logs of my cabin walls. The Parson, almost as excitedly happy as I, lent me a team to drag them to the spot where the house was to stand. They were far too heavy for me to lift, so I had to roll them into place by an improvised system of skids. Construction was a toilsome work; I was not skilled at it, I handled my ax awkwardly, and squandered much energy in "lost motion." But how I sang and shouted at the task! Never could Kit Carson nor any other pioneer have exulted at his building as I did! No wonder the deer paused in the aspen trails and peered timidly out from their leafy retreat in amazement! No wonder those sages, the mountain sheep, watched from the cliffs above with sharp, incredulous eyes. Never before had the ring of an ax echoed in Silent Valley!

My cabin grew, as fast as young shoulders and eager hands could build it. Log walls snugly chinked, and log rafters boarded and sodded; two windows, "lazy" windows we maligned them, because they lay down instead of standing, one sash above the other, and opened by sliding past each other. The few dollars I had saved from my original stake and made from the sale of hides, I spent, extravagantly, it seemed then, for boards to make a door and lay a floor. That lumber cost nine dollars per thousand feet on the job, and had to be hauled eleven miles

NEVER BEFORE HAD THE RING OF AN AX ECHOED IN
SILENT VALLEY!

from a local sawmill—an exorbitant price that made a lasting impression on my thrifty mind and left my old leather pouch flat; That same lumber sells to-day for fifty-two dollars a thousand! Shades of Kit Carson! How fortunate I lived near your time!

Built-in furniture is nothing new, "we pioneers" always used it! From the odds and ends of planks left from the door and floor, I built a wall seat, a chimmey corner, a shelf cupboard and a bunk. My scanty furnishings were all homemade—a rough, pine-board table, which served for kitchen, dining and library purposes, and a bench which I always "saved," using the floor before the hearth instead. "Aunt Jane" insisted on giving me a featherbed to put on the rough slats of my bunk, and some pieced quilts; I used my camp blankets for sheets. She gave me, too, a strip of old rag carpet she had brought from her Eastern home.

The crowning architectural feature of my mansion was the corner fireplace, raised of the native granite bowlders. With what care I selected the stones!—choosing those most richly encrusted with green lichens, fitting each into its place, discarding many, ranging afar for others to take their place. Chimney building is a job for an artisan, and even then much of a gamble. Imagine my delight, then, when, the last stone in place, I built a fire on my hearth, and it roared like a furnace, and all the smoke went up, and out, the chimney! Later, the eddying winds sometimes shot prankishly down it and playfully chased the smoke back into the room, but this only blackened the stones, giving my fireplace an air of antiquity.

My open fire was cook stove as well as heater. I added to my camping utensils a Dutch oven, an iron pot with a heavy, deep-rimmed, tight-fitting iron lid, and a tin basin. My furnishings were complete!

Long evenings I sat on the floor before my hearth, dreaming. Sometimes I read, but the windy days outdoors, tramping and climbing, left me relaxed and drowsy. I possessed, perhaps, a dozen books; among them "Treasure Island," which I read over and over, with my door bolted. My imagination gave piratical significance to the sighing of the pine trees and the scampering of the pack rats over my roof.

Yes, my dream cabin was come true. There it stood on its lofty vantage, watching over me as I fared forth on my explorations, waiting faithfully for my return, never reproaching me for my absence, its snug walls always ready to welcome me like sheltering arms, its quickly blazing hearth cheering me like a warm, loving heart. So high was it perched, that I could see it, while on my excursions, from many miles away. It was a beacon to my wandering spirit, a compass and a guide to my wandering feet.

From it, as my knowledge of woodcraft, which I came to know was nothing more than common sense and resourcefulness applied to outdoor living, increased, I ranged farther and farther, into the wilder, more remote regions, which, except for an occasional trapper, no other white man had ever penetrated. The country around my homestead, Long's Peak, and the adjacent mountains, which have since been made a part of Rocky Mountain National Park, is itself exceptionally high and rugged. There, in a comparatively small area, are more than sixty peaks over twelve thousand feet high, Long's, of course, being over fourteen thousand feet. As the years passed my wanderings took me along the Continental Divide, from the Wyoming line at the north to the southern boundary of Colorado.

The vastness of the Rocky Mountains is beyond comprehension, they sprawl the length of the continent. No one can hope to see all their beauty, all their grandeur and awesomeness in a single lifetime. From the crest of the Divide, north, west, and south, stretches a world of rugged peaks. Range on range, tier on tier, like the waves of a solidified ocean in a Titanic storm they roll away to the distant horizon shore.

Always, as a boy, that compelling panorama fascinated me. On pleasant, sunny days, those rugged slopes, from a distance, looked safe and plushy, for all the world like deerskin; the dark green cañons mysteriously beckoned to me, the myriad lakes sparkled knowingly, intimately, the swift brooks chattered incessantly, urging action, adventure. On stormy days, when violent winds swept over the Divide and hid the heads of the peaks beneath the scuttling clouds, that overwhelming vista, with its tremendous, deep-gashed cañons, its towering, forbidding cliffs, still challenged even while it repelled me.

To explore every mile, vertical and horizontal, of that uncharted sea of peaks! That was my boyish ambition! that was what led me westward, that was what lured me on and on! And my field of exploration was limitless—one peak conquered, there was always another just beyond, a little higher, a little harder, waiting to be climbed. The wilder the region the greater was its fascination for me. No matter how difficult, how slow my progress, it never became tedious— there was always the unexpected, the mysterious, as a guarantee against monotony.

Timberline always interested me and those vast, naked plateaus above it never ceased to move me to wonder—miles and miles of great, granite desert, up-flung into space. The very tip-top of the world. I used to marvel that so much of the earth was waste. It was an everlasting enigma.

Timberline was not all grotesque trees with

bleak winds forever scourging them.   In late
summer, it was a veritable hanging garden.
Sweet blue and pink forget-me-nots hid in the
moss of its bowlders, Edelweiss starred its stony
trails, King's crown, alpine primrose, and many
other flowers nodded a gracious welcome.

And just below it, what a riot of bloom there
was! I had learned, oft to my inconvenience,
that the higher the altitude the greater the precipitation.   Around and just below timberline
are many lakes, and miles of marshy, boggy land.
On those first winter excursions to the heights I
marveled at the deep snowdrifts banked in the
heavy Englemann forests just below timberline.
Long after the last white patch had melted or
evaporated from the exposed slopes, these sheltered drifts would lie undiminished and when
summer really came, they gave birth to scores of
trickling rills.   Vegetation sprang up in that
moist, needle-mulched soil as luxuriant as any
in the tropics.   From the time the furry anemone
lifted its lavender-blue petals above the dwindl-
ing snow patch, until the apples formed on the
wild rose bushes and the kinnikinic berries turned
red, it was a continuous nosegay.   Indian paint-
brush, marigolds, blue and white columbines as
big as my hand and nearly as high as my head,
fragile orchids, hiding their heads in the dusky
dells, thousands of varieties I never knew or
learned.   Some few I recognized as glorified

cousins of my Kansas acquaintances. The dense, towering spruce forests sheltered them, conserved the moisture, and scattered their needles over their winter beds.

In spite of the Parson's experienced advice, on my first trips, boylike, I ladened myself with blanket roll, cooking utensils and an unnecessary amount of food. I soon found, however, that besides tiring me early in the afternoon and robbing me of my zest for scenery, my pack limited the scope of my operations, for with it I did not dare attempt many precipitious slopes where a single slip might land me in eternity. I found, too, that without it I could practically double the length of a day's journey, and arrive at the end of it still fresh enough to enjoy things. So I soon simplified my camp equipment. Campfires took the place of blankets, a pocketful of raisins, a few shelled peanuts, some sweet chocolate bars provided satisfying feasts. Eventually, when I became adept at snaring game, I made a spit of twigs and roasted the game over hot coals.

Sometimes this primitive method of camping was inconvenient, but it was lots of fun. It was pioneering! What boy has not wished himself Robinson Crusoe? Somehow, in this way I retrieved that early frontier period passed before my birth. So I met the challenge of the mountains, met whatever emergencies arose, with such resourcefulness as I could muster; made my own way with what ingeniousness I possessed, and lived off the land. Indians could do no more!

Having given up my gun, I learned other, and for me, at least, more reliable methods of taking game for food. Setting snares was an intriguing sport, but when I did not have time for it, I resorted to a more primitive method, stone-throwing. Of course there were days when neither of these methods succeeded, when the meal hour had to be postponed, while I whetted my appetite, rather superfluously, with more miles of tramping. I was surprised to find I could go foodless for several days and still have strength to plod ahead and maintain my interest in the scenery.

The cottontail of the Rockies is the commonest and easiest source of meat, not only to the camper, but to the rabbit's cannibalistic neighbors. He is a sort of universal food—a sort of staff of life to the animal world. But for him famine would stalk the big killers. Fortunately for himself and for his preying foes, he is most prolific, and holds his own, in numbers at least, despite man and beast. Occasionally some ravaging disease carries his kind off by the thousands, then starvation faces those dependent on him for food. The killers have to seek other hunting grounds, frequently far from their home range, and often they become gaunt and lank, driven to take desperate chances to save themselves from starvation and death.

As you can easily imagine, it keeps Bunny Cottontail moving to outwit his many enemies. He has no briar patches in that rugged country, though the jumper thickets might serve as such, so he lives beneath the rocks, usually planning a front and back door to his burrow. In this way he has a private exit when weasels or bobcats make their uninvited visitations. A whole Rooseveltian family of bunnies live in congested districts. Learning this, I usually set a number of snares in their runways, or at likely holes beneath the rocks.

Part of the game of making nature yield one a living is keeping an eye out at all times for possible food supplies. If a rabbit scurried across my path, I marked the spot of his refuge. If he dodged beneath a certain slab, I set my snare there. Then I poked about, hoping to scare him into the snare. I did not always succeed in this, though, for my stick could not turn the corners of his burrow, and he often appeared out of some other exit, laughing at my stupidity, no doubt. Sometimes, when very hungry, I tried smoking him out. The stone porch of his burrow usually sloped, so a small smudge started at its lower side would travel up-hill, into the tunnel. Mr. Rabbit, thinking the woods were on fire, would make a dash for the open and fall victim to the

snare. But despite the fact that rabbits are
credited with little wit, I have often known them
to nose aside my traps and escape.

Cottontails I found up to eight or nine thousand feet, but even higher I ran across their
cousins, the snowshoe. He quite excelled me in
manipulating his "webs"—his tremendous hind
feet with long, clawlike toes, covered with stiff
and, I judged, waterproof hairs. He made his
way nimbly over the soft, deep snow, while I on
my webs often floundered and fell. Like the
ptarmigan and the weasel, the snowshoe rabbit
changed to a white coat for winter. In the
spring, he was bluish, though underneath he still
retained his arctic snowiness. In the fall, with
good taste and a sense of the fitness of things, he
put on a tan coat, and then, as the winter snows
began to drift, he once more donned his ermine
robes.

Grouse were plentiful, except during the winter months. Usually I found them between six
thousand and nine thousand feet altitude, but as
the fall coloring painted the mountain slopes, and
the juniper berries ripened, they moved to the
higher, exposed wind-swept cliffs. Above timberline were the ptarmigan, always easy targets
for a well-aimed stone.

Rabbits, grouse and ptarmigan were all available and filling, but the most abundant and most
easily caught food in all the Rockies at that time

were the mountain trout. When I was a boy, every stream, even as far down as the plains, was alive with them. Like salmon, they swam upstream till they came to rapids or cataracts which they could not leap. Those in the lakes were exceptionally large, but too well fed to be interested in my bait. In the valleys were deep pools made by beavers' dams and in these the trout "holed up" for the winter. Fishing through the ice was common sport years ago. I remember that one of Jim Oss's neighbors brought a mess of trout to him when he gave his homesteading dance in January. With fish so abundant and unwary, and fishermen few, fishing was easy. It took me only five or ten minutes to catch all the trout I could use. Usually a few feet of line, a hook, and a willow or aspen rod, was all I found necessary. Sometimes I used bait—grasshoppers, bugs or worms.

Campfire cooking is an art comparatively primitive and elementary, but it requires experience and intelligence to master. Like most accomplishments worth learning, it takes application, and a world of patience. Since I did not carry any utensils with me, I invariably roasted or broiled the game I cooked, using hot rocks like the Indians. I heated stones in my campfire, dug a shallow hole, and when the stones were hot lined it with them, then put in my meat, covering it with a hot flat stone. From time to time, I renewed the cooled first stones for fresh ones, hot from the fire. Sometimes I intensified that heat of my "fireless" by covering its top with moss or with pine needles.

If I decided to broil my bunny or grouse, I got out my short fishing line and tied one end of it to a limb of a tree or to a tripod which I made by fastening three poles together, setting them over the fire. The other end I fastened to a green stick, three or four feet long, which I skewered into the meat. Then I gave my "broiler" a spin which wound up the line. When it was twisted tight, it reversed itself, unwinding, and so revolving my cookery, exposing all sides to the fire. Of course it gradually lost its spin, then I gave it another twirl. Given plenty of time, over a slow fire of glowing coals, my bird would be done to a queen's taste—a much too delicious dish to waste on any king!

During dry, warm weather, I raked pine or spruce needles together for a bed, but in the winter I used green pine or spruce boughs, putting heavy, coarse ones on the bottom, planting their butt ends deeps in the snow. Upon these I placed smaller twigs, which gave "spring" to my couch, and finally I tufted it with the soft, tender tips of the branches. Never have I rested better on mahogany beds than I did on such pungent bunks! Lying there, physically weary, mentally relaxed, drowsily gazing into my campfire, I lived over the day's adventures, and would not have changed places with any man alive!

I found making camp in temperate weather was no task at all. It was when it was cold or wet that the real test of my woodcraft came. I learned that the first requisite in camp-making was the selection of a suitable camp site. It had to be chosen with thought of the accessibility to fuel and water. It had to be sheltered from the wind, which was not always easy to manage in high altitudes, for though the prevailing winter wind in the Rockies blows from the west, it swirls and eddies in the cañons, coming from most unexpected and unwelcome directions and often from all points of the compass in turn. Usually ready-made camps, overhanging cliffs, were available. When they were not, my ingenuity rose to the occasion and I thatched together twigs of willow or birch, or even spruce or pine, though the latter were stiffer and more difficult to fit tightly together. Beginning at the bottom, I worked upward, lapping each successive layer over the one beneath, as in laying shingles, and pointing the tips of the leaves or needles downward, so they would shed water.

Sometimes I had difficulty in starting my fire. If there had been daily showers for weeks, and the needles and the deadwood, as well as the ground itself, were soaked, or if in winter the deadwood were buried beneath snow and the dead limbs of standing trees difficult to break off, it was a discouraging task. Sometimes after what seemed like eons of struggling, I would get a sickly little flame flickering, when, puff! along would come a blast of wind and smother it out with snow. I did learn eventually that pitch knots were so rich in gum or resin that they would always catch fire, and so I shaved off splinters with my trusty hunting knife and used them for tinder. One night as I lighted a candle in my cabin, it came to me that a piece of it would be handy to tuck in my pocket for emergencies. Ever afterwards I carried several short, burned-down ends along on my excursions. I discovered that one of these stubbs, set solidly on the ground and lighted, would start my fire under the most adverse conditions. But for them I would have had many a cold camp.

I had read of the Eskimo igloos and I tried to make them. But the snow at hand in my mountains was never packed hard enough to freeze solid so building blocks could be cut from it. It is blown about and drifted too much. I did get an idea from "Buck" in Jack London's "Call of the Wild," that I adapted. On winter explorations I always carried snowshoes, even though not compelled to wear them at the outset. These made handy shovels. When ready to make camp I selected a snowdrift three or four feet deep, and with my web shovel dug a triangular hole, about seven feet long on each side. In the angle farthest from the wind I built my fire. It soon assisted me in enlarging the corner. Opposite it, I roofed over my dugout with dead limbs, thatching them with green boughs, and finally heaping the excavated snow over all. I had a practically windproof nest which a little fire would keep snug and warm. True I had to fire up frequently throughout the night, for a big blaze is too hot in a snow-hole, but I soon learned to rouse up, put on more fuel, and drop back to to sleep, all in a few minutes.

But the smoke nuisance in my early dugouts was terrible. Pittsburgh had nothing on me! Many a morning I crawled out smelling like a smoked ham, my eyes smarting, my throat sore and dry. Years later, my rambles led me to Mesa Verde and the kivas of the cliff dwellers. Those primitive people built fires deep underground, with no chimneys or flues to conduct the smoke outside. They ingeniously constructed cold air passages down to the floor of the kivas near the fire bowl. These fed the fires fresh air, causing the smoke to rise steadily and pass out through a small aperture in the roof. I tried this, and to my delight, found it rid me of the strangling plague.

I had discarded my gun, but my camera was with me always. Frequent dashing showers are common in the mountains. Often, too, I had to

"See All Fools Ain't Dead Yit," He Observed.

cross swollen streams, and sometimes got a ducking in transit. Matches, salt and camera plates were ruined by wetting, so I had to contrive a waterproof carrier for them. I hit upon a light rubber blanket, which added practically no pounds or bulk to my pack, and in it wrapped my perishables. It saved them more often than not, but even it could not protect them in some predicaments.

There was no month of the year I didn't camp out. Naturally I was caught in many kinds of weather. In severe storms I learned to stick close to camp, lying low and waiting for the furies to relent. In the early days, as in my first camp, I attempted to return home at once, but traveling over the soft, yielding snow only sapped my strength and got me nowhere. I learned that by remaining inactive by my campfire, I conserved both food and energy and had a far better chance to reach the shelter of my cabin without mishap.

Being young and inexperienced, I was the recipient of much free advice, the most common being warnings about the imminent weather or the oncoming winter. Most of these prognosticators used the cone-storing squirrels or the beavers, working busily on their dams and houses, as barometers. But I found the old adage that only fools and newcomers could forecast weather to hold true in the mountains. I got so I didn't believe in signs. I saw the squirrels and the beavers make preparation for winter every fall. I took each day, with its vagaries, as it came and made the best of it.

Returning from one of my midwinter trips to the wilds, one day I coasted down a very steep slope and shot out of the woods into a little clearing—a snug log cabin stood there, buried in snow up to its eyes. In a snow trench, not far from the door, an old trapper was chopping wood. As I burst upon the scene he dropped his ax and stared at me. Then he found words.

"See all fools ain't dead yit," he observed with a grin. Then, as I started on he yelled after me.

"But I bet they soon will be!"

So I spent the days of my boyhood—tramping, climbing, exploring! Was ever another mortal so fortunate as I in the realization of his dreams? Was ever another lad so happy?

CHAPTER SEVEN

GLACIERS AND FOREST FIRES

W HEN I first came West, with my imagination fired by the reminiscent tales of my mother and my father, and our pioneer neighbors, I looked only for mountains made of gold, for roaming buffaloes and skulking savages, for fierce wild beasts and mighty hunters. That the mountains were golden only in the sunset, and the Indians and bison alive only in the immortal epics of the frontier, somehow did not disappoint me. So wonderful were those rocky upheavals in the reality, so intriguing were the traces of redskin and buffalo, I forgot my fantastic misconceptions. To my enthusiastic youth, everything was extraordinary, alluring, primitively satisfying. Parson Lamb said the big game were gone, but there were enough left to give me many a thrill.

Naturally, at first, I saw only the more obvious wonders of the wilds, but as time passed I discovered other sources of interest, hitherto unheard of. High and dry upon the meadows and lower mountain sides were smooth, round bowlders, undoubtedly water-worn. The granite walls of many of the cañons I climbed were curiously scored—here and there were inlaid bands of varying colored stone. Running out from the loftier ranges were long, comparatively narrow heaps of earth, which resembled giant railroad fills as flat on top as though they had been sliced off by a titanic butcher knife. They were covered with forests, and small, jewel-like lakes were set in their level summits. At the foot of Long's and many other peaks were more lakes, with slick, glazed, granite sides. The water in them was usually greenish and always icy. There were immense, dirty "snowdrifts" that never diminished, but appeared to be perpetual.

Following my trapline or trailing the Big-horn or watching the beaver, I noticed these things and wondered about them. How came those bowlders, round and polished, so far from water? What made those scratches upon those granite cliffs? What Herculean master-smith fused those decorative belts into their very substance? What engineer built those table-topped mounds? Who had gouged out the bowls for those icy lakes? Why were some snowdrifts perennial? I puzzled over these conundrums, until, bit by bit, I solved them. The answers were more amazing than anything else I encountered in the wilds.

I learned that those sand-coated drifts were

not drifts at all, but glaciers, probably the oldest
living things in the world. For they were alive,
moving deposits of ice and snow, the survivors
of the ice age. Eons ago, they and their like
had gouged out the huge bowls which later became lakes, had gashed the earth and scoured its
cañon walls, leaving in their wakes those square-
topped dumps or moraines; débris, once solid
granite, now ground into rocks and sand and
gravel by their slow-moving, irresistible force.

Most of the glaciers I found were upon the
eastern slope of the Divide. This is because the
prevailing winter winds are from west to east.
Glaciers are formed by thawing of the exposed
snow on top of the huge deposits, the water
trickling down through the moss, and freezing
solidly. Gradually, through continued thawing
and freezing, the whole drift is changed into a
field of ice. The first sign of movement comes
when the mass of ice breaks away from the cliffs
at its upper edges. There is an infinitesimal
downward sagging, as with incredible delibera-
tion it moves on with its cargo of rock and sand.
But, slowly as it moves, its power is overawing.
A glacier is the embodiment of irresistible force.
Its billion-ton roller cuts a trench through the
very earth, with cañon-like walls; these latter
turn upon their master and imprison him. It
tears immense granite slabs from the cliffs and
carries them along. It grinds granite into pow-

der. I have seen water emerging from glaciers, milk-white with its load of ground-up rocks.

By setting a straight line of stakes across the ice, I measured the movements of some glaciers. Some progressed several feet in a year, others traveled scarcely more than a few inches. All moved farthest nearest the center; for, as is true of streams, there the friction of the side walls does not retard them. They varied in width from a hundred feet to half a mile, in depth from forty to a hundred feet.

During my first years in the Rockies, the winters were severe, with heavy snows, and the summers unusually rainy. The low temperature and great precipitation prevented the usual amount of thawing on the glaciers. But there came a season as arid as any in the Sahara desert.

"It's miserable droughty," grieved the Parson one day when I met him on top of Long's Peak. "Springs are going dry and the streams are terrible low. See that drift down there?" Standing on Long's overtowering summit he pointed down the Divide. "The one with black rock at its edge. Well, sir, I've never seen that drift so small before—not in all the thirty years I've watched it. The glaciers will be opening up with all this hot weather! the crevasses'll widen and split clear down to the bowels of the earth. Wal; it's an ill wind that blows no good. This drought will make it easy for the tenderfoot to get a good look into 'em."

I took the Parson's tip and next day packed a horse and started for Arapahoe glacier which lies south of Long's Peak. On the second day out, having taken my pack-horse as far up as possible, I unpacked him, hobbled him and turned him loose to crop what grass he could find. Then I set up camp.

Camp made, I began the last lap of my climb up the glacier. Along the way, below snow-banks, wild flowers grew head-high, but in the woods beside the game trails they were scarce and stunted. As I plodded slowly up the steep slope I heard loud reports, as though some one were setting off heavy blasts. They echoed and reëchoed among the cliffs. A roaring stream dashed frothily down the slope, rocks rolled past. I climbed a pinnacle overlooking the glacier and looked down upon it.

The Parson was right. All the snow which ordinarily hid the icy surface was melted away. the glacial ice lay uncovered. Its surface was split by numberless yawning crevasses. Water drenched their sides. Every little while ice would break away, and then reports, similar to the ones I had heard on my way up, would nearly deafen me.

I climbed gingerly down and edged out upon the glacier, testing each foothold. I peeped into

the crevasses, and dropped stones or chunks of
ice into them to sound their depths. I ventured
into a shallow crack and followed it until it
pinched beneath a wall of solid ice. Then I tried
another, a larger one. Gaining a little courage
by these explorations, I ventured yet farther and
climbed down into one of the deeper crevasses.
Water showered down upon me, from melting
walls above. I crept on down until I was about
fifty feet below the top of the glacier. I paused;
before me gaped a dark cavern fenced off by
heavy icicles as large as my body. I peered
through this crystal lattice into the darkness beyond. From somewhere came the tinkle of water,
I decided to investigate. A stream pouring into
the crevasse from above, had washed down a
stone. Using it for a sledge, I set to work to
break into that barred vault. I shattered one of
the glassy bars and crawled inside. A ghostly
blue light filled the place. With lighted candle
I moved away from the entrance, turned a corner
and plunged into the blackest darkness I have
ever experienced.

The silence was eerie, frightening. Just then
it was shattered by a muffled report, followed
almost at once by another that seemed to rend
my cavern walls asunder. Bits of ice dropped
about me. I suddenly remembered a number of
things I wanted to do outside, I turned and
sought the guarded cavern of the ghastly light.

I mistook the way and turned aside into a blind alley for a moment. I grew panicky—my flesh went clammy—but that momentary delay no doubt saved my life. As I reached the opening, there came a rending crash, a splintering of ice, and broken blocks came hurtling into the crevasse just outside my cavern door. An inrush of air snuffed out my candle.

My hands trembled as I relighted the candle. Ice still bombarded the opening. Somewhere water splashed. Before I had descended into the crevasse I had been perspiring freely, for the sun shone hot upon the surface of the glacier; now I was shivering, my feet were soaked with ice water, a dozen little streams trickled down from the cavern roof. I would soon be warm in the hot sun outside; then . . . I discovered the crevasse was blocked with ice.

I lost my head and shouted for help. There were none to hear. I pushed against the barriers. I pulled myself together and began to search for a passage among the blocks of ice. The candle gave a feeble light. Without waiting to feel my way, I edged into a crack, wriggled forward and stuck tight. Cold sweat oozed as I wiggled backward into the cavern again. I had difficulty relighting the candle. Again and again I attempted to squeeze out among the pieces of broken ice; I climbed up the smooth wall, lost my footing and tumbled back. At last I found a larger opening among the ice blocks and squeezed into it like a rabbit into a rock pile. I knew I must hurry because these jumbled pieces would soon be solidly cemented together when the water pouring over them froze.

I surged desperately against the pressing ice, held my breath and squeezed my way through into the sunshine at last—safe. Late that evening I reached my camp, my interest in glaciers chilled.

Since that experience I have usually looked long before leaping into a crevasse and then have not leaped.

The next morning I broke camp. I had had enough of close-ups of glaciers. I followed the crest of the Continental Divide northward, satisfied with such distant views of those treacherous juggernauts as could be had from the rim rocks.

That was how I came to be camped at timberline above Allen's Park when the big forest fire set the region south of it ablaze. From my lofty station I watched a thunder shower gather around Long's Peak and move southward, tongues of lightning darting from it venomously. It was perhaps ten miles wide. It circled Wild Basin, then faced eastward toward the foothills, its forked tongues writhing wickedly. Those to the south struck repeatedly; I counted three fires they started, but two of these the shower extinguished; the third was miles beyond the edge of the rain, and began spreading even as I watched. Smoke soon hid the doomed forest, filling the cañon and boiling out beyond it.

Everywhere in the mountains, I had found burned-over forests; ancient trees that had stood for centuries, had endured drought, flood, storm and pestilence, only to be burned at last by a fiendish flash and left, charred skeletons of their former green beauty.

I hurried down from the heights as the fire spread upward along both sides of the gorge. Upon a bare, rocky ridge, several miles north, inside the edge of the shower limits, I deposited my pack and turned the horse homeward, alone. I hoped that I might be able to put out the fire before it spread too far.

As I hurried in its direction I saw two deer standing in a little opening watching the smoke intently. They showed no fear, merely curiosity. But as I approached closer to its smouldering edge, I met birds in excited, zig-zagging flight. Along a brook I found fresh bear tracks. Bruin had galloped hastily from the danger zone.

The fire was confined to the heavy timber near the bottom of a cañon, but was licking its way up both slopes, the backfire eating slowly downward while the headfire leaped upward. Trees exploded into giant sparklers. The heat of the approaching flames caused the needles to exude their sap, combustion occurred almost be-bore the actual fire touched them. Black acrid smoke arose visible a hundred miles out on the plains.

Not a breeze stirred where I stood, but the fire seemed fanned by a strong wind, that swayed it back and forth. It did not travel in a set direction; one moment it raced westward, paused, smoldered, then burst forth again, running south-ward. A little later a flood of flame would come toward the east. These scattered sorties cut narrow swaths through the forest, flaming lanes that smoldered at the edges, widened and com-bined.

The smoke cloud grew denser. My eyes streamed with tears, my throat burned, I began to cough. I descended the ridge to cross the cañon—in the bottom I found little smoke and fairly good air.

Flocks of panic-stricken birds veered uncer-tainly about. They would flee the fire, en-counter dense smoke, and turn straight back toward the flames. They circled and alighted at the bottom of the gorge. No sooner safely there, then they'd take wing again and flutter back into the trees near the fire. Many dropped, overcome by the smoke, whole flocks disappeared into the roaring flames to return no more. They lost all sense of direction, all instinct for self-preser-vation.

But the birds were not alone in their distress; the animals, too, were on the move. Down the slopes came deer, does with their young, bucks with tender, growing horns. To my surprise, they paid no attention to me. Whether they were unable to get my scent because of the fumes of burning woods, or whether the fire filled them with a greater fear, I could not decide. A coyote trotted calmly down a game trail, eyed me for a moment, and went on his way toward safety. He was the only one of the wild folk able to keep his wits about him.

Occasionally one of the deer would break away from the refugees, head up or down without apparent reason, the rest of the band instantly following his lead. In less than a minute all would return. They feared to desert their usual haunts in time of trouble. The smoke robbed them of their sense of smell, the noise of the fire was too loud for their usually alert, big ears to catch the smaller, significant sounds. As their confusion grew their terror mounted; they bundled nervously away in all directions, rushing back together, heading upstream toward the fire, and leaping wildly over smoldering needles of the forest floor.

The fawns were deserted, their mothers dashed about frantically as though unable to recognize their own offspring; they snorted wildly to rid their noses of the biting fumes that robbed them of scent. A fawn stopped within a few feet of me and stared about with luminous, innocent eyes. Its hair was singed and its feet burned. It lifted its left hind foot and stared at it perplexed; then I saw beween its dainty, parted hoofs a burning stick.

Other animals passed. A badger waddled slowly down the trail, pausing to grin at me comically. Two beavers splashed downstream, following the water, diving through the deeper pools and lumbering through the shallows of the brook. Other animals crashed through the woods, but I could not recognize them.

A little brook sizzled down through the burning land. I stopped and, cupping my hands, scooped up some water and drank thirstily. The first swallow nearly strangled me, it was saturated by the fumes of the burning forest. I drank on nevertheless; it was wet and cooling to my parched throat. I soused my head in the brook and soaked my handkerchief in case of need.

A faint breeze sprang up. Circling the fire, I moved up the slope, with the wind at my back. The needle-carpeted forest floor was a smoldering mass—the squirrels' hidden hoards were afire. Young trees, just starting from those stored-up nurseries were destroyed by tens of thousands.

On raced the head fire, setting the dead trees

THE MEMORY OF THAT RACE FOR LIFE IS STILL VIVIDLY
TERRIFYING.

and stumps furiously aflame, touching the needles of the living trees with swift, feverish fingers, igniting insidious spot-fires as it went. Its self-generated draft roared thunderingly. It snatched up countless firebrands and sent those flaming heralds forth to announce its coming to the trembling forest beyond. As it topped the cañon walls it seemed to leap beyond the clouds that hovered overhead and burn asunder the very heavens.

Of a sudden I was enveloped by one of its serpentine arms. It writhed everywhere around me, hissing, striking at my face, singing my hair, scorching my frantic hands that would ward it off. My eyes could not face that venomous glare. My lungs were choked by its searing breath. I found a stick and, feeling my way with it, fled, like the beaver, to the brook for sanctuary. That flaming serpent pursued me. Its breath grew more acrid, more deadly. I coughed convulsively, strangled, stumbled, fell: when I regained my feet, I was dazed, confused. But I retained consciousness enough to know I must keep moving. I must reach the fire's immemorial enemy and enlist the aid of that watery ally to escape it. I took leaps over the ground, but blindly, with no such brilliant eyes as my relentless foe.

The memory of that race for life is still vividly terrifying; blinded, choking, crashing into trees, falling, struggling to my feet, fighting on and on and on, for what seemed endless hours. In reality it was—it could only have been—a few moments. I plunged into the brook and submerged my burning clothes, my tortured body. I hurried on as fast as I could, downstream, halting now and then to dive beneath the grateful waters of the deeper pools, but never stopping, until, staggering, gasping, sobbing, I reached the safety of the cañon.

CHAPTER EIGHT

IT was my boyish ambition to find some corner of those rocky wilds where no human being had ever set foot and to be the first person to behold it. What boy has not felt that Columbus had several centuries' advantage of him: that Balboa was a meddlesome old chap who might better have stayed in Spain and left American oceans to American boys to discover? Oh! the unutterable regret of youthful hearts that the Golden Fleece and the Holy Grail and other high adventures passed before their time!

In searching for my virgin wilderness, I saw many spots that bore no trace of human existence, wild enough, remote enough, calm enough, to justify my willing credulity.

But I had another notion which even my young enthusiasm had to acknowledge was in error. I fancied that the animals in such a spot as I have described, unwise to the ways of man, having had no experience to teach them fear and caution, would be gentle and trusting, and approachable. I was doomed to disappointment. I found that no matter how remote the region, how primeval its forests or how Eden-new its streams, its beasts were furtive, wary, distrustful.

But after all, though these ideas, like many of my other youthful dreams, did not "pan out" in following them up, I found other leads which yielded rich experiences.

When I first came to the mountains, the beavers were extremely wild. Rarely did I glimpse one or even see signs of their activities. True, all along the streams were deserted beaver homes, merely stick frames with most of the mud plaster fallen off, and through the meadows were a succession of dams which might easily have flooded them for miles around. No doubt large colonies had once lived there. Once in a while I found a fallen aspen, with the marks of a beaver's keen chisels upon it. But as for the beaver's renowned industry—it wasn't!

"I thought beavers were busy animals," I complained to the Parson. "I've heard industrious folks called beavers all my life. I don't see how they got their reputation. Why, it wouldn't be hard for me to be busier'n these beavers!"

The old man laughed.

"Now, you're rather hard on the little critters," he defended. "They're not so indolent, considering their chances." Then he went on to explain.

A horde of trappers, he said, had followed Kit Carson's successful trip into the region in 1840. They visited every stream and strung traps in all the valleys. Beaver fur was taken out by pack-train load. In twenty years the trappers had reaped the richest of the harvest; in ten years more they had practically "trapped out" all the beavers. They left only when trapping ceased to be profitable; and even so, the early settlers had found some small profit in catching a few beavers every winter.

The survivors, my old friend said, were wiser if sadder animals than those the first trappers found. Many beavers had maimed or missing feet, reminders of the traps that caused their trouble. They deserted their ponds, neglected their dams and houses and sought refuge in holes in the banks of streams. Their tunnels entered the bank under water, thus making it difficult to locate their runways, or to set traps after the discovery of the runways.

So that was the reason for the beavers scarcity and wariness! Few were the chances they gave me, on my early rambles, to observe their habits. But just when it seemed they were doomed to suffer the fate of the buffalo, Colorado and a few other states woke up to the fact that beavers were threatened to be classed with the dodo, and feeble measures were taken to protect them. Slowly their numbers increased, they returned to their normal habits of living, and rebuilt their dams and houses.

Down in the valley below my cabin, within a few rods of the spot where the ruins of Kit Carson's cabin still stand, are two small streams along which I early found numerous traces of beaver. At the confluence of these streams were dams and houses that were not entirely deserted; for occasionally the beavers did some repair work. Since they were within five minutes' walk of my cabin I visited them frequently during all seasons of the year. Five times I saw the beavers return to the old home site, repair the dams and rebuild the houses. Four times I saw them forced to desert their home, once because a fire burned the surrounding trees which were their source of food, the other times to elude trappers.

I discovered that this colony consisted of a trap-maimed old couple and their annual brood. The male had lost a portion of his right hind foot, his mate had only a stump for her left front one. I early dubbed them Mr. and Mrs. Peg, and came to have a real neighborly affection for them. Their infirmities made it easy for me to keep track of them, and to keep up with their social activities. Neighborly interest must be kept alive by the neighbors' doings, you know!

They certainly showed no inclination to become dull from overwork! About the time the ice on their pond began to break up, they would take their youngsters and start upon their summer vacation. Upon a number of occasions I found their familiar tracks along the streams eight or ten miles below their home site; once more than fifteen miles away. On their rambles they met other beaver families, and stopped to visit; the young people of the combined families played and splashed about, while their more sedate elders lay contentedly basking in the sun.

But late August or early September always saw Mr. and Mrs. Peg back home; usually without their youngsters. Those precocious paddlers had set up homes for themselves or had wedded into other tribes. The old couple at once set to work, toiling night and day, taking no time off for rest. They repaired their dam to raise the water to the desired level, replastered their house inside and out with mud, and in addition cut down a number of aspen trees, severed their trunks into lengths they could handle, and brought both trunks and limbs down into the pond. They towed the heavy green wood down first and piled it in the deep water near their house, the rest they piled upon these until their larder was full. They ate the whole of the smaller limbs of the aspen, but only the bark of the larger boughs and trunks. They used the wood for house and dam construction.

Trappers have told me that the streams beaver live in are poor fishing places because the furry inhabitants eat the fish. By careful observation, I proved to my own satisfaction at least, that quite the opposite is true. For the deep ponds made by the dams they build are literally spawning pools for the trout, breeding grounds and hatcheries. They are also pools of refuge, to which the fish flee to elude the fisherman, and in their warmer depths the finny tribe "hole up" when the streams are frozen over in winter. I have lain motionless upon a bowlder overlooking a beaver-inhabited stream and watched large trout lazing about almost within reach of a pre-occupied paddler, apparently in no alarm over his nearness. Neither paid the other "any mind." I am sure that beavers eat neither fish nor flesh.

Which reminds me that early in my mountain experience I happened upon an old trapper's log cabin and stopped to visit him. Mountain hospitality generously insists that guests be fed, no home or hut is too poor to provide a bite for the chance visitor. Upon this occasion I was handed a tin plate with some meat on it.

"Guess what it is," my host urged.

I tasted the meat, examined it, smelled it and tried to make out what it was. It tasted somewhat like venison, yet not quite the same. It had something the flavor of cub-bear steak broiled over a campfire, but it was sweeter and not so strong. I guessed wrong several times before the trapper informed me.

"Beaver tail," he laughed, pleased at outwitting me.

Still chuckling he went outside to a little log meat house and returned with a whole beaver tail for my inspection. The tail was about ten inches in length, nearly five inches wide at the broadest part and perhaps an inch thick. The skin that covered the tail was dark in color and very tough, suggestive of alligator skin. The meat of the beaver tail was much prized by explorers and trappers, and visitors, such as I, were often given this meat as a special treat.

The old fellow talked at length about the wise ways of the beaver he had caught. Though I made note of a number of his observations for future reference, I was skeptical of their authenticity. As years passed and I talked with many men, I found that their observations varied greatly. They were not always unprejudiced observers, their observations were colored by their personal point of view, under diverse conditions.

I early learned that trappers and hunters, as a rule, are not real nature students. They are killers, and killers have not the patience to wait and watch, to take painstaking care and limitless time in the study of an animal. They will spend only a few minutes watching an animal that a man without a gun might study for days, or even weeks. They are prone to snap judgment.

Then their over-active imaginations supply ready misinformation for missing facts.

"A beaver has as many wives as he can git," my host informed me as we sat before his fire. "There's some that don't have many, and agin there's some that have a lot, and that's the reason we find some ponds with only a little house an' others with mighty big ones."

A Brigham Youngish sort of conception of beaver domestic economy!

That same summer another trapper in Middle Park, not many miles from the first, gave me his version of a beaver's domestic life.

"Don't think they mate at all," he told me; "they're always working to beat time or else they're wanderin' off somewhere lookin' up good cuttin' timber and dam sites."

Now, I am sure that Mr. and Mrs. Peg were mated, and for life. Indeed, I believe all beavers mate for life. They are by nature domestic, home-loving and industrious, and provident, storing up food for the winter, making provision against the time food will be scarce because of snow and ice. They have the coöperative instinct and often combine their efforts, constructing a house large enough for the whole colony in the deepest water of the pond, all joining in the harvesting of green aspen or cottonwood.

Every fall I watched Mr. and Mrs. Peg at their repairs. Their tribe increased as the years

EVERY FALL I WATCHED MR. AND MRS. PEG AT THEIR
REPAIRS.

passed, and the shielding laws of the state protected them. I called their group the "Old Settlers" colony.

One fall the Old Settlers abandoned their pond and constructed an entirely new dam above it, thus solving a number of problems. Sand and gravel carried down by the swift little stream had settled in the still water of the pool and almost filled it. The ever-increasing family outgrew the old house. All the near-by aspens had been cut; this necessitated the dragging of trees too great a distance before they could be pushed into the water and floated down. Coyotes had surprised and killed a number of the Old Settlers' kin as they worked on the long portage to the stream, and I am sure that the moving of their home was partly to overcome this danger.

Then it was they earned the title, "Busy Beaver"! How they worked! That was before the days of ubiquitous automobiles and the beavers had not become nocturnal in their habits. They swarmed everywhere. Certain ones were detailed to inspect the dam, make necessary repairs and maintain the water at the same level all the time. Others worked at the new house, piling sicks and mud into a heap. It grew, the dam was raised, so the water was maintained within a few inches of the top of the unfinished wall. Occasionally I caught a glimpse of some workers in the deep water or near the shores of the ponds; they were digging safety-firsts, water escapes for emergency use. These canals led from the house to either bank and connected with tunnels that had their openings concealed beneath the surface of the water. Thus, should their pond be drained suddenly, they could escape by the canals to their emergency homes beneath the bank.

Other beavers worked in the aspen grove, felling trees and cutting them into lengths that could be pushed or pulled or rolled to the bank and floated down the stream. Their work was impeded by the jamming of the logs in a narrow rocky neck down which they had to be skidded into the water.

Then the engineers decided upon the construction of a canal around the rocky falls. They started digging at a point upstream, beyond the troublesome neck, swung outward, away from the water to the fringe of aspens, then back again to the stream below the rocks. In all the canal was two hundred feet long, about two feet wide and averaged fifteen inches deep. For a time all other work was suspended, and night and day the whole population toiled on the canal. Apparently each beaver had his own section to dig, and each went about his work in his own way. With tooth and claw they worked. Often they cut slides or runways down the sides of the canal giving them roads up which they carried their loose dirt.

For thirty-seven nights they toiled in the dry ditch, then turned water in, and completed the work of deepening the canal. This transportation system saved them much labor and delay, and provided a safe route to and from the grove, for they could dive into the water when their enemies attacked.

I suspected Mr. and Mrs. Peg directed the storing away of that wood, for it was piled in the deep water beside the house, now rising majestically several feet about the level of the pool, just as they always did theirs. The green wood was almost as heavy as the water, and required little weight to force it under. Thus they always had some food in their icebox, where they could reach it handily when the pool froze over. I have observed other beavers on larger streams come out of their tunnels in the banks and find food along the shores throughout the winter months. But the smaller the stream the closer the beaver sticks to his pond. This I believe is a matter of safety for beavers are slow travelers, and if they venture far from their pool they fall easy prey to such enemies as bobcats, coyotes, wolves and mountain lions.

One day while following one of the small tributaries of the St. Vrain River south of Long's Peak, I heard a loud explosion just ahead of me, and when I emerged from the fringing woods I discovered two men busy dynamiting the largest of the three beaver dams in the valley.

"Mining didn't pan out much," one of them replied in answer to my question, "so we callated we'd take sum beaver fur to tide us over the winter."

They were prospectors, out of grub, up against starving or getting a job in the foothills town below, until with their golden promises, they could again talk some sympathetic listener out of a grub stake. Not content with obtaining beaver by the usual but slower method of trapping, they had decided to blow up the dam, drain the pond and shoot the animals as they sought to escape. Their rifles lay ready to their hands.

For hours I lingered, to see what luck they would have. They set off three heavy charges before the dam was shattered. When the water was nearly drained out—it took but a few minutes—they grabbed their guns. Not a beaver did any of us see.

They then set a charge of powder against the house and blew a gaping hole in its side—but there was nobody home! Evidently all had escaped by the canal in the bottom of the pond to the tunnel beneath the bank.

The men would not admit defeat, but set about to dig the beavers out of the bank. Darkness saw their task unfinished so they camped for the night at the entrance of the tunnel; they piled heavy stones at its mouth hoping to trap the animals within.

Next morning I watched them resume their work, feeling sympathy for the beavers, but not daring to interfere. Shortly after noon the quest ended quite unexpectedly. The diggers had discovered a hidden exit that was concealed among the willows, the beavers had followed the canal, which could not be drained, to their refuge tunnel in the bank; and when their enemies destroyed the tunnel, they had used the hidden exit, and had in all probability made good their retreat during the night.

As more people settled in the valleys, there was an inevitable overlapping of claims. The settlers claimed both the water and the land, and they had government deeds to back them up in their claims. But the beaver had prior rights, and gamely adhered to them. A feud arose that is still unsettled between the Old Settlers and the newcomers. In my rambles I continually came upon homesteaders striving to drain the valleys and raise grass for their cattle, while simultaneously the beavers were working to maintain high water. Many of them lost their lives for their cause, but rarely did they forsake a home site once established. In the same sections, where the homesteaders had used aspen for their fence posts, the beavers, no doubt mistaking them for trees, cut them down. Sometimes their pluck and persistence won them the admiration of their enemies. In most cases they won out.

One day, far up near the headwaters of the Cache la Podre River in Colorado, I came upon a rancher trying to drain a number of beaver ponds to secure water for irrigation; it was a very dry season and water was scarce. During the day he tore gaps in the dams, during the night the beavers repaired the breaks. When after opening the dams the rancher hurried down to his fields to regulate the flow of water, the beavers, even in the daytime, would swarm forth and plug up the holes.

Finally in desperation, the man set traps in the gaps he had opened in the dams. He caught a few beavers and decided that his troubles were over. But the survivors met the emergency. They floated material down from above and wedged it into the breaks, without going near the traps.

At this stage of the struggle an old prospector came down from the higher mountains, driving his burros ahead of him. Hearing of the rancher's predicament, he suggested his own panacea for all troubles, dynamite. Enthusiastically, the rancher accepted his proposal. Soon the dams were in ruins.

A mile below where the dams had been destroyed an irrigation ditch tapped the river and carried a full head to the green fields. I saw the rancher standing in the middle of the field, water flowing all about him. He looked upstream and chuckled, then leaned triumphantly on his shovel handle. For a long time, he leaned thus, lost in dreams of prosperity.

Suddenly he awoke and hurried along his supply ditch. Barely a trickle was coming down it. The beavers had dammed the intake.

I once worked for a rancher who had a homestead on the North Fork of the St. Vrain River, which heads south of Long's Peak. He had just finished clearing a patch of ground to raise "truck" on.

"We've got to get rid of some beaver," he told me the very first day. He shouldered his shovel and walked down to the dam that sprawled across the meadow for several hundred feet.

"I cut her loose," he informed me on his return. "She'll soon dry out so we can put in the crop."

Next morning, whistling happily, he started out for the meadow. His whistle died away as he caught sight of the water in the pond. It was as high as usual. The beavers had repaired the break.

Day after day he cut the dam, night after night, the beavers repaired it. He trapped five of them before they became "trap-wise." After that they either turned the traps over or covered

them with mud. After trying a number of ruses
to frighten them away, the man hung a lighted
lantern in the break he had opened in the dam.
The next morning his whistle piped, merrily, the
break was still open. But his joy was short-lived,
for on the following night the beavers constructed a new section of dam above the break,
curving it like a horseshoe.

"Hope they appreciated my givin' 'em light
to work by," he laughed; and gave up the contest.

Beavers seem to possess sagacity in varying
degrees. The old animals are wise according to
their years; the stupid and lazy die young. They
adapt themselves quickly to changed conditions;
they outwit their enemies by sheer cunning, never
in physical combat; rarely do they defend themselves—and not once have I known one to take
the offensive side of a fray. Watching them
waddling along, one wonders how they accom-
plish their great engineering feats in so short a
time. Of course, they can move more rapidly in
water than on land, but I suspect its "everlasting
teamwork" that accounts for their achievements.
They are prolific and, unlike the bees, drones are
unknown to them. Coöperative industry—there
lies the secret.

I was absent from my cabin for more than a
year; and upon my return at once visited the
Old Settlers. Like any other thriving commun-

ity, they had made several improvements—two new ponds and houses had been built. Tracks in the edge of a small new pond showed that my pioneer friends, Mr. and Mrs. Peg, had removed to a new home. Whether the increasing number of beavers in the larger pond got on the old folks' nerves, I do not know; but whatever the reason, they were living alone. I walked rapidly toward their home, instead of approaching slowly and giving them a chance to look me over. As I neared the edge of the road, one of them, I presume Pa Peg, smote the water a mighty whack with his tail. Both disappeared. I watched for their reappearance, for I knew that they were watching me from their concealment among the willows. I sang, whistled, called to them to come out—that I was their old friend returned. My persistence was at last rewarded. Shyly they came to the surface, watching me sharply the while, diving at my slightest movement, reappearing on the farther shore, cautious and canny as ever.

It was spring. Within a few weeks after my homecoming the Pegs would permit my near approach as they had done before I went away. Though they worked mostly at night, they did venture out in daytime. If they were working at separate tasks, the first to discover me would thump the ground or give the water a resounding whack.

One morning Daddy Peg was missing from the pond. Downstream I picked up his tracks and discovered that he was hastening away from home. As it was springtime, I was not concerned lest he was deserting his faithful wife. It was his habit to leave home when Mrs. Peg was "expecting." I knew he'd come waddling back in a few weeks to give the babies their daily plunge.

Sure enough, Mrs. Peg came forth with four midgets in fur; a happy, romping family that splashed about the pool for hours at a time. Like all their kin, they had been born with their eyes open and were much "perter" then other animal infants. They swam, and ate, and took the trail at once. If Mrs. Peg showed fear of anything, the youngsters took quick alarm, and forever afterward shunned the object. Of me, Mrs. Peg took little notice, merely giving me the right of way if I intruded on one of her trails, or stopping work to watch me curiously whenever I came near. The beaver babies accepted me as a friend, permitted me to sit or stand near them as they played.

One morning, as I approached the pool, I discovered the four youngsters in great agitation. They were not playing. They swam about restlessly, circled the pool, visited the dam, swam out to their house, dived inside it, only to reappear almost at once. I searched around the pond, and found their mother's fresh tracks leading to-

ward the aspen grove.   Near it she had been
overtaken by a coyote.

In vain I tried to catch the motherless waifs,
but they eluded me.   I went home, made a rude
sort of dip-net from an old sack, and returned
to the pool.

During my absence a strange beaver mother
with a brood of five babies had visited the pool
where the orphans lived.   She immediately
adopted the wee bereft babies.   Shortly the pool
was merry with the rompings of the combined
families.

CHAPTER NINE

MOUNTAIN climbing is the reverse of the general rule of life in that the ascent is easier than the descent, and much safer. Most climbers underestimate the time required to make a chosen trip, and, starting out with the day before them, ascend at their leisure, making frequent and unnecessarily long stops to rest, drinking in the beauty of the prospect from each rise attained, forgetting to allow themselves sufficient time for the even more difficult descent. Consequently the return trip is crowded on the edge of darkness, a dangerous condition on any trail any time, but especially hazardous when the climber is weary and, therefore, not alert. It is impossible for him to see the slight footholds or handholds on which he must put his trust, and weight.

One day, as a boy, I came to grief because I was so absorbed by the interesting things about me that I took no note of the passing of time or of the altitude to which I had climbed. From my camp at Bear Lake I had followed the old Flat-

top trail to the Divide, from which I could see
a hundred miles or more in all directions; to
the north the mountains of Wyoming peeped
through purple haze; eastward, the foothills
dropped away to the flat and endless prairies,
with gleaming lakes everywhere. West and
south, my own Rockies rose, tier on tier, to
snowy heights. Gay and fragrant flowers beckoned my footsteps off the trail; friendly conies
"squee-eked" at me from their rocky lookout
posts; fat marmots stuffed themselves, making
the most of their brief summer. A buck deer
left off polishing his new horns on a scraggly
timberline tree to look at me. Overhead an eagle
swept round and round in endless circles.

From the rim of the cañon, between Flattop
and Hallett, I viewed the spot where I had
blundered over the edge of the snow-cornice on
the way to the dance. Beneath lay Tyndall
glacier, its greenish ice exposed by the summer
thaw. I circled the head of the canon and
climbed to the top of Hallett. From my eerie
height, I got an eagle's view of the world below
—a hazy, hushed world where the birds called
faintly, the brooks murmured quietly and even
the wind spoke in whispers. From near by came
the crash of glacier ice; falling rocks that thun-
dered down the cliffs.

All the afternoon I traveled along the crest
of the Divide, wandering southward, away from

familiar country into a new maze of peaks and glaciers, deep cañons and abrupt precipices. Suddenly a gale of wind struck me, blinded me with penetrating snow. In that instant, without preliminary or warning, summer changed to winter, and forced me off the heights. It was impossible to thread my way back over the route I had come; for it twisted in and out, around up-flung crags and cliffs.

My compass showed that the wind was driving eastward, the direction in which I wanted to go; so I headed down wind, secure in the thought that I would soon be off the roof of the world. Lightning and heavy thunder accompanied the snowstorm, the clouds came down and blotted out the day; twilight descended upon the earth.

A band of mountain sheep started up from their shelter behind an upthrust rock and ran ahead of me. I followed them, partly because they ran in the direction I was going, and partly because they are apt to select the safest way down the cliffs.

But they turned aside the moment they were out of the wind, swung up on a protected ledge and there halted to wait out the storm. My compass had gone crazy. A dozen times I tried it out. It would point a different direction whenever I moved a few steps. However, the compass mattered little; the chief thing that concerned me was getting down off the roof of the world.

Snow swirled down the cliffs, plastering rocks and ledges until both footholds and handholds were hidden. Still I had to go down, there was nothing else to do. The hardy sheep, with their heavy coats, could wait out the storm. But night, with numbing cold, and treacherous darkness in which I'd dare not move, would soon o'ertake and vanquish me.

For an hour the ledges provided footing. By turning about, twisting and doubling, there was always a way down. Of a sudden the clouds parted; a long bar of sunshine touched the green forest far below me, focused for a moment upon a single treetop, then vanished as though the shutter of a celestial camera has snapped shut.

At last I came to a ledge beneath which the sheer cliff dropped away into unfathomable snowy depths. After short excursions to right and left I discovered that a section of the cliff had split off and dropped into the cañon, leaving only sheer rock walls that offered nothing in the way of footholds. Irresolutely, I faced back the way I had come. Overhead the wind roared deafeningly; the snow came piling down. No hope of retracing my steps. I was tired; that upward climb would be slow and tortuous, would require great strength and endurance. I faced about and began a thorough, desperate search for a downward route. I stood marooned in the cañon wall shaped like a crude horseshoe. At its toe water had leaped down and eroded a slight groove in the solid rock. This was my only chance. It was not inviting, but I had no alternative. It led me down a hundred feet, then tightened into a sort of chimney. Just below I could see the swaying top of a big tree. Firewood must be near at hand! Wider ledges must lay close beneath!

Fifty feet down the chimney, just as it deepened into a comfortable groove with rough, gripable sides, I came to a sudden halt, for the rock was broken away; the cleft bottom of the chute overhung the cliff below. Sweat streamed down my face, in spite of the cold wind. Visions of a leaping campfire died out of my mind.

The Engelmann spruce swayed toward me encouragingly, as though offering to help me down. But its top was many feet from the wall. There was an abandoned bird's nest in it; a little below that was a dead limb with a woodpecker's incision at its base. By leaning out I could see, a hundred feet or more below the bottom of the swaying tree.

In my extremity I shouted, even as I had done in the glacier crevasse, though there was no one to hear. The echo came back sharply. "There must be another wall angling this one," I thought.

"It's got to be done, there's no other way" I spoke the words out loud to boost my courage.

The tip of the old spruce rose to almost my level; but there was that intervening gulf between it and the rock on which I stood. How wide was that gulf, I wondered. Five feet? Ten? Too far!

A score of times I surveyed the tree-top, tried to estimate the distance, sought a foothold in the cramped rock chute, and worked into position for the leap.

No sharpshooter ever aligned his sights more carefully than I did my feet. My coat was buttoned tightly, cap pulled down. When at last I was all set, I hesitated, postponed the jump and cowered back against the wall. A dozen times I made ready, filled my lungs with deep breaths, stretched each leg out to make sure it was in working order, but every time my courage failed me.

Suddenly resolute, not giving myself chance to think, I tensed, filled my lungs, leaned away from the rock, and launched headlong.

As my body crashed into the treetop my fingers clutched like talons, my arms clasped the limbs as steel bands. I was safe in the arms of that centuries-old spruce.

Never since that day have I taken such a chance. The thought of it, even now, sends cold, prickly chills along my spine.

That time trouble came out of a clear sky, but sometimes a bit of innocent curiosity betrays one. Thus one day, with sunshine overhead and peaceful murmurs below, I stood upon a rock spire upthrust from the slope of Mount Chapin, watching a band of Bighorn sheep above timber-line. The Fall River road now runs past the spot where they were feeding. When I climbed up toward them, they gathered close together, some of them scrambling up rocks for vantage points, all watching me interestedly. They were not excited. They moved away slowly at my near approach, stopping now and then to watch me or to feed. For several hours I kept my position below them; sometimes edging close to one of them, keeping in sight at all times, and being careful not to move quickly.

The band worked its way to the foot of the steeper slopes, above the tree line, hesitated, eyed me, then started up a narrow little passage that led up between two cliffs. A rock-slide cluttered this granite stair. Stable footholds were impossible for the loose rocks slipped and slid, rolled from beneath the sheep's feet and bounded down the slope.

Of a sudden something frightened the Bighorn, just what I had no time to learn. Instantly every one of those nineteen sheep was in full flight up the rock-slide. They bounded right and left, tacked across it, turned, scrambled up, slipped back, tumbled, somersaulted, but always regained their balance and made steady headway.

They seemed to have lost their wits, for they scattered, each selecting his own route, all striving with great exertion to make speed up the steep slope.

A barrage of stones fell all about me. Dust-puffs dotted the slide. Then the whole thing seemed to move downward, like the rapids of a river, dashing rock spray everywhere. The air was filled with flying granite, as hurtling rocks struck and exploded into smoky fragments. Bits, the size of wine-saps, scattered like bird-shot; larger pieces, the size of bushel baskets and barrels, bounded and danced, leaped away from the slope, out into space, and dropped like plummets. Huge bowlders (sleeping Titans that they were) stirred, roused themselves, and came crashing down, plowing through the forest below, furrowing the earth and cutting a swath through the trees as clean as a scythe through grass. What was first merely the metallic clink of rolling stones changed to a steady bombardment, and then into a sullen, ominous roar as the giant bowlders got under way.

For me the scene had changed abruptly; a moment since I had been following the wild sheep with ready camera, stalking them, entertaining them with antics, occasionally hiding for a moment to excite them. Now pandemonium reigned. The first few stones I dodged; then they came too thick to be avoided. I dived headlong behind a bowlder, partly buried in the slide. Like a rabbit I hid there, clinging as the stones hailed about me, afraid to lift my head. Rocks struck close, filling my eyes with gritty dust, choking me. Then a gaint slab came grinding downward. I could hear it coming, its slow thunder drowned out all other sounds. The whole mountain heaved. My rock fort shook, flinging me backward amidst a deluge of smaller stones. Over and over I rolled, with the loosened rocks, fighting frantically every instant.

Inside a few short, busy seconds the giant slab shot past, my bowlder had halted it for only a second. As I leaped aside I was pelted by a score of stones, battered, bruised, knocked half unconscious, eyes filled with sharp, cutting grit. At last I gained the outer edge of the whirlpool, where the movement was less rapid, where only the smaller stones trickled down. Dazed, bleeding and breathless, I was flung aside, too blinded to see and too stunned to avoid the projectiles shooting my way.

The slide lessened; its roar diminished; only occasional rocks came down. Then came silence, vast, still and awesome after the uproar. But it was broken by the belated descent of tardy stones, loath to be left behind. Miniature slides started, hesitated and scattered.

Like a battered bark I lay half submerged at the edge of the slide. My cap was gone, my camera lost, my clothes torn; in a score of places I was scratched or bruised. I crawled farther from the danger line, found a trickle of water below a melting snowbank, where I drank and laved my bruises. At length I started down the mountain, safe, but not sound; somewhat wiser, thrilled tremendously at the experience that had come unannounced.

It is always thus in mountain climbing—the unexpected is the rule!

The habit of estimating time by the number of miles to be traveled goes by the board in mountain work. A mile stood on end ceases to be a mile and becomes a nightmare. Trail miles, or those that stretch across the mountain tops, are not even related to the miles of straight, smooth highway of the lower levels. A new unit of measurement should be created for alpine climbers, to conform to the haughty attitude of the mountains. At times, upon the crest of the Continental Divide, and at an altitude of from ten to twelve thousand feet, I have covered from three to five miles in an hour. And again, while breaking a snow trail, creeping up treacherous glacier ice, or edging along the ledges, I have often reversed the digits, taking several hours to gain a single mile.

Then, too, no trip is taken twice under the

same conditions. The mountains are never the same: the weather, the wind, snow or rain conditions may alter decidedly the footing upon their slopes. Thus a climb that was accomplished on the first of June in one year without serious obstacles may, on the same date another year, be found to be impossible. Experienced mountaineers intuitively know when to proceed, or to turn back; and though they may not be able to explain why they abandon or continue a trip, they "feel" their actions imperative.

So climbing tests a man's judgment, his physical endurance, and tries his soul. It brings out his true character. The veneer of convention wears through inside a few miles of trail work and reveals the individual precisely as he is, often to his shame but usually to his glory. Thus a silent, backward boy one day became a hero by diving headlong across smooth ice to rescue a trio of climbers who had lost their footing and had started to slide across a glacier. Again, upon a certain climb, two husky men who gave promise of conquering the ascent without trouble, turned out to be the weakest of weaklings, abusing all the party, demanding all the guide's help for themselves.

"You can't never tell how fur a toad'll jump!" the Parson said disgustedly as he heard the tale of these two huskies who had turned babies; "nor which way neither."

One of the things which I have found most helpful on hard climbs, is mental preparation. If there are certain, lurking dangers to be overcome, I have found it a decided help to admit the facts freely before attempting the climb; picturing as far as it can be done the situations that may arise. In this way it is possible, to a certain degree, to anticipate emergencies before they happen and to prepare for them. It also helps one to act with imperative promptness.

It is less easy to prescribe for physical preparation. Equipment must vary with needs and these are as varied as the climbers themselves. However, I have found that it is well to dress lightly, for this permits freedom of movement. Personally I prefer light, low shoes that reach just above the ankle, the soles studded with soft-headed hob nails, not the iron ones. A change of socks is sometimes a life-saver, for frequently the footing leads through ice water or soft snow. Numb feet are always clumsy and slow, and dangerous besides. I have found it best to wear medium-weight wool underclothes and just enough outer garments to keep one warm. A staff is a handicap on rockwork, but helpful on glaciers or other ice climbing.

On the mountain tops, as well as upon the highways, speed is dangerous. Haste on a mountain brings grief of various kinds, nausea, needless exhaustion, injuries. Never sprint!

Climb slowly, steadily, like a sober old pack-horse. You will make better time, and reach the summit in condition to enjoy your achievement.

I came to distrust, and to test out, every rung in my rocky ladders. I found that even the most secure-appearing "stepping stones" were often rotten and treacherous, weathered by the continual freezing and thawing of the moisture in its seams. Often a mere touch was sufficient to shatter them, but sometimes it was not until I put my weight upon them, holding to a shrub or an earth-buried bowlder the while, that they gave way.

I learned, too, that the wise selection of a route up and down is the crucial test of a good guide. In such selection there are no rules; for every climb presents problems particularly its own, and what worked out well on the last climb may turn out to be dangerous on the next. Thus, on one ascent of the cliffs of Black Cañon, my companion suggested that we follow a "chimney," a water-worn crack that offered convenient toe-holds. We ascended by the selected route without difficulty. But an hour later, when a similar ascent confronted us, we selected the same sort of route and came to grief, finding our way blocked by an overhanging wall impossible to surmount.

The actual climbing of difficult places becomes

a habit, so far as the physical effort is concerned, leaving one free to inspect the precipices above, and to feel out, instinctively, the possible routes to the top.

The selection of a way up difficult places calls for the sixth sense, instinct, which cannot always be acquired by experience. Wild animals possess this "instinct" to a great degree; but human beings are not so unerring. One man may be blest with it, but another, with equal experience, will be unreliable. There is no accounting for the wide difference in their accuracy, it exists—that is all we know.

There are times when even with this guiding instinct, one comes to grief; though I have noted that grief came to me most often when I was tired, less alert, and more prone to take chances or needless risks. Sometimes, under stress of haste to get off a dangerous place before darkness overtook me, I have had to leap without looking. No climber may expect to survive many such reckless steps. It is the rule of the mountains that you look—then do not leap. In most of life's experiences we may make a mistake and, if wise, profit by it. But in mountain climbing the first mistake is liable to be the last.

Mountain climbing is a game, a big game; divided as are other sports into minor and major divisions. The minor climbs include the lesser peaks, safe, well-marked trails that lead to comfortable night camps: the major division includes almost everything from peeping into an active volcano to getting imprisoned in a glacier crevasse.

Colorado offers wide variety of experience in both divisions. It has forty-odd peaks above fourteen thousand feet, with hundreds of others almost as high, yet unknown and unmapped. The peaks that are most widely known, and most often climbed are Pike's Peak near Colorado Springs and Long's Peak in the Rocky Mountain National (Estes) Park. Pike's has long been easily accessible by way of the famous cog road, and more recently an automobile road has reached its top. But Long's has no royal road to its summit. Only a foot trail partly encircles it.

There are many other than these two peaks to challenge the climber. The Flattops, in western Colorado, are not necessarily low or smooth, though flat. The San Juan Mountains are extremely rough and rugged. The Sangre de Christo Range is at once rarely beautiful and forbidding. The Never-summer and Rabbit Ear ranges invite exploration, and the great Continental Divide has no peers.

Every mountain offers its peculiar attractions and difficulties. All mountains entice the bravehearted and the adventurous. Occasionally men lose their lives in conquering them and not infrequently women die heroically scaling their slopes.

Long's Peak was early the objective of experienced mountain climbers. For a number of years it defied all efforts to scale it. From 1864 to 1868 a number of unsuccessful attempts to reach the top failed. In the summer of 1868 a party in charge of W. N. Byers, who had led the first unsuccessful party, reached the top. Since that time each year has seen an increasing number of successful climbers. Most climbers go in small parties, for large ones (more than five) are dangerous. Dogs are dangerous companions on a climb, because they start rock-slides.

As a boy I lived at the foot of this forbidding Sphinx, climbed it every month in the year, and thus came to know its mighty moods, the terrific fury of its storms, the glory of its outlook.

Miss Carrie J. Welton lost her life upon the Peak in 1884. She gave out near the top and her guide, Carlyle Lamb, son of the Parson, made heroic efforts to save her. But he, too, became exhausted and had to leave her alone while he went for help.

But when help arrived, Miss Welton was dead, having perished from exhaustion and cold.

Other casualties have occurred on this towering mountain. A boy left his parents in camp at the foot of the Peak and disappeared. Late in the summer, as the snowbanks diminished, his body was found, lying at the base of the three-thousand-foot precipice. One man was killed by the accidental discharge of a pistol. A doctor was killed by lightning. In January, 1925, occurred a double tragedy. Miss Agnes Vaille perished near the spot where Miss Welton lost her life, and under similar conditions. Herbert Sortland, member of the rescue party, became lost and perished in the storm that was raging over the heights. His body was found many weeks afterward within a few minutes' walk of home.

CHAPTER TEN

BACK on the farm of my childhood, the names of Kit Carson, Jim Bridger, Buffalo Bill and other renowned frontiersmen were ever on the lips of my parents. Their reckless bravery that took no thought of self, their diplomatic cunning that cleverly kept the Indians friendly, their unlimited resourcefulness, equal to the most unprecedented emergencies, were the subjects of many a heroic tale. When I came West, no matter how far I penetrated into remote regions, if there were trapper or prospector about, I found the immortal fame of these intrepid pathfinders had traveled into those mountain-guarded wildernesses.

They became the heroes of my boyish dreams, the patterns of my conduct, the inspiration of my ideals. I seized upon every written word concerning them and plowed through thick, poorly-printed volumes on the frontier for one brief sentence about these gallant scouts. I longed to emulate their fearless, immortal deeds. They left an indelible impress upon my character, even as they had upon the romantic annals of their country.

My growing familiarity with the Rocky Mountain region opened up one trail in which I could follow their footsteps. Tourists were finding out the country, guides were in demand. In the early days, before the creation of the National Park, guides were unlicensed. Any experienced old-timer or climber could take parties up the Peak or on other alpine trips. I began guiding by taking occasional visitors up Long's. I furnished my horse, and on most trips, supplies, wrangled the pack-horses, made camp, cooked the meals, and gave invaluable advice and "first aid" all for the munificent wage of five dollars a day! That sum made the replacement of climb-shattered cameras, the purchasing of a few coarse, cheap garments, and the acquiring of a Montgomery Ward library, all such riches, possible.

The work afforded none of the opportunities for fame and glory that had lurked in the trails of my heroes; I did not creep steathily from a wagon train in the dead of night to thwart the redmen in a fiendish massacre; I was not compelled to kill game to furnish food for my charges; I did not have to find fords across wide, deep and treacherous unknown rivers, and steer panic-stricken cattle or heavily laden oxen across them. But even though the work lacked the glamour of the pioneers' primitive, golden day, it was not without engrossing interests. It was filled with drama, relieved by comedy, sometimes fraught with tragedy.

Yes; styles in guides have changed since Bill Cody scouted the plains, even as they have changed since I piloted my first party up Long's Peak. A new breed has sprung up since the people have made such wide use of their National Parks. Not only the modern guides outwit the savage elements, but, under the National Park administration, they are required to have a fund of general information, especially nature lore, to be able to identify the thousands of varieties of wild flowers, the birds, animals and trees; to conduct field classes in geology, and to explain every phenomenon of weather and climate. Such a guide must have the patience to answer numberless questions. All this in addition to watching his charges, as a nurse watches her patients, feeling their pulses, so to speak, and taking their physical and moral temperatures. He must keep up their morale with entertaining yarns, he must restrain their too ambitious experience, must protect them from their own foolhardiness. He must have the charity to forbear deriding their stupidity. He must be as courageous and resourceful as the old-time guides, though his trials may not be so spectacular. A guide soon plumbs a man's character and fathoms its weakness and its strength.

As a boy guide I trailed far into the wilds with hunting parties, and camped through the summers with fishermen, geologists, explorers and mountain climbers. The reaction of individuals to the open spaces has ever been interesting to me. I have seen voluble women silent before the awesome beauty. I have seen phlegmatic business men moved to tears. There was no way of anticipating people's reactions.

Nearly all climbers dread the altitude of the high country. It is the "Old Man of the Sea" to most "tenderfeet." It has as many forms as the clouds and changes them as readily. It pounces upon the innocent but not unsuspicious wayfarer in the form of nosebleed, short wind, earache, balky watches, digestive troubles, sleeplessness and oversleeping.

As guide one day for the wife of a well-known geologist, I secured a new idea regarding altitude. We were to spend the day above timberline, where we hoped to identify the distant mountain ranges, observe the wild life close at hand and collect flower specimens. We left the valley at dawn, let our horses pick their way slowly upward. We halted occasionally to watch a scampering chipmunk or to explain our harmless errand to a scolding squirrel.

Near the timberline we emerged into a little

grassy glade beside a rushing stream.   Far above and deep below us grew a dense forest of Engelmann spruce.   In the glade stood a detached grove of perhaps a dozen trees, dead and stripped almost bare of limbs and bark.

My lady stopped abruptly and stared at these. She shook her head sadly, murmuring to herself. At last she spoke:

"Isn't it too bad?" she grieved.

I agreed sympathetically, then peered about to learn the cause of our sudden sadness.

The lady pointed to the dead trees, wagged her head, and said:

"Isn't it too bad the altitude killed them?"

There were green trees a mile farther up the mountain above the dead ones in the glade.   Yet my lady insisted that the altitude had singled out and killed the little grove in the midst of the forest—so we let it go at that.

Of course, some persons really are affected by altitude, but weariness, lack of muscular as well as mental control, often creates altitudinous illusion.   Of this condition I had an example while guiding a party of three women and one man to the top of Long's Peak.   We climbed above timberline, headed through Storm Pass, and finally reached Keyhole without a single incident to mar the perfect day.   The ladies were new, but plucky, climbers; the man rather blustery, but harmless.

Beyond Keyhole lies rough going, smooth, sloping rocks and the "Trough" with its endless rock-slides that move like giant treadmills beneath the climber's feet. The pace I set was very slow. The man wanted to go faster, but I called attention to Glacier Gorge below, the color of the lakes in the cañon, in short, employed many tactics to divert him from his purpose.

My refusal to travel faster excited him, he became extremely nervous and made slighting remarks regarding my guiding ability that ruffled me and embarrassed the ladies. Hoping to convince him of his error, I speeded up. He remonstrated at once, but when I slowed down to our customary pace he still objected, saying we'd never reach the top before dark.

Suddenly he developed a new notion. Climbing out upon a ledge he lifted his arms and poised, as though to dive off the cliff.

"Guide," he called, his voice breaking, "I must jump."

After some confusion we were on our way again, the man within clutch of my hand. All progressed without further trouble until we reached the top of the trough, where we halted to rest and to look down into Wild Basin, memorable scene of my first camp! My charge craftily escaped my clutches, walked out on a promontory, and again threatened to jump. Secretly I hoped he would carry out his threat.

Before we began scaling the home stretch, I tried to persuade the erratic idiot to remain behind, but he refused. However, we all made the top safely. He relapsed into glum silence, which I hoped would last until we were safely off the peak. But as we stood near the brink of the three-thousand-foot precipice overlooking Chasm Lake, we were startled to hear his voice once more, raised to high pitch.

"I must jump over, I've got to jump," he screamed.

He waved his arms wildly, as though trying to fly. The ladies begged me not to approach him lest he totter from his precarious perch. Summoning all the authority I could command, I ordered him to come down off the rock. My commandment unheeded, next I humored him and tried to coax him back upon the pretext of showing him something of special interest. But he stood firm, mentally at least, if not physically.

Pushing the ladies ahead, I hurried on toward the trail. As I started, I waved good-by, and shouted:

"Go on, jump. Get it over with, coward!"

He turned back from the edge, swearing vengeance against me. In abusing me, however, he forget his obsession to jump.

During the summer of my experience with the man who wanted to jump, I guided a party of three men who behaved in a totally different, but in quite as unexpected, manner. They were three gentlemen from New York, who wished to make a night climb up Long's Peak. It was a beautiful moonlight night. Our party left the hotel at the foot of the Peak at eleven o'clock. Proceeding upward through the shadowy, moon-flecked forest, we sang songs, shouted, listened to the far-away calls of the coyotes in the valley below, and from timberline saw the distant lights of Denver. At one o'clock we reached the end of the horse trail. In two hours the horses had covered five miles and had climbed up thirty-five hundred feet. We were on schedule time. Though the sun would gild the summit of the Peak soon after four in the morning, we would arrive sufficiently ahead of it, to watch it rise.

All at once my troubles began. The three men wanted to race across bowlderfield. It was sheer folly and I told them so, and why, but failed to convince them. They raced. They kidded me for being slow, dared me to race them, and gib-ingly assured me that they would wait for me on top and command the sun not to rise until I got there.

They would have their little joke. They waited for me at Keyhole and we moved slowly along the shelf trail beyond. On that they raced again, but not far, for the steep slope of the trough with its slippery stones stood just beyond. Right there they insisted on eating their lunch,

an untimely lunch hour for there was hard climbing yet to do. Not satisfied with emptying their
lunch bags, they drank freely of some ice water
that trickled out from beneath a snowbank.

I got them going at last and we had gone only
a short way when two of them fell ill. They felt
they just had to lie down, and did so, and became
thoroughly chilled, which added to their pangs
of nausea. After awhile we proceeded very
slowly. No longer their song echoed against
the cliffs. They broke their pained silence only to
grumble at one another.

Midway of the rock-slide of the trough, they
stopped, and like balky mules, refused to go forward or turn back. In vain I urged them to start
down, assuring them the lower altitude would
bring relief. The sick men didn't care what happened; they craved instant relief by death or any
other instantaneous method, as seasick persons
always do. Their more fortunate friend looked
at them in disgust, as those who have escaped the
consequences of their deeds often look at those
who have not. He upbraided me for not keeping them from making fools of themselves. I
knew argument with him would be futile in his
quarrelsome frame of mind. I kept still. His sick
companions crawled beneath an overhanging
rock, and lay shivering and shaking, too miserable
to sleep. Presently he joined them, sputtering
at me as the author of all their troubles. His

sputterings grew intermittent, ceased. He was audibly asleep.

After a long time one of his pals demanded.

"Who in the — proposed this — — trip anyway?"

The conduct of these men was not unique. Most climbers start out exuberantly, burn up more energy than they can spare for the first part of the trip, and find themselves physically bankrupt before they've reached their goal. The rarefied air of the high country seems to make them lightheaded! The most disagreeable character to have in a party, as in other situations, is the bully, or know-it-all, who spoils everyone's fun. A guide is a trifle handicapped in handling such people, in that his civilized inhibitions restrain him from pushing them off the cliffs or entombing them in a crevasse. I was too small to do them physical violence anyway, so I had to resort to more subtle weapons, the most effective being ridicule. If a joke could be turned on the disturber he generally subsided. The rest of the crowd were profuse in their expressions of gratitude to me for such service rendered.

Such an individual was once a member of a fishing party I guided to Bear Lake. The trip was made on horseback and we hadn't gone a mile before he urged his horse out of line and raced ahead, calling to some kindred spirit to follow. They missed the turn and delayed the whole party more than an hour while being rounded up.

"Lanky," as the party dubbed him out of disrespect, blamed me for their getting lost, but dropped behind when he saw the half-suppressed mirth of the others. Along the way were many inviting pools, and occasionally we saw a fisherman. "Lanky" soon raised the question of trying out the stream, but was outvoted by the others. He was inclined to argue the matter, but we rode up the trail, leaving him to follow or fish as he desired.

At Bear Lake at that time was a canvas boat, cached twenty steps due west of a certain large bowlder that lay south of the outlet. The boat was small, would safely hold but two persons. As it was being carried to the water, "Lanky" appeared and insisted on having the first turn in it. To this the others agreed, much against my wishes. To save the others from the annoyance of the fellow, I went out with him in the boat.

The trout were too well fed to be interested in our flies, though "Lanky" and I paddled around and across, and tempted them with a dozen lures.

My passenger became abusive and blamed me for wasting a good fishing day by bringing the party to the lake. In the midst of his tirade the boat tilted strangely. For a few minutes he shamefully neglected me while he gave his whole attention to righting it.

By sundown the party had caught a few small fish, and were ready to quit. They had gladly let "Lanky" monopolize the boat so as to be spared his society. To "Lanky's" disgust we had caught only two six-inch fish. Just as we started for the shore he made a farewell cast.

Something struck his spinner; his reel sang, his rod bent, and he stood up in the boat, yelling instructions at me. The rest of the party quit fishing to watch him land the fish. The trout was a big one, and game, but we were in deep water with plenty of room. From the shore came excited directions: "Give him more line!" "Reel him in!" "Don't let him get under the boat!" "Head him toward the shore!" "Lanky" turned a superior deaf ear.

After a tussle of ten minutes a two-pound trout lay in the boat, and "Lanky" raised an exultant yell in which the cliffs of Hallett joined. Now, indeed, was justice gone astray, when the one disagreeable member of the party had the only luck.

When the last triumphant echo died away, I picked up his prize, inspected it critically, held it aloft for the others to witness. "I'm a deputy warden," I snapped at him disgustedly, "and you don't keep small ones while I'm around." With that I tossed the trout into the lake.

Just as I finished, the boat mysteriously upset, and "Lanky" and I followed the fish.

The early trips I made with parties were mostly short ones for game or fish, but as more and more visitors came each succeeding summer, longer trips became popular. From fishing, the summer guests turned to trail trips, camping en route and remaining out from five to ten days. To cross the Continental Divide was the great achievement. Everyone wanted to tell his stay-at-home neighbors about trailing over the crest of the continent, and snowballing in the summer.

The route commonly chosen was the Flattop trail to Grand Lake, where camp was pitched for a day or two; then up the North Fork of the Grand River (known farther south as the Colorado River) to Poudre Lake, where another camp was made. From here they made a visit to Specimen, a mountain of volcanic formation which rises from the lake shore. This peak has ever been the home of mountain sheep. One can always count on seeing them there, sometimes just a few stragglers, but often bands of a hundred or more.

However interesting the day's experience had been, the climax came after camp was made, supper served and cleared away, when a big bonfire was lighted and all sat about it talking over the happenings of the day, singing and putting on stunts. In the tourists' minds the guide and the grizzly were classed together; both were wild, strange and somewhat of a curiosity. Nothing delighted them more than to get the guide to talking about his life in the wilds. Most of them looked upon him as a sort of vaudeville artist.

When several parties were out on the same trip they all assembled around a common campfire. The guides were given the floor, or ground, and they made the most of the occasion. Such competition as there was! Each, of course, felt obliged to uphold the honor of his party and out-yarn his fellows. Their stories grew in the telling, each more lurid than the last. There were thrilling tales of bear fights; of battles with arctic storms above timberline; of finding rich gold-strikes and losing them again.

At first the guides stuck to authentic experiences. But as the demand outgrew their supply, they were forced to invention. They had no mean imaginations and entranced their tenderfoot audiences with their thrilling tales. Around the campfires of primitive peoples have started the folklore of races. These guides were more sophisticated than their rustic mien hinted, the points of their yarns more subtle than the city dwellers suspected.

One evening I reached the Poudre Lake camp at dusk, to find two other parties ahead of mine. The others had finished supper and were gathered around the campfire, with North Park Ned the center of attraction.

"I was camped over on Troublesome crick, an'

havin' a busy time with cookin', wranglin' the hosses and doin' all the camp work. The fellers, they was all men, were too plumb loco to help, everything they touched spelt trouble. They admired to have flapjacks, same as we et, for supper, an' they watched jest how I made 'em, an' flipped 'em in the frypan. Then they wanted to do the flippin'."

Ned chuckled quietly to himself and went on: "I hadn't realized afore that a tenderfoot with a pan of hot, smeary flapjacks is as dangerous as he is with a gun. He's liable to cut loose in any direction. He ain't safe nowhere. One of them I had out was called Doctor Chance; guess he got his name cause other folks took chances havin' him round. Well, Chance was the first flipper. I'd showed him the trick of rotatin' the frypan to loosen the jacks so't they wouldn't stick an' cause trouble. The doctor got the hang of flippin' 'em 'an did a good job 'til he wanted to do it fancy. The plain ordinary flip wasn't good enough for him, no siree. He wanted to do it extra fancy. Instead of a little flip so's they'd light batter side down, the doctor'd give 'em a double turn an' they'd come down in the pan with a splash. He got away with it two or three times; then he got careless—flipped a panful without loosen'n 'em proper—them jacks stuck at one edge, flopped over and come down on doc's hands. We had to stop cookin' and doctor the doctor.

"Then another one of 'em thought he'd learnt how from watchin' the doc, so I set back an' let 'im have all the rope he wanted. It was their party, an' they could go the limit so far as I was concerned. But the new guy slung 'em high, wide an' crooked as a sunfishin' bronc. First thing I knowed there was a shower of sizzlin' flapjacks rainin' where I set, an' I had to make a quick getaway to keep from bein' branded for life. Then he heaved a batch so high they hit a dead limb over the fire an' wrapped aroun' it.

"It was then the next feller's turn, and he started in, while Number Two shinned up the tree to get the jacks offen the limb. Number Four hadn't came to bat yet, so the performance was due to last some time. I got up on a big rock, outta range.

"Number Two was in the tree; Number Three flippin'; Number Four was a rollin' up his sleeves an' gettin' ready for his turn. The third chef was sure fancy! He juggled them cakes just like a vodeville artist does. Of a sudden he cuts loose a batch that sailed up high an' han'some, turned over an' cum down on the back of Four's neck—him bein' entertained at the time by the feller in the tree."

Ned had acquitted himself well, his story had the tang of reality in it, and he told it with rare enthusiasm. He was so clever, in fact, that the younger guides, including myself, decided not to enter the story contest that night. But there was one in camp who did not hesitate; Andrews was his name. I had not seen this man on the trail before, so listened as eagerly as the others to what he had to offer.

"Remember the mountain sheep we saw on Flattop?" Ed recalled as he put aside his pipe. "Well, them wild sheep always has interested me. They're plumb human some ways, I reckon. They sure got a whale of a bump of curiosity, an' they beat country kids in town when it comes to starin' at strange sights. Reckon there ain't nuthin' short of a neighbor that's got more curiosity than them sheep. The old rams git so wise they live two or three times as long as the foolish ones that don't never seem to learn nothin'.

"Ole Curiosity, up in back on Specimen, is the biggest ram I ever saw. He's sure curious, an' smart along with it. If trouble shows up around Specimen, why Old Curiosity just ain't home, that's all, but hid away somewheres in the cliffs. An' once when there was shootin' he went over to another mountain till the hunters was gone. That there ole ram got so famous that the fellers used to devil the life outta him. They'd make a show of takin' their gun up the mountain jest ter see the old feller hide out.

"One day I was guidin' a party up toward Lulu Pass. We was down in a deep gully, with high walls. All to onct I looked up an' saw a bunch of sheep. They hadn't seen us yet on account of our bein' in the aspens. I flagged the party an' told 'em to watch.

"Guess some one was after the sheep, for they was in a hurry to git across the gully. One at a time they jumped off the cliff an' landed in the sand along the river. Must have been fifty feet anyhow, maybe more; but that didn't phase 'em. Of a sudden out walked Ole Curiosity, lookin' as big as a house, with circlin' horns three feet long. The ole feller jumped last; and jest as he jumped I rode out of the woods."

Ed eyed the circle of eager faces; his listeners tensed and leaned forward breathlessly. Then he continued:

"When the ole ram was about halfway down he seen me. An' what do you reckon he did?"

His hypnotized audience were too spellbound to hazard a guess.

"He turned aroun' and went back."

The story of the ram that turned back is still told around the campfires of the Rockies, and it has not grown leaner in the repetitions. But the old-time guides are giving way to younger ones, more scientific but not so entertaining. The Indians who have turned guides are unexcelled when it comes to following trails that are dim, or in tracking down runaway horses. Indians have a subtle sense of humor, even during the most serious situations. "Injun not lost, trail lost," one said when adrift in the woods.

To prevent "trails from getting lost," the Park Service requires all to pass examinations on packing, making camp, handling horses, first aid, familiarity of the region and general aptness for the calling before granting them a license entitling them to conduct parties on the peaks and trails of Rocky Mountain National Park. When the first superintendent was giving these examinations he invited me to assist him.

In order to focus the attention of the would-be guides upon certain important essentials, the questions started out by asking:

"What is the first consideration of a guide?"

"What is the second consideration of a guide?"

The answer expected to the first, of course, was the safety of the party, and to the second the comfort of the party.

The superintendent and I strolled about the room where a dozen or more young fellows were laboriously writing out their answers. One chap in particular attracted my attention, for he was from the woods, a big strapping fellow with clear eyes, and an eager, honest face.

I peeped over his shoulder. Beneath "What is the first consideration of a guide?" he had written in unmistakable brevity: "HAM." Beneath "What is the second consideration of a guide?" in a clear, legible hand was the kindred word: "BACON."

CHAPTER ELEVEN

OFF THE TRAIL

THAT same youthful ambition to emulate the early explorers and discover new worlds which had led me West also tempted my boyish feet off the beaten, man-made trails. I was told that trails were the safe, the sure routes into and out of the wilds, but their very existence proclaimed that other men had been there before me. I was not the first on those narrow, winding high roads. I preferred the game trails to them, but I liked better still to push beyond even those faint guides, into the unmarked, untracked wilderness. There I found the last frontier, as primitive as when bold Columbus dared the unknown seas, and my young heart thrilled at such high adventure.

Late one fall, I climbed high above timberline on the Long's Peak trail, and, following my adventurous impulse, left the cairn-marked pathway and swung over to the big moraine that lay south. From its top I peeped into the chasm that lies between it and the Peak, then angled down its abrupt slope to a sparkling waterfall,

and, following along the swift, icy stream above
it, was climbing toward Chasm Lake, when an
eerie wail rose from the gorge below. Somewhere down there a coyote was protesting the
crimes committed against his race. His yam-
mering notes rose and fell, ascending and descending the full run of the scale, swelled into a
throaty howl and broke into jerky, wailing yaps
like a chorus of satyrs. The uninitiated could
never have believed all those sounds came from
one wolfish throat; it seemed that it must be that
the entire pack, or at least half a dozen animals,
raised that woeful lamentation.

Facing, first one way and then another, I tried
to locate the brokenhearted mourner. But
Long's sheer, precipitous face and the lofty
cliffs around me formed a vast amphitheater
about which echoes raced, crossing and recross-
ing, intermingling. For a full minute the coyote
howled, his sharp staccato notes rising higher and
higher, the echoes returning from all directions,
first sharply, then blurred, faint, fainter. The
higher the sounds climbed the gorge the longer
were the intervals between echoes, for the cañon
walls sloped back and were wider apart toward
the top. I counted seven distant echoes of a
single sharp bark before it trailed off into numberless indistinguishable echoes. The varying
angles and heights of the walls altered their tones,
but just as they reached the top they came in uni-

form volume, and then overflowed the lower north rim and were lost.

For ten minutes that coyote howled, and I tried to locate him by the sound. I knew it would be impossible to sight him for his dun-colored coat blended perfectly with the surrounding bowlders. At last I decided he was due west of me. Cautiously I started toward him, but as soon as I moved he materialized from the jumbled pile of slide rock a hundred feet north of where I stood. The echoes had fooled me completely. I wondered then, and many times since, why he howled with me so near. He surely saw me. Was he familiar with the echoes of the gorge? Did he know their trickery? Did he lift his voice there to confound me? He is somewhat of a ventriloquist anywhere, perhaps he liked to howl from that spot because the abetting echoes deluded him into thinking his talent was increasing and he excelled all his rivals in the mysterious art! Or perhaps like some singers I have known, he enjoyed the multitudinous repetition of the sound of his own voice! After more than a score of years I am no nearer a solution of the riddle.

Twenty miles from the spot where the music-fond coyote sang, near the headwaters of the Poudre River, I rode one day in pursuit of a pair of marauding wolves. As soon as they discovered me tracking them, they took to an old game trail that climbed several thousand feet in ten miles distance and headed toward the timberline. From their tracks I could tell the country was strange to them, for animals, like men, are uneasy in unfamiliar surroundings.

Somewhere a prospector set off a blast. The sound rolled around and echoed from all about. The wolves were startled at the repeated reports, as they thought them, and at sea as to the direction from which they came; so they hid away in a dense new growth of Engelmann spruce. When I rode in sight with rifle ready across my saddle, they lay low, no doubt fearing to blunder into an ambush if they took flight.

A campbird sailed silently into the tops of the young trees and peered curiously downward. Its mate winged in and together they hopped from limb to limb, descending toward the concealed animals, and conversing in low tones of their discovery.

My horse stopped at my low command; I raised my rifle and fired into the undergrowth beneath the trees. The wolves sprang out at a run, with lightning bounds, crossed a small opening and disappeared into the heavy forest beyond. I continued firing at them, without effect. Just before they vanished into the spruces, I fired a final salute. To my astonishment, they turned tail and came racing back, straight toward me, but glancing back fearfully as they came. For a foolish instant I thought they meant to attack,

THEY TURNED TAIL AND CAME RACING BACK, STRAIGHT
TOWARD ME.

then the reason for their action dawned on me. A sharp echo of each shot had been flung back by a cliff beyond the grove. The fleeing animals on nearing the cliff had mistaken these echoes for another pursuer. They feared the unseen gun more than the gun in the open.

I killed them from the saddle. An echo had betrayed them. But they were in unfamiliar country. I doubt if they would have been misled at home, for animals are commonly familiar with every sight, sound and scent of their home range, and wolves are uncannily shrewd.

Thus I learned that the same phenomenon that had confounded me deceived the animals. Echoes make an interesting study and add mystery to the mountains. But animals, and most woodsmen, have a sixth sense upon which they rely, an intuitive faculty we call instinct. It is more infallible than their conscious reasoning or physical senses of sight, sound, smell, taste and touch. It leads them unerringly through unblazened forests, during blinding storms or in the darkness of night. It helps them solve the enigma of echoes, and sometimes when the vagrant breezes trick their sensitive noses, and bring scents to them from the opposite direction of their sources, it senses the deception, and, setting them on the right path, delivers them from their enemies.

I suppose I must have had this instinct to some

degree or I would surely have been lost in those mountain mazes. Not that anticipation of such a possibility would have deterred me—it would really have added allurement to the adventure. As it was, I did get lost, but always succeeded in finding my way home again.

But even with this instinct, people are often lost in the high country of the Rockies. Mountain trails twist and turn, tack and loop around unscalable cliffs. Let a stranger step off a trail for a moment to pick a flower blooming in the shade of the surrounding woods, and, unless he be an outdoor man, he is liable to be confused as to the trail's location when he tries to return to it. The sudden changing weather of high altitudes also causes the climber to lose his way. A sky which at sunrise is as innocently blue as a baby's eyes, may be overcast by lowering clouds by noon, or even sooner. A fog may settle below the summits of the peaks, and cloak all objects more than a few yards distant, distorting and magnifying those mistily discernible. A turn or a detour to survey the vicinity and attempt to get one's bearings almost invariably brings disaster. A fall that dazes one even for a few minutes is liable to befuddle one as to direction and cause one to lose one's way.

Few persons lost in the mountains travel in a circle. The typography of the country prevents them, high ridges confine them to limited areas.

They are as apt to travel in one direction as in the opposite, but they may usually be looked for and found in a shut-in valley or cañon.

I was lost one day within a mile of home, almost in sight of the home buildings, upon a slope I knew well. It came about through my following a band of deer on my skis. The day was windy the snow blowing about in smothering clouds. I came upon the deer in a cedar thicket. At my approach they retreated to a gully and started up the slope. The snow grew so deep that after floundering in it a few yards, they deserted the gully, tacked back close to me, and cut around the slope about level with my position. I gave chase on skis, which almost enabled me to keep up with them. When they altered their direction and headed down hill, I easily outran them. Soon I was in their midst, but had difficulty in keeping my balance.

All at once the animals indulged in queer antics. One lay upside down, his feet flailing the air; another stood on his head in space; two does on my left whirled round and round as though dancing with a phonograph record for a floor. The next instant I joined their troupe. In the flash that followed I remembered seeing the tops of small trees beneath me, remembered my skis whipping across in front of my face.

In their panic to escape me, the deer's instinct had deserted them, and they had dashed full speed across a slope where a spring overflowed and froze, and the ice was coated with snow.

When I regained my feet I was lost. Everything was unfamiliar. I set my course toward a prominent thumb of rock, but when I reached it, it had either changed its shape or moved. The whole valley was strange.

After skiing for several hours, I topped an utterly foreign ridge. Below me were houses. I coasted down to the nearest that had smoke rising from its chimney. A neighbor, living just a mile from home, came to the door. Then I realized where I was, and recognized the "strange" valley, the "unfamiliar" ridge and my neighbors' houses. I had traveled in a ten-mile circle. The fall with the deer hadn't exactly dazed me—I wasn't unconscious—but it had jarred shut the window of my memory, and though almost at my own door, there was "nobody home."

The best example of storm causing one to lose one's way is the experience of Miss Victoria Broughm, the first woman to climb Long's Peak alone. She started one September morning from a hotel at the foot of the Peak, taking a dog as her companion. She tethered her horse at bowlderfield, where horses are usually left, and without difficulty, or delay, made the summit. Just as she reached the top, a storm struck the mountain and, inside of a few minutes, hid the trail. Pluckily Miss Broughm worked her way down, tacking back and forth, mistaking the way but making progress. She was afraid to trust the dog to guide her. Late in the evening she descended the trough, a steep rock-filled gully that extends far below the timberline. The trail goes only part way down this slide, then tacks across to Keyhole. In the storm she could not distinguish the cairns that marked the turn-off, and continued on down the trough far below the trail and was lost.

That evening when she did not return to the hotel, a searching party set out to find her. But a terrific hundred-mile gale was raging upon the heights. The searching party found it almost impossible to battle their way above the timberline and after many ineffectual attempts, they returned, nearly frozen, without tidings of the lost girl.

William S. Copper, Carl Piltz and myself set out at midnight for the Peak. The wind that met us at the timberline halted our horses, even jolted them off the trail. Just above the timberline my horse pricked his ears toward a sheltered cove and gave a little whinny. We hurried forward hoping to find Miss Broughm. But only her horse was there, dragging its picket rope. We proceeded to bowlderfield.

The night was moonless and half cloudy. The wind shrieked among the rim rocks and boomed against the cliffs. Our lantern would not stay lighted. Time and again we crept beneath a rock slab and relighted it only to have it snuffed out the instant we emerged into the wind. Across the rocks we crept, crouching like wary wrestlers. When sudden blasts knocked us off our feet, we dropped flat and clung to the rocks. But even with all our caution we were toppled headlong at times, or bowled over backward as the wind struck us.

It was after three in the morning when we reached Keyhole, the pass in the knifelike ridge that separates bowlderfield from Glacier Gorge. The wind forced up the slope from below tore through Keyhole like water through a fire hose. One at a time we attempted to crawl through, but it hurled us back. Together, each holding to his fellow, we braced against the side walls, clung to little nubs on the floor, and edged forward an inch at a time. Even so we were blown back like so much chaff.

We dropped back down below Keyhole and, creeping beneath some rocks, waited for daylight. No matter how far we crawled beneath the jumbled slabs the wind found us out. We shivered, all huddled together for warmth, and waited for dawn to light our way and to calm the hurricane.

At daybreak we managed to get through Keyhole and made our way to the trough, where we separated, Cooper and Piltz following the trail to the top while I descended the trough toward Glacier Gorge. We had agreed to watch for silent signals, since it was impossible to hear even the loudest calls more than a few feet.

In a little patch of sand not much larger than my hand, I discovered a human footprint, with a dog's track imposed upon it. I wigwagged to my companions, received their answering signal, and went on down the trough, whistling to the dog and shouting his name though I could not hope he would hear me above that gale. I searched beneath every likely slab as I went.

Suddenly the dog appeared atop a huge rock. He howled in answer to my call; the wind blew him off his post and he disappeared. I hastened forward; then paused. What would I find beneath the rock? Resolutely I started to crawl beneath it— and met Miss Broughm coming out. She was cold, her lips were blue and cracked, but she had not given up hopes or lost her courage. With her hair blowing like the frayed remnants of a flag, she stood beside the bowlder and smiled a brave if twisted smile. She was too cold to walk unaided, so as soon as the others came up, we all supported her and started upon the return trip. We reached the hotel between ten and eleven o'clock in the morning with our lost lady still smiling wanly but rapidly recovering the use of her limbs. She retired for a few hours and reappeared in time for luncheon, little the worse for her night out on top of the world.

A compass is limited in its usefulness partly because it is sometimes, though rarely, affected by mineral deposits and goes wrong, but mostly because a lost person seldom thinks he is lost and traveling in the wrong direction, but instead doubts the accuracy of the compass. At most he will admit he is off the trail, but he does not think that is synonymous with being lost. His tracks will record the uncertainty of his mind, wavering, haphazard, indefinite, but he will not admit, even to himself, that he is lost.

There are a few general rules followed by searchers for lost people. If the proposed destination or general direction in which they disappeared is known, the rescuers take the trail and track them. Every trail, even across windswept bare rocks high above the timberline, as is the Long's Peak trail, has occasional deposits of soft sand in which footprints may be imprinted. And as I have said before, the area which must be searched is restricted by confining cliffs and ridges. A lost person who cannot find his way back over the trail he has come, shows wisdom in following down a stream which will eventually bring him to habitations in the valley below.

Whether or not searching parties start out at once for the unfortunate climber depends on the character of the country he was bound for. If his goal is the summit of a high, bleak peak like Long's, or a glacier, it is imperative to start at once as the temperature above the timberline is often below freezing, even during the summer months. But if the country is not so menacing, the searchers delay, hoping the lost person, like Bo Peep's sheep, will come home unsought, as indeed he generally does.

Most of the lost are found, but a few persons have vanished never to be seen again. The Reverend Sampson disappeared supposedly somewhere along the Continental Divide between Estes Park and Grand Lake, and though parties made up of guides, rangers and settlers searched for more than a week, they found no trace of the missing man. I was in the town of Walden, North Park, late one fall when a woodsman came down from the mountains west of the Park with some human bones he had found near the top of the Divide. By the marks on its barrel, the rusty rifle lying near the bones was identified as one belonging to a man who had been lost while on a hunting trip thirty years before.

One moonlight night I had an extraordinary and ludicrous experience with a lost person, though at the time it seemed only exasperating. I had stepped outside my cabin to drink in the "moonshine" on my superb outlook. Across the valley, as clearly as in daylight, Long's Peak and its neighbors stood out. The little meadow brook shimmered like a silver ribbon. I walked out to Cabin Rock, a thousand feet above the valley, and sat down. Coyotes yip-yipped their salutations to the sailing moon. The murmur of the little brooks rose to my ears, subdued, distant. I listened for each familiar night sound as one does for the voices of old friends. I sat entranced, intoxicated with the beauty of the hour, refreshing my soul, at peace, content.

A strange cry startled me from my reverie, a human cry, faint, as though far off.

"Help!" Then a pause. "H-e-l-p!" Then more urgently: "H-E-L-P!"

For a few minutes I sat still upon my crag, puzzling. Some one has stumbled into a bear trap, I thought, or been injured in a fall. After marking the locality from which the calls came, I ran down my zigzag trail, and hastened down the valley toward the spot whence the cries had come. Whenever I came to the open, parklike clearings, I stopped to listen. The floor of the wide valley had been burned over scores of years before, and a new growth of lodge-pole pines covered it. These trees were of nearly uniform height, about fifteen feet, and in places too dense to permit of passage.

Three miles were covered in record time. Then, thinking that I must be close to the spot from which the calls had come, I climbed an upthrust of rock, searched the openings among the trees near by, and listened intently. I shouted; no reply. For perhaps ten minutes I waited. Then from far up the valley, close below my cabin, the distressing calls were repeated.

"He's certainly not crippled," I thought. "He's traveled nearly as far as I."

I set off at a run, for I know every little angle of the woods in the vicinity. But when I arrived, breathless and panting, there was no answer to my shouts. I gave up the chase in disgust, and started up the trail toward my cabin. I decided some one was having fun with me.

Midway up the trail to my cabin, I heard the cries again, agonized, fearful. They came from across the valley, toward the west. Heading for the peaks! I must stop him! It certainly sounded serious. I'd have to see it through.

I hurried across the valley, shouting at intervals, stopping to listen and to look for the person in distress. There was no answer, no one in sight. As I reached the steep slope, leading upward to the high peaks, I heard terrified, heartrending cries, southward, toward the spot from which the first call had come. It was strange, and maddening, that I could hear him so distinctly, yet he could not hear me. He was certainly deaf or very stupid, for he continued calling for help, when help was pursuing him and yelling at the top of its lungs.

Again calls. This time straight south of my position. It was a riddle; annoying, yet interesting. Never in my mountain experience had I encountered such a mystifying situation. However, with grim determination, but little enthusiasm, I turned south. My curiosity was aroused. I wanted to see what sort of fool ran around in dizzy circles yelling for help, yet not waiting for an answer to his supplications, nor acknowledging my answering shouts.

I was in prime condition, and well warmed up with ten miles of travel. My endurance was too much for the will-o'-the-wisp. As, for the second time, I neared the spot from which he had first called, he shattered the silence with lusty appeals, then broke cover within a hundred yards of where I followed, hot on his trail. He looked able-bodied and goodness knows he'd been active, so I withdrew into the shadows of a thicket to watch what he would do.

After his outcry, he kept mumbling to himself —his words were inaudible—lost his voice— don't wonder! Some rooter he'd make at a football game while he lasted! After muttering a minute, he stopped and listened intently, as though expecting an answer. Good heavens! He thinks he can be heard! He moved on, staggering crazily, stumbling, stopping to look at the shining peaks; then going on aimlessly. "Loco," I decided.

I circled ahead of him and concealed myself behind an old stump. I wanted to hear what he was saying. Twice he had crossed the road that ran down the valley, the only road in that vicinity. From Cabin Rock I had seen a tent beside it.

As he came toward me, I stepped from behind the stump.

"What in time ails you?" I roared.

He stared at me and walked completely around me before saying a word.

"Huh," he grunted then. "Where'd you come from?"

I explained with considerable emphasis that I had come from almost every point of the compass.

"Will you tell me why in Sam Hill you are yelling for help when it's as light as day?" I demanded hotly.

"I'm lost," he said meekly.

"Lost!" I yelled.

He nodded shamefacedly.

"Went fishing and couldn't find my camp again," he confessed.

I recalled the tent beside the road, I'd seen from Cabin Rock. It was the only camp, on the only road in the vicinity.

"Why in thunder didn't you follow the road?"

"Didn't know which way to go," he defended.

"There's the Peak!" I gibed, pointing upward;

"plain as day. Your camp is straight east of it—didn't you know that?"

He winced, but did not answer.

"Couldn't you see the Peak?" I insisted. "You couldn't help but recognize it."

"Yes," he admitted. "I saw the Peak, but I thought it was in the wrong place."

CHAPTER TWELVE

WHAT with my hunting, trapping, exploring, cabin-building and guiding, my boyish dreams of striking it rich and sending home trainloads of glittering nuggets to my parents, who had been frustrated by illness in their trek across the plains to the golden mountains of Colorado, began to fade into the background. I was engrossed in getting acquainted with my wild neighbors, in learning their habits and customs, and in trying to photograph them in their natural habitat. Moreover there was no rich gold ore in the vicinity of my cabin. Though I was greatly disappointed in this fact at the time, I have since become reconciled to it. After seeing the naked, desolate, scarred-up country around Central City, Cripple Creek, Ouray and other mining localities, I am thankful that no such madness will ever tempt men to despoil the beauties of the region around Estes Park.

But if there was no paying gold in the vicinity, there were plenty of prospectors. The slopes above the Parson's ranch were "gophered" all over by them. There were miles of outcrop showing and all bore traces of gold. Every summer some wanderer came probing among the countless holes sure he'd find riches where others had failed. The most persistent one was called "Old Mac" who returned repeatedly. Late one fall he took up his quarters in a log cabin belonging to a mining company. The cabin stood near Long's Peak trail, at an altitude of about ten thousand feet. There they had cached some left-over supplies. Old Mac, forever dreaming, stumbled on to the cache and decided to take up his residence there.

Through October and November I saw Old Mac frequently as he pottered about the mine or picked up ore samples from the dump. He staked half a dozen claims, marked their locations, and dug some new holes to test the mineral. In December, when deep snows came, I left the region.

When I returned in the spring the snow lay deep and undisturbed about the old cabin. Evidently Old Mac had got out before winter set in. However, I shouted his name, more in the spirit of talking to myself than of expecting a reply. I was surprised to hear a faint reply. From inside the cabin came a creaking as though some one were getting out of bed. Then the door opened and the old man, blinking owlishly, stood before me. His long white hair was unkempt and tangled. He yawned and stretched like a bear emerging from its winter hibernation.

"Came up to bring them papers?" he asked, expectantly. I recalled then, when I last saw him in December, that he had asked to borrow some Denver papers that contained information about the Reno gold rush. I had forgotten about them. I explained and apologized.

"What sort of a winter have you put in?" I asked by way of diverting him.

He looked at me in a sort of maze.

"Winter?" he mumbled perplexed. "It's sure settin' in like it meant business. But I'm plannin' to start a tunnel—got a rich vein I want to uncover—think come spring I'll have her where somebody'll want to build a mill an'——"

"But you told me you were going to Reno," I recalled.

"Yep; I am, come spring," he earnestly assured me.

"Do you know the date?" I shot at him.

He looked at me sheepishly.

"No-o-o, don't reckon I do," he admitted, scratching his head and eying me quizzically.

I waited.

"Must be about Christmas, ain't it?" he guessed at length.

It was the eighth of May!

Old Mac was a typical prospector. They are

all queer, picturesque characters, living in a world of golden dreams, oblivious to everything but the hole they are digging, the gold they are sure to find. They have a fanatical, unshakable, perennial faith in every prospect hole they open, no matter how many have been false leads. They are incorrigible optimists, the world's champion hopers. Unkempt, unhurried, dreaming, confiding, trustful, superstitious, they wander the length of the Rockies, seeking the materialization of their golden visions. They are seekers, far more concerned with finding gold than with digging it out. Like hunting dogs, their interest ceases with the capture of their quarry.

They do not care whether the region they propose to search has been scientifically tested and thought to contain gold. They adhere to the miner's adage, "Gold is where you find it"; and they seem to have some occult power of divination for they have uncovered fabulous fortunes in regions which, like Cripple Creek, had been declared "barren of gold." Yet, as the old settlers say, "Prospectors never get anything out of their finds." Having struck it rich, they take to the trail again, to search endlessly, to probe ceaselessly, with patient faith, the inscrutable hills.

In addition to their seemingly occult power of divining the location of earth's hidden treasure, these rugged old men of the mountains possess a mysterious means of learning news of gold strikes. Let a bonanza strike be made and every prospector in the region will be on his way to the new camp within a few hours.

"How did you know that gold had been struck at Caribou?" I asked an old man whom I met on the trail, driving his pack burro ahead of him, hurrying considerably for a prospector.

He looked at me, scratched his head, spanked the burro and started on. No doubt regretting his discourteous silence, he turned, "I knowed they was agoin' to," he told me.

Nearly every prospector has a little pack burro, that seems to absorb all the patient philosophy of its master. To his shaggy burden-bearer, he gives his last flapjack, tells his golden dreams, confides the location of rich veins of ore, and turns for comfort when the false lead plays out. The knowing animal provides that rarest of companionship, a sympathetic, silent, attive listener.

Most of the prospectors I have met on the trails were old men, working alone, but two do sometimes cast their lot together, and become partners.

The story I heard told once around a campfire, of two old prospectors who were always quarreling, is characteristic. Many times they separated, each to go his own way; sometimes they merely set up separate camps a few yards apart, refusing to speak or to take any notice of each other. Thus they bickered, fought and made up, close to forty years. They staked claims wherever they discovered promising outcrop. They were familiar with a hundred miles of ragged mountain ranges.

After all those years, old and failing, they fell out over some trivial thing and separated for good. One traveled north, the other south. Both struck fine mineral that promised to make their dreams come true. But neither was content. Each wanted the other's companionship and yet each feared that pride would keep his poor partner from accepting his advances. They grew morose, and finally both blew up their holdings to conceal their riches and headed back along the Divide to meet, face to face, the partner they had deserted.

Prospectors are philosophers, without hurry or worry. They meet each situation as it arises calmly, and let to-morrow take care of its own. When food and dynamite give out, they make a pilgrimage to the foothill towns and with alluring tales of leads, lodes and veins of hidden treasure soon to be revealed—just as soon as they have time to do a little more development work—they secure another grub stake and are on their way to high country again. They always find willing listeners, for the heart of many a less daring, conservative business man is in the hills. The listeners are easily inveigled into staking these old beggars, hypnotized and hypnotizing with dreams, and do it again and again, gambling on the next strike being a lucky one. The man who furnishes a grub stake shares half and half with the prospector he equips.

No matter how little they have, prospectors will share with anyone who comes their way. Their hospitality is genuine, though perforce limited. They invite you first, and learn who you are and what your business may be later.

One day I was picking my way down the bogs and marshes of Forest Cañon. All at once it narrowed, boxing up between high walls. To go on I had either to climb the walls or back-track for some distance. I elected to climb. After the struggle up the face of the rock I sat down to rest.

"No one within miles," I panted as I sat down.

"Don't look like there's ever been anyone here," I added as I recalled the way I had come.

"What ya take me fur?"

Ten feet away, standing motionless beside an old stump, stood a cadaverous fellow whose rags suggested the moss that hung from the trees.

"Hungry?" he shot at me before I recovered from my surprise. "Camp's right hyar."

He led the way with all the poise of a gentleman.

But his camp! Beside an old tunnel that

plunged beneath the side wall of the cañon was a lean-to. Upon green boughs were spread a single pair of ragged blankets. His campfire still smoldered. Upon its coals were his only culinary utensils, an old tin bucket, in which simmered his left-over coffee, and a gold pan containing a stew. The pan had seen better days —and worse ones, too, for one side of its rim was gone, and the bottom had been cleverly turned up to form a new one, making it semi-circular with a straight side.

"Prospectin'?" my host ventured, eying me dreamily.

"No, lookin,' " I told him.

"Humph." Then, "Hope you find it."

But his curiosity ended there.

"Say, if you're wantin' ter see sum'thin' good, looka that."

He tossed over a piece of quartz.

"Got er whole mountain uf it," he jerked his head toward the tunnel. He lowered his voice, glanced around, beckoned me to follow, and led the way inside his mine.

At the edge of the darkness he halted, returned to the entrance and peered about. Then he leaned close that none might hear, and whispered the secret; the old, old secret no prospector ever keeps. Not that prospectors have anything to keep!

Another time, in the rough region west of

Ypsilon Mountain, I came upon a lean, wiry little old man leading a burro. He jerked at the lead rope in vain attempt to hurry the phlegmatic animal.

"Com' on, durn ye," he squeaked as he tugged at the rope. "Don't ye know we're tracin' the float? Lead's right close now."

But the burro was of little faith. He had lost his youthful enthusiasm. He carried all his master's possessions (except his golden dreams) on his back, but his pack was light.

So engrossed was the old man that he passed within fifty yards of where I sat without seeing me. He was oblivious to everything but what might lie hidden on the mountainside. The float would lead to a bonanza strike, a mill would be built to handle the ore, a town would spring up —his town, named in his honor as the discoverer of the lead! He mumbled of these things as he worked. Sometimes he paused, looking abstractedly at the peaks above, without apparently seeing them at all. He babbled incoherently of leads, floats, lodes and veins.

His actions were like those of a dog puzzling out the faint trail of a rabbit that had crossed and crisscrossed its own trail until nothing could track it down. Somewhere on the mountain above was the source of the float. The old man edged up the slope, tacking back and forth across the line of scattered quartz. He located the vein at last by trenching through a carpet of spruce needles.

He set up camp and started digging, so I dropped down the cañon towards the Poudre River. But a week later, upon my return, he was still there. He had located his claim and staked his corner. His location notice, laboriously written with a blunt pencil, was fastened to a tree. The burro lay in philosophical contemplation in the grass beside the stream; while his master sat beside the shallow hole that perhaps marked the beginning of a mine. His pose was that of a sentinel. He watched the hole with an expectant air, as though from it something important would presently emerge, and he was waiting to pounce upon it.

Years later when I passed that way again, the hole was no deeper, but the frayed remnants of the location notice flapped in the breeze.

Only once in a quarter of a century have I seen a prospector hurry. It was while I was guiding a party of Eastern folks across the Rabbit Ear range that we met a gangling fellow named "Shorty," by way of contrast. I say he was hurrying, because he held a straight course across the mountains without paying heed to numberless diverting leads he ordinarily would have "sampled."

Shorty was heading for Central City, where mining had been in full blast for forty years.

He had no burro, he had cached his tools at the scene of his last camp. He had had a dream that revealed to him the location of a rich vein, right in the midst of miles of mines, but unsuspected and undiscovered. Every prospector has dreams by day as well as by night.

My party "loaned" Shorty some grub and watched him disappear toward the Mecca of his dreams. Just before he left, Shorty confided to us that his dream vein lay just below a big bowlder and above some tall trees; that he knew the vein was right there—and it was.

To my cabin one day, came Slide-Rock Pete, who dwelt in a realm of unreality. Pete was superstitious after the manner of his tribe. He knew all the luck signs, all the charms (good or bad), and he had conjured up counter-charms against ill omens. As he approached my cabin a visiting cat, a black one, crossed his path. Pete promptly turned around three times in the opposite direction to that in which the cat had gone and calmly entered, secure in his belief that he had broken pussy's dark spell. He was afflicted with rheumatism, which prevented him from prospecting. At length he figured out the cause of his trouble and a cure for it. It wasn't dampness, or rainy weather, he told me, but came from camping near mineral deposits. If he chanced to pitch his camp near mineral, especially iron, it caused his "rheumatics" to "come on."

For protection he bought a compass with which we went over proposed camp sites. If the compass showed variation or disturbance, he abandoned the site. And once when the compass was out of order, he camped, unconsciously, at a spot where there was iron. Then as his rheumatism developed he found that his watch had stopped. Later when his aches at last left him, his watch started ticking of its own accord. His watch was so sympathetic that it couldn't bear to run when he couldn't walk! But when he felt good, it was so joyous it ran ahead to make up for lost time. Then he set it right by squinting at the sun!

No matter what queer beliefs prospectors have they are never disgruntled.

I had camped near the old Flattop trail at a spot where, sometime before, I had cached some food supplies. It was early in September. No wind reached the bottom of the cañon where I slept beside my fire. I awoke at the sound of a voice and sleepily I opened my eyes. No one would be traveling at night—surely I had been dreaming. But no—there was movement.

"If I kin git the hole ten feet deeper before snow flies, I'll have something to show that ole skinflint at the lake."

I sat up wondering. Then I remembered the voice. It was old Sutton, a prospector I had known for many years—one of the typical, plodding, babbling old fellows who live only in their dreams.

My camp was in the shelter of small spruces while my visitor stood in the open. Playfully I picked up an empty tin can and tossed it into the air, that it might fall close beside him. At the fall of the can, the man spun around suddenly, and, walking over to it, prodded it with the stick he carried.

"Gosh dern!" he exclaimed; "funny how things happen."

He stood in silence, looking down at the can.

Then I dropped another close to him. He muttered something unintelligible. The third and fourth cans made him hop around like a surprised robin beneath an apple tree, with fruit pelting the ground near it. At length he hobbled off, talking to himself about a new lead he had found, without solving the mystery of the tin cans dropping from a clear night sky.

CHAPTER THIRTEEN

F OR days I had been on the trail, or, rather, off it, for there were no trails in the high country through which I was traveling, excepting those made by game. I was hungry. The region lacked charm. It is difficult for a boy to appreciate scenery on a two-day-old empty stomach, which he has been urging up mountains and joggling down valleys. Had the bunnies been more accommodating and gone into their holes so I could snare them or smoke them out, or the grouse had been less flighty when I flushed them, and remained near enough so I could reach them with my stones, I might have stretched my food supply over the extended time of my unexpectedly prolonged travels. But no such good luck attended me on that excursion. The very first day I slipped off a foot-log while crossing a saucy little mountain brook and bruised my shin, tore my trousers and injured my camera. Like most small boys, I regretted that gratuitous bath. I began to wonder if Slide-Rock Pete was so crazy after all.

Now the clouds were pinning themselves up to dry on the pointed summits of the peaks, and were already beginning to drip on the world below. Darkness threatened to set in early. I knew I ought to stop and make camp while it was still light enough to see, but I kept on going, hoping something might turn up. My empty stomach growled its disapproval, but I stubbornly ignored its protests. While my better judgment, my stomach and myself were all three arguing, I thought I glimpsed a building, far down on the slope below. Too excited to say "I told you so" to my companions, I quickened my steps and headed toward it. "A prospector! If he has any grub at all he'll share it, and I'll be protected from this downpour." By that time the celestial laundresses were emptying out their wash tubs and sloshing water all over the earth.

When I drew near the shack, I discovered it was one of a group of straggling houses scattered along the sides and bottom of the gulch. A settlement! It was dark by then, yet not a light could I see. "Must go to bed with the chickens," I mused. "I hope they won't mind being gotten up to give a wayfarer shelter and a bite to eat."

On my way down the slope, I passed two or three log cabins but these were silent, apparently empty, and I hastened on to the main group which faced on the single, grass-grown road that ran along the bottom of the gulch, intending to knock at the first which showed signs of life. I walked the length of the sprawling road, looking sharply at each house, listening for voices, a chance word or a peal of laughter. Not a sound greeted my ears except the thud of rain upon sod roofs, the drip of water through stunted, scraggly trees.

Here was something queer; I thought of Slide-Rock Pete and his luck charms. I regretted more than ever that I had not got a single bunny. I felt the need of a rabbit's foot.

Shaking myself to shed rain and forebodings, I crossed the street and knocked boldly upon the door of the nearest house. There was no response. Again I knocked, louder and more insistently. My raps came echoing back emptily. I knocked again. A door, creaking on rusty hinges, swung slowly inward, but no one peered out, inviting me to enter. I backed away from the yawning cavern, blacker than the starless night, into the open road. A little saw-whet owl, seeking, as I was, supper, swooped by on muffled wings, and sawed wood, saying nothing. I jeered back at him, and felt my courage rising. I stepped up resolutely to the next house and beat upon its door. There was instant commotion, a rattling of pans, the clink of dishes as though some one hurried to the door. Straightening up and facing the door expectantly, I smiled in anticipation of a hospitable welcome. Then the

sounds ceased. My courage oozed away—an
unreasonable fear crept over me. I lost my desire for food and rest—I would as soon have
rested in a grave.

Once more I stood in the rutted street, searching its brief length for a human form. I had the
feeling that the inhabitants of the town were
somewhere about, that they had just stepped
out, leaving their doors unlocked against their
early return. Perhaps there was a dance or a
celebration of some sort in the neighboring village. Strange some one didn't stay behind.

The sudden eerie notes of a coyote caused
my hair to lift—why couldn't the brute respect
the silence? The wind stirred uneasily, doors
banged about me. The uncanny spell of the
place overcame my last shred of courage—my
feet started down the road of their own volition.
I found myself breathing hard, running fast. I
jerked to a standstill, laughing sheepishly at my
fears—ashamed. Then I faced about, determined to stay.

Something touched my elbows. I sprang ten
feet and whirled, on the defensive. A dark,
horned form stood before me. My muscles
tensed for another sprint, I held my breath. The
thing moved; I made out the outline of a burro.
I breathed again, relieved. Here at last was
something alive, something natural in this desert
of silence. I wished the animal would bray, but

he only nosed my pockets suggestively. I laid my hand upon him gratefully, and found he too was in sore straits, his coat as ragged as my own, his sides corrugated like a huge washboard. My spirits rose, my forebodings were forgotten.

"Hello," I called joyfully. "What are you doing here?"

Again he smelled my pockets, wagging his great ears the while, then waited expectantly.

"Sorry, pal," I apologized.

The little beggar's attitude expressed such dejection I laughed.

"Never mind, old fellow. We'll go find something. There must be somebody here."

I started out to renew my search and he followed at my heels. So, together, we wandered down the street on a tour of investigation. His coat was so black that often I could not distinguish him from the darker shadows that filled the street. At every door he crowded forward expectantly, focusing his long ears as though to catch the first longed-for salutation.

Nearly every door was ajar. The log cabins were small, two or three rooms at the most, and easily searched. Their owners had apparently taken only their most portable and necessary possessions, for nearly every cabin contained something of value, bed springs, bunks, suspended by wire from the rafters, tables, chairs, dishes, cooking utensils, even miners' tools. One had a row of books upon its stone mantel. When we came to the one where sounds had answered my knocking, I paused before the door, hesitating to intrude. That first creepy feeling stole over me. I put my hand on the burro's neck. I jerked the latchstring and pushed open the door. The room was dark and silent. When I struck a match, there was a rapid scurrying of rats, darting for shelter.

My burly bodyguard never once left my side. He waited patiently for my report, when I emerged from each cabin, and accepted with philosophical resignation my decision to postpone further search till daylight.

Early next morning I was up and out, further to explore the village. No one had returned home, there was no doubt now that it was deserted. In one of the cabins I found some salt which I divided with the burro. Another yielded a little flour. I prepared a sticky mixture of flour and water, seasoned with salt, and cooked it in one of the fireplaces. When baked, it had the firmness of granite, but my appetite had a cutting edge, and the burro, no more particular, accepted the hardtack, and crunched it greedily.

After breaking our fast, to say nothing of our teeth, we continued our—yes, excavations; for out of the dust and neglect of years of desertion, we dug the history of a buried past, of a forgot-

Out of the Dust of Years, We Dug the History of a
Buried Past.

ten civilization, where men had worked, women had loved and sacrificed, and little children had laughed and played.

One of the houses had evidently held the post office, for in it was a small cabinet holding a few pieces of uncalled-for mail addressed to various persons. There were unopened letters and papers, bearing the postmarks of towns back East; there were packages, showing marks of long journeys, still intact, their cords still tightly knotted. Many of the letters had been forwarded from other Western post offices, and had followed the men to whom they were addressed to this, then alive, town named Teller.

The postmaster had apparently been a notary public. His book of records lay dusty on the shelf, near what had been the post office. Upon it, too, were filed copies of mining claims. "The Grizzly King," "Decoration Day," "Lady Forty," "Queen Victoria," "Tom Boy," "Last Chance," "Deep Water," "Black Mule," "Hope Ever," fantastic, picturesque names, suggesting many a tale of romance and adventure, revealing the hopes and fears of daring hearts.

Something of these was hinted at in an open letter lying on the floor of one of the cabins. It was worn thin where it had been creased, as though its owner had long carried it around in his pocket, the better to read and reread it. The wind had pried into it, leaving it spread open for the next intruder's convenience. Somehow, I felt those frank spirits would not mind my reading it:

Dear Fred:

Hope you strike it rich in Teller, the new town you wrote about. Most anything out there would beat what we have here. Corn is all dried up in Iowa, and there's little to live on. Quite a lot of the neighbors have "pulled up stakes" and moved to Kansas. Ten wagons left last week, following the road west which so many have taken for better or worse.

The last and smallest cabin in the town was as clean and tidy as though its owner might have been gone but a few days. Upon the table was a worn and frayed little book, weighted down by a rough piece of ore, a sort of diary, and yet it seemed to be written to some one. I copied extracts from it into my own notebook:

My dear Katherine—I believe I've struck it rich at last. There was a rush up here three months ago, and I came in soon as the news reached Cheyenne. Must have been several hundred in the race to get here first—about twenty of us won out. I filed on several claims and tried to hire men to help me do assessment work; but no one would work for wages. Everyone is raving crazy, bound to strike it rich, and working double shift to hold as many claims as possible.

Katy, dear, it's been a month since I started this letter. Things have settled down here now, and the fly-by-nights have vanished. But there's a few of us sticking to our holes with the notion if we go deep enough they'll pan out rich. But there's no way of . . .

They came for me to help with a poor fellow who got hurt when his tunnel caved in on him. Guess he'll make a die of it too. Seems terrible, just when he thought he had struck a bonanza, to be killed that way. Makes me lonesome to think how things turned out for him.

I've got a secret cache straight west of my cabin, forty-eight steps. Under a big rock I've hid a buckskin sack with the golddust another fellow and I panned from a bar in the Colorado river. It's not so very much; but it'll help out in a pinch.

Kate, this camp's played out. I'm quitting, disgusted. After all the hard work here there's nothing rich; just low-grade stuff that won't pay freighting charges. Maybe if we had a mill—but there's no use talking mill, when every fellow here is in the same fix—on his last legs. We got to get out or starve; we're all living on deer and wild sheep, but its getting so we can hardly swallow it much longer. I'll let you know as soon . . .

It was unfinished.

The sides of the gulch were "gophered" with prospect holes, most of them very shallow, with little mounds of dirt beside them, like the graves of dead hopes. Occasionally a deeper hole had picked samples from the ore vein it followed piled near its opening. Likewise, outside, some of the cabin doors were little heaps of choice ore which hopeful owners had brought in against the time when shipments would be made, or an ore mill set up near by.

I had chanced upon an abandoned mining town, left forever as casually as though its residents had gone to call upon a neighbor. There are many such in the mountains of Colorado. During the early gold rushes, when strikes were made, mining towns sprang up overnight, and later when leads played out or failed to pan out profitably, or rumor of a richer strike reached the inhabitants, they deserted them to try their luck in new fields of promise. Often they were eager to be the first ones in on the new finds and left without preparation or notice, trailing across mountains and through cañons, afoot, each anxious to be the first man on the ground, to have his choice of location, to stake his claim first. They could not carry all their household goods on their shoulders, nor pack them on a burro's back, and to freight them over a hundred miles of mountain trails cost more than the purchase of new goods in the new town. So they departed with only such necessities as they could carry, and abandoned the rest to pack rats and chance wanderers such as I.

So these towns, born of their high hopes, died, as their dreams flickered out, and were abandoned when new hopes sprung up in their breasts.

I forgot my hunger in unraveling the mysteries of the silent village, but my companion showed no such inclination. Being a pack burro, and having a prospector for a master, he had come to look upon tragedy with a philosophical eye. No doubt he had seen deserted towns before, and been the innocent victim of the desertion. He grew bored as I lingered over letters and the other evidence of bygone days and nudged me frequently to remind me of our original object in searching the cabins. At last he protested with a vigorous, "Aww-hee-awwhee, a-w-w-h-e-e —" Remembering his loyalty of the night before, to appease him I left off rummaging in those dust-covered cabins.

"All right, pal, I'll come. We'll leave this grave-yard right away and try our luck at fishing."

He seemed to understand for he capered about like a playful puppy.

I knew of several small streams below the town, alive with trout. I headed for the nearest one, the burro plodding patiently behind, silent, expectant.

The smell of smoke, coffee, and other camp odors came up the trail to meet us. Soon we came abruptly in sight of two prospectors who were eating a belated breakfast.

"Reckon you better have a bite with us," invited one of the men as he set the tin-can coffee pot upon the coals of their fire.

"Thet thar burro bin a pesterin' you?" asked

the second man, fixing the burro with a searching gaze.

"Oh, no!" I denied, remembering my debt to
the animal. "We put in the night together, and
he even ate some of my hardtack this morning,"
I ended laughing.

"He's the tarnationist critter, always a gala-
vantin' roun', an' a gittin' inter somebody's
grub."

The burro chose to overlook these insults and
drew near the fire, unostentatiously. The old
prospector slipped him part of his breakfast.

"Which way you headin'?" asked the first man,
plainly puzzled because I carried neither gun
nor mining tools.

"To climb Arapahoe peak."

"Climb the peak," he repeated, much mystified.

"What's the idear?" the second wanted to
know. "Goin' way off thar jes' to git up a
mountain, when thar's plenty right hyar, higher
ones too?" He indicated the ranges to the east.

"Any place up that way to get out of the rain?"
I asked, for the clouds were dropping again with
the threat of gathering storm.

The men exchanged glances. Abruptly the
small one got to his feet and led the burro out of
sight among the willows. The other man faced
me.

"Better take a friend's advice and keep outen
there," he swept a grimy hand westward.

"What's up?"

"Better do your climbin' round hyar," he replied suggestively.

"But I want to climb Arapahoe; I have heard the Indians used it for a signal mountain and . . ."

He beckoned me to follow, and led the way into the grove mysteriously. At length he stopped, peered about uneasily, then whispered.

"There's an ole cabin up yonder"—he faced toward Arapahoe—"that's ha'nted."

"Haunted?" my interest quickening, my fears of the depressing night forgotten.

He nodded—dead earnest.

"Are you sure about that? Did you ever see the, the——"

His look silenced me.

"Ole feller died up thar," he declared; "nobody knows how." His tone was awesome.

I made a move down the trail, thanking him for the meal.

"Wouldn't go, if I wus you," he persisted, following me as far as his camp.

Then, as I took the unused trail that led down toward North Park, he called after me:

"Remember, I've warned you!"

Fishing was good in the stream a few miles below their camp, and I soon had all the trout I wanted and was on my way to the round dome of Arapahoe peak, jutting above some clouds

that were banked against its lower slope.
Through the willow flats and a dense forest of
spruce, the way led up between parallel ridges
over a game trail, deeply worn and recently used.
I was right upon a log wall before I knew it.
Then I circled and saw that the wall was part of
an old cabin built in a little opening of the forest.

A section of the roof had fallen in and the
fireplace had lost part of its chimney; the slab
door had a broken hinge, and swayed uneasily on
the one remaining, and the dirt floor bore no
traces of recent habitation.

Having gathered wood for the night, for I
had no blankets and must keep the fire burning,
I broiled several trout for my supper. How I
relished that meal!

Supper over, I climbed upon a cliff behind the
cabin and watched the moon rise silently above
a ridge to the eastward, and listened to the faint
clamor of the coyotes far below. Shadows crept
closer to the cliffs as the moon climbed higher,
while from the peaks above came the moaning of
the wind. Never had been such a night!

It was late when I went inside the old cabin,
and the fire had burned low. I put on fresh
wood, removed my shoes, and stretched out before the comforting blaze. I was asleep almost
instantly. From time to time, as had become

my habit, I roused enough to feed the fire; then quickly dropped off to sleep again.

Just when, I am not sure, but I think about midnight, I awoke with a strange feeling that an unseen presence was in the room. The prospector's warning came to me vaguely, and I tried to rouse up to listen, but I dropped back to sleep almost immediately.

Later, coming awake suddenly as though some one had shaken me, I sat up and, rubbing my eyes to open them, glanced around, but the interior of the cabin was dark, only the stars sparkled close above the broken roof. I yawned expansively, rolled nearer the low fire, and fell asleep.

The next I knew I heard a thud close to my head, and I was wide awake upon the instant. I lay still, trying to convince myself that there was nothing in the cabin but myself; when a hot breath struck my face. I got up on end—so did my hair. I started for the door.

A bulky shadow moved between it and myself. I postponed going in that direction for the moment and, turning, felt my way to a dark corner back by the fireplace. From the corner across the hearth came a faint sound. Thinking the time propitious for a prompt exit, I felt my way along the wall, turned the corner and made for the door.

Unfortunately, my uninvited guest had the same thought, for as I sprang for the opening,

I bumped into him, and the creaky slab door banged shut, leaving the cabin blacker than ever.

An idea shot through my head. If the visitor, whatever it was—ha'nt or otherwise—wanted the location near the door, it could have it. Far be it from me to be discourteous. I groped my way back to the fireplace, stumbling over my wood as I went. I had a fleeting notion to fling fresh wood on the fire which had almost burned out. Again I collided with my dusky visitor.

I hesitated no longer. I would vacate the cabin instantly, for good and all, without stopping to gather up my few belongings. Across the dirt floor I dashed, grabbed the creaky door and jerked it open.

But before I could dart through I was shoved aside. In panic I sought that exit, but was buffeted about, and finally knocked headlong on the ground.

Thoroughly scared, I leaped to my feet, ready to run.

Standing a few feet in front of me, big ears thrust forward inquiringly, was the friendly burro of the night before.

CHAPTER FOURTEEN

I N my childish estimation, bear stories rivaled the tales of mad gold rushes, thundering bisons and savage Indians. No chore was so hard nor so long but that I managed to complete it in time to take my place in the fireside circle and listen to accounts of those huge animals that lived in the Rocky Mountains and were fiercer than any other bears in the world. "Ursus horribilis," my father called them, and a delicious little shudder would run down my back at the sound of the words. There was talk, too, of hunters who had tracked these monsters to their lairs and overcome them.

Early I decided that when I went West, I would become, besides other things, a mighty bear hunter. The cows I drove to pasture were "ursus horribilis" (how I reveled in those words!) fleeing before me, and I was stalking them through the wilds with rifle upon my arm, and pistol and hunting knife in my belt! I planned to discard the ragged overalls and clumsy "clod-hoppers" of the farm, as soon as I reached the

mountains, for smoke-tanned, Indian-made buckskin suit and moccasins, all beaded and fringed.
I wondered if the Indians wore coonskin caps
like Davy Crockett—I felt it absolutely necessary that I should have one to wear to meet my
first bear.

My first venture into the woods below the
Parson's ranch I remember vividly, because I
was filled with eager, yet fearful anticipation. I
expected to meet a grizzly around every bowlder. I kept wondering how fast a bear could
run; I halted frequently beside trees, for I remembered my father's saying grizzlies did not
climb, so I planned to shin up the tallest tree
in the woods should one come in sight. In my
dreams back on the farm, my only fear had been
lest all the grizzlies be killed before I reached
the Rockies; barring such dire calamity, I had
never had a doubt of my prowess. But somehow, when at last I found myself alone in the
dark forest, it seemed the better part of valor
to postpone the actual encounters until I should
become more skillful with my old black-powder
rifle. So obsessed was I by the thought of bears
that on my first excursions into the wilds, a rock
never rolled down a slope nor dropped from a
cliff, a crash sounded in a thicket, but that I was
sure a bear was mysteriously responsible. I
dreamed of them, day and night, until they became bugbears, grizzly bugbears!

Considering my long-avowed intentions, my first camp alone in the Wild Basin country was not entirely unfortunate, for there, that first exciting afternoon, I met a bear face to face. Of course, I gave him the right of way. Was I not the intruder and he the rightful resident? Though years have elapsed since I dropped my rifle and sped in instant flight down the mountain side toward camp, I still like to think that my marvelous speed discouraged "ursus horribilis" and, therefore, he turned tail.

During my first summer in the mountains, I saw bears several times, in each instance going about their business and making no move to attack me. After these glimpses of them I gathered courage and decided to postpone my career as a hunter no longer. Bears were the objectives of my hunting expeditions, but they always succeeded in eluding me. Many times in stalking them I came upon fresh tracks showing they had broken into flight at my approach. One day I turned homeward, empty-handed, and learned later I had been within gunshot of one without catching sight of him.

Gradually my respect for them grew. The one I had watched stalk the marmot increased my admiration of their cunning. I eventually learned that they are extremely alert and agile, despite their seemingly stupid lumbering about, that they employ keen eyes and sensitive ears and high-power noses to the best advantage. As my respect for them grew, my ambition to become a mighty hunter of them gave way to a desire to learn more about them, to observe them in their natural state and study their habits. Just as they had inspired the most heroic dreams of my childhood, so they came to interest me more than any other animal of the wilds.

To the south of the Parson's ranch lay a wild, rugged region, which I called the "bad lands" on account of its jungle of woods, streams, swamps and terminal moraines, where bowlders of all sizes had been deposited by an ancient glacier. Through this tangle it was impossible to move without making noise, for a fire had swept over it and young lodge-pole trees had sprung up so close together that it was impossible to move without crashing into them. It was while on hands and knees in one of these thickets of new growth that I came upon bear tracks. The tracks were the largest I had even seen, so I gripped my gun tightly and peered about warily. The tracks pointed west, so I headed east, crashing through the trees ponderously, giving an occasional yell to help the bear keep out of my way.

I had gone about a hundred yards and was congratulating myself on my escape, when, to my horror, I discovered fresh tracks paralleling mine. Altering my course I went on, shouting vigorously, but with less confidence of scaring the bear out of the region.

In this extremity I recalled a bit of advice the Parson had given me.

"Don't ever let on you're afraid," he cautioned me one day, "because if you do the animal may turn on you."

With this in mind I faced about, took up the bear's trail, and with ready rifle, followed it. I kept looking behind me, to the right and to the left. The wind was blowing snow off the high peaks above and it made the tracks easily followed, for it kept them fresh. They turned aside, angled off, tacked and came back close to their first line. Around and around I trailed. A dozen times I stopped with my heart in my mouth, the rifle at my shoulder, but my alarm was occasioned by some other denizen of the wilds. Twice deer crashed away and left me rooted fast; and once, a cock grouse took the air from a rock just above my head, and nearly precipitated a stampede.

Finally I gave up the chase and started home, still watching warily for the bear. Better to guard against attack I climbed a little ridge that overlooked the irregular openings through which I had been trailing; and up there, paralleling my course, were bear tracks. Bruin had been craftily looking me over from his higher position. I at once advised that bear, by every

means at my command, that he was no longer
being hunted, and I made tracks for home as fast
as my legs would let me, watching warily, or
bearily, in all directions.

The Parson laughed heartily when I told of
my experience that night as together with Aunt
Jane we sat before the glowing fire of his hearth.
Despite Aunt Jane's gentle excuses for me, I
felt ashamed and determined to return next day
and take up the bear's trail. Running away from
an unseen bear was ludicrous, not to say cow-
ardly. But I comforted myself with the assur-
ance that even the Parson might have no other
chance to run, if the bear saw him first!

The "bad lands" became the scene of many
a hide-and-seek game, with the animals slipping
silently away as I blundered along behind, puzzling out their trails, and imagining I was stalking them unawares. My many failures, while
discouraging, were fruitful of experience, for I
learned to hunt up-wind, thus discounting the
high-power noses of the bears and muffling to
some extent my clumsy movements from the deer.
Repeated trips into that rough region informed
me that one or two bears lived there, and that
though they often left it to explore some other
region, they eventually returned to their own
home range. In tracing their movements I kept
a sort of big-game Bertillon record; only instead
of taking finger-prints, as is done with criminals,

I measured footprints sketching them in my notebook, noting any slight peculiarity that would distinguish one track from another, and thus made positive identification possible.

I was compelled to get my information concerning the bears' movements mostly from their tracks, for they were far too crafty to be seen "in person"! They evidently moved on the assumption that vigilance was the price of life. They used their wits as well as their keen senses, seemed to reason as well as to have instinct. Moreover they made use of other animals for their own defense. They were ever alertly watching the significant movments of their neighbors, for signals of dangers beyond the range of their own senses. The quiet retreat of a fox or coyote apprised them of something unusual in the wind; the sudden up-winging of magpies and jays warned them of the approach of an enemy. They distinguished between the casual flight of birds and their flying when bound toward a kill of mountain lion or other beasts of prey. They were tuned-in on every animal broadcasting station on their range.

I learned that contrary to the lurid tales of the early explorers and hunters, they were peace-loving, deeming it no disgrace to run away from danger and leaving the vicinity as soon as man appeared in it. True, their curiosity sometimes tempted them to circle back and watch a man from some secure retreat, and at such times they slipped as silently from one thicket to another as a fox, sampling the air for tell-tale odors, standing erect to watch and listen.

Bit by bit, as I learned more about them, I came to revise my early, gory opinion of them. My impression had been formed chiefly from tales of Lewis and Clark's expedition; when they made their memorable trip across the continent, grizzlies were not afraid of men because the arrows of the Indians were ineffective against them. Whenever food attracted them to an Indian camp they moseyed fearlessly among the tepees, helping themselves to it and scattering the redskins. Their attempts thus to raid white men's camps gave rise to blood-curdling stories of their savagery, and their fearless, deadly attacks on men. These tales, while pure fiction, led to the belief that all bears were bad and should be killed, at every opportunity; and ever since Lewis and Clark saw the first one, men with dogs and guns, traps and poison have been on their trail. While I do not believe bears guilty of the many offenses charged them, I am sure that they had been the "life of the party" at many a camp, having been led out of their retirement by their small-boy curiosity.

In the region where first I followed a bear, or where it followed me, there ranged two of these animals, each recording a different track and displaying individual traits which I came to recognize. The smaller track had short claws that left their prints in the sand or soft places. In following this track I found that the maker was inclined to be indolent; that if the digging after a chipmunk was hard he left the job unfinished and sought easier sources of food. Thus the black bear that frequented the "bad lands" loafed across his range, living by the easiest means possible and rarely exerting himself. Twice when Blackie's trail crossed that of other black bears, the tracks showed that all stopped to play, romping much as children romp and showing a sociable disposition. It was usually late in November before the black bear denned up for the winter, commonly adapting the shelter beneath some windfall to make a winter home by enlarging and improving it and perhaps by raking in some dead pine needles.

At the approach of fall Blackie left off distant wanderings, conserved energy by little exertion, and thus waxed fat. In the thickest of the rough jumble I found two of his deserted winter dens to which he never returned, and once in midwinter I found him out, asleep beneath some brush over which the snow had drifted. It was the thread of rising steam from a tiny hole above the den that first attracted my attention to it, but my nose gave me additional information.

Blackie's tracks showed he had unusually large

feet for his pounds, so I called him "Bigfoot."
There was a marked difference between Blackie's
and the other tracks I found in the "bad-lands."
The other tracks were those of a grizzly, a fact
I determined after collecting evidence for several years, and by sight of the animals themselves.
There was a wide difference, too, in the actions of
these animals whenever anything unusual happened. Blackie, commonly, ran away without
waiting to learn what had caused the alarm. The
grizzly displayed extreme caution, usually standing erect on his hind feet, remaining motionless,
watching for silent signals of other animals and
the birds, swinging his head slowly from side to
side, training his high-power nose in all directions, cocking his ears alertly as a coyote. When
he located the enemy he slipped away noiselessly,
followed a trail with which he was familiar and
left the vicinity, perhaps traveling ten or twenty
miles before stopping.

Unlike Blackie, too, the grizzly was a prodigious worker. No job was too big for him. Often
he spent an hour or more in digging out a
tiny titbit such as a chipmunk, and several times
in his pursuit of a marmot he excavated in rock-
slides holes large enough for small basements.
Daily he traveled many miles, foraging for food
as he moved, sometimes eating swarms of grasshoppers, or stowing away bushels of grass or
other greenery, or uprooting the ground for dog-

tooth violets of which he was very fond. Such spots, when he had finished his rooting, resembled a field which the hogs had plowed up.

In one respect the black bear and the grizzly were alike: they never seemed to have enough to eat, but had the insatiable appetites of growing boys; never showing any signs of being finicky, but devouring everything edible. Ants, hoppers, chipmunks, marmots and rabbits, comprised their fresh meat; while roots, shoots, bulbs, grass, berries and practically everthing growing served for vegetables. They both were inordinately fond of honey. Early one fall the grizzly left his home range and headed for the foothills. More than twenty miles away he found a bee tree, an old hollow cedar which he tore open. He devoured both bees and honey, then went lumbering home. Mountain lions made frequent kills about the region, leaving the carcasses of deer, cattle, horses and burros, which the bears located with their noses or by the flight of birds, and gorged themselves; afterward lying down in some retreat and sleeping long, peaceful hours.

It was because of their scavenger habits that they came to be blamed for killing the animals upon which they fed. But not once did I find evidence that they had killed anything larger than a marmot. The grizzly was always working industriously, from dawn to dark, or at night; while Blackie dallied, even though making a "bear living." He preferred to go empty rather than to work for food.

Three winters in succession the grizzly climbed to a den in an exposed spot on the northern slope of Mount Meeker. It was a low opening beneath a rock, the entrance to which was partially stopped with loose rubble, raked from inside the cave, and every fall he renovated it by chinking the larger cracks and by pawing together loose bits of rock for a bed. As fall approached, his tracks led to it; apparently he napped inside occasionally to try it out. His ultimate retirement for winter hibernation depended upon the weather and the food supply; if the fall were late, with plenty of food, he would still be about the woods as late as December, while one fall when snow came early and deep, and so made food unavailable, he disappeared at the end of October.

The grizzly had many individual traits. Not once in the years I followed him, did he show any desire for others of his kind. He preferred being alone. His play consisted chiefly of elaborate stalkings of easily captured animals. If his hunger was appeased for a time he would turn to hunting grasshoppers. Marking the spot where one had alighted he would steal forward and pounce upon it as though it were an animal of size and fighting ability. Again he would take great pains to waylay a chipmunk, lying motion-

less while the unwary little spermophile ventured closer and closer, then, with a lightning-
like slap of a huge paw, he would reduce his victim to the general shape and thinness of a pan-
cake.

Though the grizzly was somewhat awkward in
appearance he could move with amazing speed,
and his strength was incredible. From glimpses
I had of him I estimated his weight at six hundred pounds, but he could move the carcass of a
cow or horse twice that heavy. Once on Cabin
Creek, not many miles from his accustomed
haunts, a lion killed a horse. As he approached
the kill, the grizzly circled warily around it,
stood erect to sniff and listen, and growled warn-
ingly, informing all would-be intruders that it
was his. When he had eaten his fill, he dragged
the carcass nearly a hundred yards uphill over
fallen timber, into a thicket, where he covered it
against the prying eyes of birds, thinking, I presume, that they would signal other animals of its
location.

The date of his emergence from his den in the
spring, like his holing up in the fall, depended
upon the weather. Commonly though, he hi-
bernated about one-third of the year. When he
came out after his long sleep he was very thin,
the great layers of fat he had taken care to put
on before denning up were gone. One year I
followed his tracks the day he came out to learn

what he first ate, and was surprised to find that he scarcely ate at all. Instead of being ravenous, as I had supposed he would be, he seemed to have no appetite, and barely tasted a green shoot or two, and a little grass. His claws had grown out over winter and the tough soles of his feet soon shed off so that, though born to the wilds, he became a tenderfoot.

Upon two occasions I found the tracks of this "bad lands" grizzly far from home; once he was at the edge of a snowbank near Arapahoe glacier, where he had gone for a frozen grasshopper feast; and another time, some years later, beyond Ypsilon Mountain, in an old sheep trail that led toward the headwaters of the Poudre River. He was more than thirty miles from home and still going.

Experience with men has made the few surviving grizzlies of the Rockies crafty, and they are instinctively wary. Their habits have been much the same wherever I have had opportunity of observing them. Their extreme caution would perhaps lead one to believe them cowards, but nothing is farther from the truth, for they are fighters of first rank, and show unrivaled courage as well as lightning-like speed and prodigious strength in combat. A fighting grizzly is a deadly antagonist, never giving up, determined to win or die.

When a grizzly turns killer, as occasionally

one of them does, you may depend upon it, there are extenuating circumstances, and any fair-minded jury would exonerate him of blame. When his home range becomes settled up and the sources of his natural food are destroyed, he is forced to seek new haunts and to eat such food as his new location affords. It is not strange that, constricted in his range by ranchers and cattlemen, with no opportunity to seek food according to his instinctive habits, he sometimes turns cattle killer.

His action brands him at once as a bad bear, a killer and his infamy quickly spreads the length of the mountains. He is blamed for the kills of mountain lions, and the death of stock killed by chance. He is hunted, becomes a fugitive from justice, and is kept so continuously on the move that he has to prey on cattle because he is not given time to forage in his former manner. Persecution sharpens his faculties; he eludes his pursuers and their dogs, poisoned bait and traps, with a shrewdness that puts their so-called intelligence to shame.

It was my rare privilege one day to witness the chase of an accused "killer" by a dog pack. I was near timberline in the Rabbit Ear mountains when first I heard their distant baying and caught sight of them far down a narrow valley, mere moving specks. Close behind these small dots were larger ones, men on horseback. A mile ahead of the pack a lone object galloped into an opening and, as I focused my glasses, stood erect, listening. It was a grizzly. He paused but a moment, then tacked up the side of the mountain, crossed the ridge, dropped into a parallel valley, and doubled back the way he had come. Occasionally I caught a glimpse of him as he ambled along, seemingly without haste, yet covering the ground at surprising speed.

Abruptly he left this second valley and re-crossed the ridge to the first, taking up the trail he had been on when the pack disturbed him. The riders were still upon the ridge when the dogs recrossed it and started baying up the first valley. When the fresh scent led them back over the grizzly's first trail, they hesitated, confused, disagreeing among themselves as to the course to follow: and while the dogs delayed, the bear abandoned the lower ridges and timbered valleys and headed toward the cliffs. Here the going was slow. Sometimes he followed old, deep-worn game trails, but more often he chose his own way. He climbed up the face of a cliff, following narrow ledges. At the top, he turned and angled back, arriving at the base of the wall again, but some distance from the place where he had climbed up, and where he crossed his own trail, he swung back and forth repeatedly.

Half an hour later, the pack came howling to the cliff, and began seeking a way up. They scattered, swung back and forth along the ledges, crossed and recrossed the grizzly's tracks, but seemed unable to follow the way he had gone, before they finally circled the cliff and picked up his trail again. The bear's ruse had succeeded, by it he gained several minutes' lead on his pursuers.

The grizzly emerged above timberline near where I sat and galloped straight for a pass that overlooked the deep cañons, dark forests and rocky ridges on the other side of the range. Just before he gained it, three of the dogs broke cover and gave tongue, wildly excited at the sight of their quarry, and instantly hot on his trail. The bear coolly kept his same gait, until just short of the pass, at the top of a steep, smooth incline between two huge rock slabs, he halted and faced about, waiting for them to come up. When the dogs, panting and spent from running, dashed up, he had got his wind and was ready for them.

The three dogs rushed pell-mell up the steep rock. With a deafening roar, the grizzly struck out right and left. Two of the dogs ceased howling and lay where they fell, the third turned tail and fled. The bear, stepping over the dead bodies of his vanquished foes, leisurely proceeded through the pass and down into the wild country beyond.

I have watched other grizzlies under similar conditions, and they have all shown the same shrewd, cool, craftiness. They appear to reason, to plan; their actions indicate forethought, premeditation. They seem to have not only the marvelous instinct of the animal world, but also an almost human power to think. They conserve their energy, bide their time, choose their position and, in short, set the stage to their own advantage. They have an instinct for the psychological moment—it seems at times that they evolve it out of the chaos of chance.

The Parson said, "You never can tell what a bear will do," and I, for one, believe him. The oddest performance of an individual bear I ever saw took place over on the banks of the Poudre River. Rambling through the forest I came, late one evening, upon the camp of two trappers. They were making a business of trapping and had extensive trap-lines set throughout the region, mostly for beavers, minks, bobcats and coyotes, but some for bears too. In a narrow, dry gulch, one of them had found fresh bear tracks—he thought of a medium-sized black bear—leading up to the scattered, bleached bones of a cow. Tracks about the skull indicated that the bear had rolled it about, much as a puppy worries a bone. One day the trapper found the skull hidden in some juniper bushes, and reasoned that the bear returned from day to day, played with it, then hid it away. So he returned to camp, got a trap and set it by the beast's toy.

I was eager to learn the outcome of this action, so I gratefully accepted the trappers' invitation to stay over with them. Next day, I went along when they visited the trap. To our astonishment, the skull was gone and the trap still set.

It was easy to trace the culprit for his tracks revealed that his left front foot was badly twisted, its track pointing in, almost at right angles, to the tracks of the other three feet, with the claw-marks almost touching the track of the right front foot. We followed his trail till we came to a sandy stretch upon which that bear had held high carnival. He had rolled the skull about, punted it with his good right paw, and leaped upon it, in mimic attack, as though it were a fat marmot. Then, playtime over, he had carried it a considerable distance and cached it beneath some logs.

The trapper returned to camp for another trap, and set it and the first near the skull, concealing the traps cleverly in depressions scooped out in the sand, and covering their gaping, toothed jaws with loose, pine needles. Then he scattered a few pine cones about, and placed dead tree limbs near the traps in such a way that in stepping over them the bear would be liable to step squarely upon the concealed pan of one of them.

Three times the bear rescued the precious cow skull, each time avoiding the traps. At last in desperation, the trapper took two more traps to the gulch and vowed that he'd pull up stakes and leave the bear alone if he did not get him with the set he purposed making.

With boyish interest, I accompanied him to the gulch, carrying one of the traps for him. We left the traps a short distance from where the bear had concealed the old skull, while the trapper looked the ground over and decided to set the traps where the skull was hidden, for the spot was ideal for the purpose. On two sides logs formed a barrier and beyond them was a huge bowlder, the two forming a natural little cove. He expected the bear to approach his plaything from the unobstructed side.

The trapper had further plans. Close beside the logs grew a stunted pine tree with wide-spreading limbs near the ground. In its crotch he placed the cow's skull, higher than the bear could reach, and fastened it there with wire. Then, after setting the traps in a semi-circle around the tree, just below the skull, and concealing them carefully, we returned to camp, jubilantly confident of catching Mr. Bruin.

Three times we visited the set and found things undisturbed. We decided the bear had forsworn his toy and run away. However, I lingered at the camp in hope that the matter would yet come to a decisive end.

Some days later, when we visited the gulch again, we came upon a surprise. From a distance we missed the skull from the tree. So we hastened forward, keeping a sharp eye out for the bear which we felt certain was in a trap and lying low. At the set we stopped short. The two traps nearest the open space had been carefully dug up and turned over, and lay "butter side down." The bear had climbed into the tree, wrenched his plaything free, and dropped it to the ground. Tracks in the sand showed that after climbing down he had cautiously placed his feet in the same tracks he had made when he advanced toward the tree.

He had carried the skull a hundred yards from the traps and hidden it again; but there were no signs that he had stopped to play with it.

The trapper was as good as his word; and after recovering from his astonishment, he sprung the traps, and we carried them back to camp.

"Some smart, that ole twisted-foot bear," the trapper told his partner. "He's smart enough to live a hundred years—an' I'm willin' to let him."

No campfire is complete without bear stories, and it was around one that I heard the funniest bear story imaginable.

A lone trapper was caught one day in a trap of his own making, a ponderous wooden coop calculated to catch the bear alive by dropping a heavy log door in place at the open end. This door was on a trigger which a bear, in attempting to steal the bait, would spring.

As this tale was told, the trapper had just completed his trap and was adjusting the trigger, when the heavy door crashed down, pinning him across the threshold, with his legs outside. The door caught on a section of log in the doorway, and saved him from broken legs, but he was a helpless prisoner.

In struggling to free himself, he kicked over a can of honey he had brought along for bait, and the sticky fluid oozed over his thrashing legs. Four hours he lay, imprisoned, shouting at intervals, with the hope that some wandering prospector or trapper might hear him. Instead a bear came his way, tempted by the scent of the much-loved honey.

The bear loitered near by some time, no doubt wary of the presence of man, but at last his appetite overcame his caution, and he started licking up the honey. Almost frantic with fear, dreading the gash of tearing teeth, the man lay quiet, while the animal licked the smears off his trembling legs. Fortunately for the trapper, the bear was not out for meat that day; so, after cleaning up the sweet, he went his way. The relieved and unharmed man was rescued shortly afterward.

The only serious injury I have suffered from a wild animal was inflicted inside the city limits of Denver, Colorado's largest city and capital. The beginning of this story dated back to the time when I discovered that another grizzly had

intruded into the "bad lands" of my bears. The
first announcement of the strange bear's arrival
was its tracks, together with those of two tiny
cubs. This was in May, while yet the snowbanks
lingered in that high country.

Across the miles of fallen timber I lugged a
steel bear trap and set it in a likely spot beside the
frozen carcass of a deer. Afterwards I inspected
it every day, though, to do so, I had to cross
boggy, rough country, fretted over with fallen
logs. I always found plenty of bear tracks—it
was typical bear country—and there were many
signs of their activities: old logs torn apart, ant
hills disturbed, and lush grass trampled.

The first week in June, I made a surprising
catch—three grizzly bears and a fox. A mother
grizzly had stepped into my trap, and her two
cubs, of about fifteen pounds each, had lingered
near by, until, growing hungry, they had ventured to their mother, and one had been caught
in a coyote trap set to protect the bait. The fox
had been caught before the bear's arrival. Mrs.
Grizzly, frantic over her predicament, had de-
molished everything within her reach, tearing
the red fox from its trap, literally shredding it,
apparently feeling it was to blame for her mis-
fortune.

Her struggles soon exhausted her, for it was a
warm day, and when I discovered her she was
about spent, and easily dispatched.

The cubs, very small, helpless and forlorn, howled lustily for their mother. I decided to tie their feet together, and their mouths shut.

With ready cord, I dived headlong upon a cub, caught him by the scruff of the neck, lifted him triumphantly—then dropped him unceremoniously, the end of a finger badly bitten. I was compelled to return to my cabin for a sack, because the amount of tying required to render the cubs really harmless seemed likely to choke them to death before I got them home. It required about an hour's lively tussle to get the two young grizzlies stowed safely in the sack. But I learned that having them sacked was no guarantee of getting them home.

If "a bird in the hand is worth two in the bush," a bear at home, chained up, is worth the whole Rockies' full in the woods.

The old grizzly's hide, paws included, must have weighed fifty pounds; the cubs, sacked, thirty—a total load of 80 pounds to carry out over rocks and fallen trees, through bog and willows. With this load on my back, I struggled to my feet and started, picking my way slowly, circling logs and avoiding soft spots. The first half mile was the best, after that things thickened up, the bog deepened, the bears wanted to get out and walk.

Where the stream emerges from between a wide moraine and Meeker Mountain, it is not broad, nor very deep, but it is exceedingly cold and swift, and the only crossing was a beaver-felled aspen, which lay top-foremost toward me, presenting an array of limbs that served as banisters. About midway over the limbs gave out, leaving the smooth aspen trunk as a foot-log. Many times I had crossed this without mishap, so I had no qualms about tackling it now. Deliberately I edged along, stepping slowly, carefully, progressing nicely until about midway. Just then one of the cubs sank his teeth into my back. I jerked away, twisted, tottered, half regained my balance, then pitched headlong into the icy water of the beaver pond beneath.

For a moment there was a grand mêlée. The cubs did not like the ice water any more than I. They squirmed and clawed, fought free of the sack, and lightened my load considerably. I spent a busy hour catching and sacking them again.

It required six hours to transport those cubs four miles! And I'm sure they were as thankful as their ferry when the trip ended at my cabin.

From the first week in June until the middle of December, they grew from fifteen pounds to forty each. Although they were interesting pets, their keep became a problem. Such appetites! They could never get enough. They weren't finicky about the quality of their food; but oh, the quantity! Then, too, I couldn't leave them and go on long trips. So I decided to part with them.

The City of Denver sent a representative to see me, for they wanted some grizzlies to show eastern tourists.

It was with the feeling that I was betraying the cubs, however, that I finally took them to Denver. They were so obedient and well-behaved that I hesitated to deliver them into unknown hands. They knew their names, Johnny and Jenny, as well as children knew theirs. At command they would stand erect, walk about on their hind feet, whining eagerly for some treat, looking for all the world like funny, little old men.

At the Denver City Zoo we were welcomed by the keeper, Mr. Hill, who courteously invited me to spend the day with him, and entertained me by taking me into many of the cages, permitting me to feed some of the animals, and telling me interesting tales of happenings at the Zoo.

When we returned to the large inclosure surrounding the cage of the larger and fiercer animals, Mr. Hill asked me to assist in transfering a brown bear and a black bear to the cage where my pets were to be housed. These other bears were over a year old and more than double the size of Johnny and Jenny. The brown bear went willingly enough into the new cage, and we expected the black bear to follow, but when he reached the cage door, he stopped. Gently we urged him forward, but his mind was made up—he had gone as far as he intended and was homesick for his old cage. The keeper was tactful, and unobstrusively tried to maneuver the bear into the cage without exciting his obstinacy further, but he wouldn't yield. At last it came to a show down. We had the option of forcing the bear into the cage, or letting him go back.

"You go inside and snub the rope around the bars," the keeper directed me. "I'll boost from behind—we'll show him a trick or two."

A crowd had collected outside the heavy iron fence. Suggestions were abundant. No young man ever had so much advice in so short a time. However, we were too busily engaged to profit by what we were told.

The keeper boosted the bear—and I took up the slack in the rope; but still the bear balked, though three times we double-teamed against him. Then, suddenly, he let go all holds and lunged through the doorway, charging headlong upon me and sank his teeth into my left knee. The bite and the force of his unexpected charge knocked me backward into the corner. Instantly the bear was on top of me, growling, biting and striking.

With my uninjured leg I kicked out savagely and thrust him away, sliding him back across the slippery concrete. Again he charged, and once more I kicked him off.

Outside the iron fence women were screaming

and men trying futilely to enter, but the fence
was ten feet high and the sharp iron points of its
pickets were discouraging—and the gateway was
locked against intruders.

At this juncture the keeper rushed to another
cage where he kept an iron bar for just such
emergencies, but the bar was away from home
that day.

At this crisis, Johnny and Jenny arrived,
Jenny collided with the bars of the cage and
staggered back, dazed. But Johnny found the
open cage door, and charged the black bear fero-
ciously. The black bear outweighed my little
grizzly three to one, but Johnny struck his sensitive snout, forcing him into a corner, and followed up, striking with both paws, lunging in
and taking furry samples of his hide.

Within a few seconds the black bear was climbing the side of the cage and howling for help.
He gained the shelf near the roof. Johnny, unable to climb, sat below, growling maledictions
in bear language, daring him to come down and
fight it out. But the black bear had had more
than enough. He stuck to the safety seat,
whimpering with pain and fright.

Thus, limping and reluctant, I took leave of
my pets. The ambulance had arrived to rush
me to the hospital where my knee was to be
treated. As long as I could see them, they looked
after me, wondering at my desertion.

CHAPTER FIFTEEN

ROCKY MOUNTAIN NATIONAL PARK

IT had been my boyhood dream to find a region unspoiled by man, wild, primitive. When I saw that rugged wilderness called the Rockies I was sure I had found it. Miles and miles of virgin forest, innocent of ax and saw; miles and miles of fertile valleys, yet to feel the touch of plow; miles and miles of unclaimed homesteads with never the smoke of a settler's chimney! Deer and elk, sheep and bear roamed the forests, beavers preëmpted the valleys, trout spashed and rippled the waters of the lakes and rivers. Yes, this was purely primeval, natural, uncivilized.

But the old-timers did not agree with me. Parson Lamb, whose nearest neighbor was ten miles away, complained that the country was being spoiled.

"It's gotten so nowadays you can't see a mountain 'thout craning your neck around some fellow's shack; cabins everywhere cluttering up the scenery."

I recalled my father's chuckling about the

pioneers always moving on as soon as a country got settled up. Surely the Parson was having his little joke!

One day when I was out looking for Mr. and Mrs. Peg, I ran upon an old trapper.

"Huh!" he said, "won't be long till they won't be no critters atall. They ain't enough now to pay for trap-bait. Game ain't what it useter be in these parts, I tell you, sonny. I'm goin' ter pull up stakes for a real game country!"

To me, lately from the thickly settled prairies of Kansas, practically destitute of game, their fears seemed unfounded. I thought they exaggerated, and could not understand their point of view. But I came to understand. I lived to see even greater changes take place, in the twenty-five years I wandered through the country, that Parson Lamb had witnessed from the day he hewed his way through the forest, that he might get his covered wagon into the valley, to that night when I fell across his threshold after pushing my bicycle over Bald Mountain.

For even as I rambled and camped, a subtle change was taking place so slowly that for some time I was unaware of it. I saw fewer animals in a day's journey. At first, when I missed bands of deer or wild sheep, or some familiar bear, from their usual haunts, I assumed that they had shifted their range to more distant mountains. All at once I realized that for a long time

I had not come upon a single elk nor even the tracks of one. I was startled. I made far excursions into the more remote regions, to verify my assumption that the game had merely retreated from the more settled parts. From the tops of lofty peaks, I looked down upon countless valleys with the hope that somewhere, surely, I would find them. I saw only a few stragglers.

The wilds were like an empty house where once had lived happy children, where there had been music and laughter, shouts and romping, but now remained only silence, freighted with sadness. A great loneliness surged over me. Despite the grumbling complaints of the old settlers, I had taken for granted that the country would always stay as I had found it, that other boys would have it to explore, and that it would thrill them even as it had thrilled me. I awoke at last to the distressing truth that few of the easily accessible spots were unspoiled, that forests were falling, that the game was almost gone.

I set out to see what could be done about it. I found others as concerned as I. Not only those in the immediate vicinity, but men of vision far removed from the scene. It seemed that similar conditions had arisen elsewhere and that farsighted men had evolved a remedy. Back in 1872, Congress had set aside the Yellowstone region as a national park, guaranteeing the preservation of its wonders for all time. Not only that, but the harassed and hunted game in the country surrounding it had by some subtle instinct sensed its immunity to hunters, and had fled to it for sanctuary—grizzly bears, migrated to it from long distances and found refuge. I recalled how scarce the beavers were when first I searched the valleys for them, and how, after the State had passed laws for their protection, they had multiplied. Here was the solution of the problem—protection; and the most permanent and effective protection could be procured by getting the government to preserve it as a National Park. But, just as nearsighted and self-interested individuals opposed and tried to thwart the building of the first transcontinental railroad, so there were persons who could see no reason for setting aside this region as a National Park, men who had for years cut government timber without restriction, or who had grazed livestock without hindrance, or who still hoped to strike rich mineral desposits in the proposed area to be reserved.

Fortunately, the men of vision prevailed, and in 1915, Congress created the Rocky Mountain National Park, setting aside 400 square miles of territory, most of it straddling the Continental Divide, and as wild and primitive as when the Utes first hunted in it. Thus the snow-capped peaks and the verdant valleys, the deep-gashed cañons and the rushing rivers, the age-old glaciers and the primeval forests are preserved forever from exploitation.

In administering the National Parks, the government takes into consideration that they are the property of the whole people, not just of those residing in adjacent or near territory. Not only does it consider them as belonging to the present generation, but to posterity. With this in mind, it has formulated certain general principles of administration applicable to all parks and has adopted special policies adapted to the peculiar needs of individual parks. For instance, it has found that in order to protect the visitors and insure their comfort, and convenience, it is necessary to have certain regulations of hotel management and transportation facilities. It has found it impossible to hold many individual concerns responsible for the enforcement of these regulations, so it has adopted the policy of granting concessions to one large company equipped to render the service required. Such a concern conducts its business under government jurisdiction, and is required to abide by the government regulations. The transportation companies, for example, are required to run their cars on regular schedule, at reasonable and approved rates. Their books are audited by the government, and they pay a certain percentage of their earnings to it.

As funds are available roads and trails are

developed, enabling thousands to enjoy the last frontier. And it is amazing, how, in this short time, wild life has increased within the borders of the park. Beavers have returned, their dams and houses are along every stream; deer and elk straggle along the trails to welcome wide-eyed visitors; upon the promontories curious, friendly mountain sheep are regal silhouettes against the sky.

Here boys and girls of every land may explore even as I explored—and, with their trusty cameras for guns, shoot more game than Kit Carson ever trapped!

THE END

NOTES

Notes are keyed to page and line numbers. For example, 1:2 means page 1, line 2.

MAP

vi–viii. The Cooper-Babcock map of 1911 was the joint product of William S. Cooper (1884–1978) and Dean Babcock (1888–1969), who surveyed the Longs Peak–Wild Basin region in 1908 (see Ch. 5, 76:7). It is reprinted here through the courtesy of David S. Cooper. A number of the names assigned by Cooper and Babcock were clearly idiosyncratic and were subsequently abandoned or replaced. The origins of Mt. Cooper and Mt. Hewes (which Cooper and Babcock named after their mutual friend Charles Edwin Hewes) are obvious enough. Cooper named Mt. Caroline, Caroline Ridge, and Caroline Creek in honor of his mother; Lake Margaret after a current girl friend. In the notes that follow I have been guided in matters concerning mountain nomenclature, spelling, and altitudes by Louisa Ward Arps and Elinor Eppich Kingery's invaluable *High Country Names: Rocky Mountain National Park* (Estes Park, Colo.: Rocky Mountain Nature Association, 1972). I have not, however, altered Joe Mills's text, even though his habit of adding an apostrophe to the names of mountains causes unnecessary confusion (e.g., Long's Peak).

CHAPTER 1: "GOING WEST"

1:2. Enos Mills Sr. (1834–1910) and his wife, the former Ann Lamb (1837–1923), came to Linn County, Kansas, in the late spring of 1857 with a number of other families, from Dallas County, Iowa, and settled on a farm near the future town of Pleasanton, close to the Missouri border. It remained their home for the rest of their lives. The date of removal to Kansas that Joe Mills provides in his father's "old diary" differs by some three years from the date provided by the elder Mills himself in the short autobiographical account of his life, dated December 26, 1909, published with his obituary in the *Pleasanton Observer* (February 25, 1910), hereafter referred to as Mills Obituary. The May 1857 date is confirmed by Elkanah J. Lamb, first cousin of Enos Mills, Sr., in his *Memories of the Past and Thoughts of the Future* (United Brethren Publishing House, 1906), p. 43. An account of life in Linn County during the turbulent period that coincided with the arrival of the Mills and Lamb families (who came from Dallas County, Iowa, together) can be found in Edgar Langsdorf, ed., "The Letters of Joseph H. Trego, 1857–1864, Linn County Pioneer," *Kansas Historical Quarterly,* 19 (May 1951), 113–32; (August 1951), 287–309; (November 1951), 381–400.

2:18. The reports of rich gold strikes in the streams near Denver in 1858 and 1859 (many of them inflated by promoters and speculators) sent hordes of would-be gold seekers to Colorado's eastern slopes in pursuit of "the new Eldorado." Many thousands came from Kansas and Missouri, where the promise of striking it rich offered an attractive alternative to bad crops, generally bad economic conditions, and political turmoil. For accounts of "the gold rush of '59," see Carl Abbott, Stephen J. Leonard, and David McComb, *Colorado: A History of the Centennial State* (Boulder: Colorado Associated University Press, 1982), pp. 50–69; Robert G. Athearn, *The Coloradans* (Albuquerque: University of New Mexico Press, 1976), pp. 7–32; Leroy Hafen, ed., *Colorado Gold Rush: Contemporary Letters and Reports* vol. 10, Southwest Historical Series (Glendale, Ca.: Arthur H. Clark, Co., 1942).

3:21. The Battle of Mine Creek, the most important Civil War battle fought in Kansas, occurred on October 25, 1864. It ended with the invading Confederate army, commanded by General Sterling Price (1809–67), being routed and driven back into Arkansas. The Battle of Mine Creek was long remembered by Linn County residents, many of whom were eyewitnesses. One of these was Elkanah Lamb, who was wounded and robbed during the battle. See his *Memories of the Past and Thoughts of the Future,* pp. 76–82. See also Edgar Langsdorf, "Price's Raid and the Battle of Mine Creek," *Kansas Historical Quarterly,* 30 (Autumn 1964): 281–306; and Lumir F. Buresh, *October 25th and the Battle of Mine Creek* (Kansas City, Mo.: Lowell Press, 1977).

4:1. In the spring of 1860, Enos Mills, together with his wife, his brother Enoch Mills (1837–83), Elkanah J. Lamb, and their relative David Lamb (b. 1838), set off for the gold fields of Colorado. They traveled by way of Lawrence, Topeka, and Manhattan, Kansas, to Kearney, Nebraska, and then west to Denver along the much-traveled Platte River road. From Denver, a town of "log houses and shanties" with a population of eight to ten thousand, Mills and his party entered South Park, where they briefly, and without great success, tried their hands at placer mining in the Tarryall district before "crossing the range" to

Breckenridge. ("Mrs. Mills had the distinction of being the first white woman that ever crossed the range west of Tarryall.") There they filed upon a claim, which yielded little more than "enough to replenish current wants." Mills peddled meat to the miners for a time before coming down with mountain fever, leaving Ann Mills to drive their mules and wagon over the mountains to Denver, from where they made their way back to Kansas. Mills Obituary; Lamb, *Memories of the Past and Thoughts of the Future,* pp. 49–73.

4:3. The famous injunction of Horace Greeley (1811–72) to the unemployed of New York City actually originated with Indiana newspaperman John Soule, who used it in 1851. As the influential editor of the *New York Tribune,* Greeley's statements (including this one) were widely quoted. Greeley subsequently followed his own advice and in 1870 founded a cooperative community, Union Colony, at what is now Greeley, Colorado.

10:2. This statement about "no relatives" is simply not true. Joe Mills was related to Elkanah Lamb on both his father's and mother's side. As noted above, Elkanah Lamb and Enos Mills, Sr., Joe's father, were first cousins. His mother, Ann Lamb Mills, was the daughter of Josiah Lamb (1817–62), another of Elkanah Lamb's first cousins. Interestingly enough, neither Joe Mills nor his older brother Enos ever acknowledged these close family ties in their accounts of how and why they first came to Estes Park. Nor is there any mention of the relationship in the 1935 biography *Enos Mills of the Rockies,* written by his widow Esther Burnell Mills and Hildegarde Hawthorne, the granddaughter of Nathaniel Hawthorne. The mother of Enos Mills, Sr., Sarah Moon (1805–62), and the mother of Elkanah Lamb, Elizabeth Moon (1807–87), were sisters. Sarah married Abijah Mills (b. 1800) on September 2, 1824; Elizabeth married Esau Lamb (1806–83) on June 15, 1826. At the time of the 1850 census the Esau Lamb and Abijah Mills families occupied adjacent farms in Union Township, St. Joseph County, Indiana. About 1852 the two families, in the company of other relatives, moved to Dallas County, Iowa, and then in the spring of 1857 to Linn County, Kansas. Tradition has it that the Lamb and Mills families arrived in Linn County in a wagon caravan numbering some fifty individuals, together with all their worldly goods and livestock. The best single printed source for the history of the Lambs and their relationship to the Mills family is C. V. Jackson, "Josiah Lamb—Inventor and Legislator," *Linn County News,* March 1, 1984, pp. 9, 13.

11:13. The Reverend Elkanah J. Lamb (1832–1915), Longs Peak's first professional guide, was born at South Bend, Indiana. As noted above, Lamb was the first cousin of Joe Mills's father, and together with his wife, Welta Jane, whom he married on August 24, 1853, was numbered among the party that moved together from Dallas County, Iowa, to Linn County, Kansas, in the spring of 1857. Following their brief interlude in the gold fields of Colorado in 1860, Elkanah returned to Kansas and remained there until May 1866, when he moved to a 160-acre homestead in Saline County, Nebraska. Following the death of his wife in 1867 and his remarriage a year later, on September 29, 1868, to Jemima (Jane) Morger, née Caldwell, a widow with three sons, Lamb decided to enter the ministry of the Church of the United Brethren. He returned to Colorado in 1871 to do missionary work as an itinerant preacher, and in August of that year made his first visit to Estes Park, where he climbed Longs Peak twice and, while boarding at Griff Evans's ranch on lower Fish Creek Road, spent "several days in this beautiful park, wandering up and down Fall River and the Big Thompson, fishing, prospecting, and enjoying primitive life in its fullness and freshness." Lamb visited the park again in 1873 while pursuing missionary work in the towns of the St. Vrain valley along the front range and two years later, in 1875, he constructed the twelve-by-fourteen-foot cabin covered by poles, brush and dirt in Longs Peak (now Tahosa) Valley that would evolve into Longs Peak House. Soon afterwards Lamb was augmenting his preacher's salary by raising cattle, putting up tourists, and guiding parties to the summit for five dollars a trip. "If they would not pay for spiritual guidance," Lamb later wrote, "I compelled them to divide for material elevation." Lamb continued to operate Longs Peak House until 1902, when he sold it to Enos A. Mills. Lamb continued to live in Estes Park at a ranch called "Mountain Home," which he built some two miles north of Longs Peak House at the head of Wind River (the current site of Wind River Lodge), until the time of his death in 1915. He left a record of his varied and interesting life in two autobiographical volumes, *Memories of the Past and Thoughts of the Future* (United Brethren Publishing House, 1906) and *Miscellaneous Meditations* (The Publishers' Press Room and Bindery Company [c. 1913?]).

CHAPTER 2: "GETTING ACQUAINTED WITH WILD COUNTRY ANIMALS"

14:3. On the morning of the Battle of Mine Creek, October 25, 1864 (See Ch. 1, 3:21), Lamb and several friends, hearing "occasional firing and skirmishing not far from our residence," rode out onto the prairie to investigate. There they were surprised by a small party of border ruffians posing as Union cavalry, and Lamb was robbed, wounded, and almost killed by a "freebooter from Missouri." See Lamb, *Memories of the Past,* pp. 76–79.

14:26. Lamb first climbed Longs Peak alone in August 1871, and for reasons not clear, having made the ascent by way of the traditional route ("Keyhole," "Trough," "Narrows," and "Homestretch"), elected to descend the sheer, three-thousand-foot East Face of the mountain. Dressed in an "overcoat" containing specimens he had gathered on the summit, lacking climbing equipment of any kind, and without any real knowledge of where he was going or what lay ahead, Lamb descended the couloir below the Notch on the south side of the East Face to the ledge now known as "Broadway," some thousand feet below the summit. From there he made his perilous way down the long snowfield leading to Chasm Lake. Since that day the snowfield has been known as "Lamb's Slide," for it was during its descent that Lamb suffered a fall that might well have ended his life had he not grabbed a projecting boulder. As Lamb later recounted the adventure in his *Memories of the Past and Thoughts of the Future,* pp. 130–33,

> Getting my knife out of my pocket, I opened it with my teeth, then reached half-way to the rocks of safety and began digging a niche in the ice for a toe hold, when my knife broke in two. This left me stranded and stopped further progress in digging. My nervous system was very much unstrung by this sliding, swinging experience, but I was compelled to decide—quickly, too. So, putting the tip of my left foot in the shallow niche I had cut, (knowing that if my foot slipped I was a lost Lamb,) then working my arm to the top of the rock, I gave a huge lunge, just managing to reach the foot of the mountain . . . .
>
> Then, on I went, finally coming to a perpendicular wall. Grooves were worn into its face by the action of water in streams and drippings for untold ages. My situation was fearful to contemplate. The mountain was perpendicular to the south over the lake; to the north, utterly inaccessible. The only alternative was to go down one of these grooves in the granite wall. Selecting one with projecting rocks sufficient for foot and hand holds, I let myself down this perilous route. . . . This descent brought me to Crater [Chasm] Lake. . . .

Lamb's adventure is also recounted in M. Matilda Moody's "E. J. Lamb, Well Known Guide, Makes a Frightful Slide Down Mount Long," *Denver Post,* August 10, 1902, n.p.

Some twenty-two years later, in June 1903, Enos A. Mills repeated Lamb's adventure. Mills's descent was subsequently described by Earl Harding (who had "arrived at Longs Peak Inn just as the mountain climber was returning from this adventure") in "Climbing Long's [*sic*] Peak," *Outing,* 44 (July 1904): 461–68.

15:25. Until the first years of the twentieth century, when the value of its water supply became recognized and a number of reservoirs were built on existing lakes, Wild Basin remained the least known area in what is now Rocky Mountain National Park. It was surveyed by William S. Cooper and Dean Babcock, who published the first detailed map of the Wild Basin region in 1911 (see frontispiece). William S. Cooper, "Wild Basin in 1904–08," *Trail and Timberline,* 558 (June 1965): 107–9.

18:12. When the first settlers arrived in Estes Park, elk were plentiful and thriving. But extensive hunting, for both sport and profit, gradually reduced the size of the once extensive elk population so that by the late 1880s elk had become rare. In 1913, Estes Park residents raised the funds necessary to purchase twenty-nine elk from Montana. (They were transported by railroad car to Lyons and from Lyons to Estes Park by Stanley Steamer automobiles equipped with special cages.) An additional herd of twenty-four elk was added in 1915. With the Rocky Mountain National Park providing a mantle of protection, the elk—or Wapiti—is once again a familiar sight in the Estes Park area, sometimes to the annoyance of local residents.

28:19. No doubt Mills Moraine, named after Enos A. Mills.

CHAPTER 3: "FIRST CAMP ALONE— EXPLORING"

35:7. This is probably the wagon road—first operated as a toll road— that Elkanah Lamb and his son Carlyle (1862–1958) cut through the timber from the lower end of Estes Park up to their Longs Peak House in the fall of 1875 and the spring of 1876. This route—which generally follows present Route 7—itself followed an older hunting trail into the park. The route is clearly visible on the map of the Estes Park area included in the *Geological and Geographical Atlas of Colorado,* published by the Hayden Survey in 1877.

36:12. Probably Thunder Lake at the upper end of Wild Basin, on whose shores archaeologists have discovered the remains of Indian encampments.

42:8. The interesting story of how and when the various landmarks within Rocky Mountain National Park were named is in the introduction to Louisa Ward Arps and Elinor Eppich Kingery, *High Country Names: Rocky Mountain National Park* (Estes Park, Colorado: Rocky Mountain Nature Association, 1972), pp. 1–11.

42:18. The pear-shaped lake is clearly Pear Reservoir as it existed before it was dammed, like several other lakes in Wild Basin, to supply water to the farms along the St. Vrain River during the first years of the twentieth century. The dam on Pear Reservoir has now largely deteriorated. "Hourglass" and "Dog-with-three-legs" are more difficult to identify, though Sandbeach Lake would qualify for the former and Bluebird Lake for the latter.

47:2. With the exception of Lulu City, along the headwaters of the Colorado across the Continental Divide north of Grand Lake, there were no extensive mining camps in the region embraced by Rocky Mountain National Park, a fact that retarded the development of the area even as it served to protect its natural beauty. Prospectors did periodically enter the Estes Park area, however, and their shafts and dumps are still encountered in various scattered places, including the Tahosa Valley. Aside from the Lulu City, the most accessible and frequently visited mining site is the Eugenia (or Cudahy-Norwall) Mine on Battle Mountain, not far from the Longs Peak trail, some two miles from Longs Peak campground, which dates from 1905. It was abandoned about 1918. The caved-in mine shaft, which once extended more than one thousand feet back into Battle Mountain, a pile of tailings, an old boiler, and the remains of several cabins serve as reminders of the dreams of bygone days.

48:26. Until the introduction of light hand-held cameras and roll film made photography readily available to the amateur, photographers were forced to rely on heavy cameras mounted on tripods and on glass plates. At first, they had to contend with a so-called "wet" plate process that required that the plates be dipped in a collodial solution immediately prior to use and then be processed in other chemical solutions on the spot. The introduction of commercially available "dry" plates during the early 1880s greatly simplified the process and reduced the time of exposure, though the plates remained fragile and the cameras, which still required the use of a tripod, remained fairly heavy.

CHAPTER 4: "DANCING ACROSS THE DIVIDE"

55:15. In 1874 the first stage line was established between Longmont and Estes Park, followed in June of 1876 by the establishment of the first post office in a small cabin north of Black Canyon Creek. Clara M. MacGregor, who arrived in the park in 1872 with her husband, Alexander Q. MacGregor (1845–96), and homesteaded Black Canyon, became the first postmistress. In 1877 John Cleave (1840–1925), an Englishman from Cornwall, became postmaster, a position he would occupy for some thirty years. Cleave's 160-acre homestead was located at the junction of Fall River and the Big Thompson River, site of the present

town of Estes Park. His post office was located near the intersection of
what are now Moraine and Elkhorn Avenues, in a building that also
served as the Cleave residence and store. Cleave sold out to C. H. Bond
and a number of others in 1905 because he did not wish to see "the danged
place overrun by tenderfoot tourists," but returned in 1917. A trip to
pick up the mail thus required a long trip from Lamb's Longs Peak House
to the valley below and back, some eighteen miles in all.

56:8. The story that Kit Carson (1809–68), legendary mountain man,
trapper, and scout, built a cabin on the side of Twin Sisters Mountain
where he spent the winter of 1842 has long been part of the lore of Estes
Park. Elkanah Lamb pointed out the ruins of an old cabin at the foot of
Cabin Rock, and it was there that Joe Mills decided to build his own.
Unfortunately, however, according to Harvey L. Carter, co-author with
Thelma S. Guild of *Kit Carson: A Pattern for Heroes* (Lincoln: Univer-
sity of Nebraska Press, 1984), the story is apocryphal. "I have never
found any evidence to support the story of Kit Carson in Estes Park,"
Mr. Carter wrote the present editor in a letter dated January 19, 1985.

> No doubt some abandoned primitive cabin once occupied the site
> you mention and speculation was that it dated back to the era of
> the trappers. Since Carson was the most well known of these it
> would be an easy step to attach it to him. But it may have dated
> only from the post-trapping era when Mariano Medina, Nick
> James, & others lived in that general area in the 1850s and 1860s.
> As you know, Carson left the mountains in 1841 and came to Bent's
> Fort. During the forties he was with Fremont much of the time
> and in the Taos vicinity otherwise, so that it can not be at all prob-
> able that he was trapping anywhere near this location at any time
> after 1840–41.

The chief perpetrator of the Kit Carson story apparently was none other than Enos Mills, who was fond of pointing out the sign marking the
spot to his guests at Longs Peak Inn. "I asked Mills as to the authenticity of the Kit Carson cabin site," Charles Hewes recorded in his journal on November 23, 1919,

> and he said that some very old man, a former witness in the Col-
> orado-Kansas Water case, had claimed to be here with Kit in the
> winter of 1853–54; that he had drawn a sketch for him which
> readily identified the spot so that Mills felt certain, at least as to
> his having been there. He said that old man Lamb knew of the

place but did not know who occupied it. The cabin was standing until burned by some careless campers. It had a door to the south, was built of logs, and a pole and gravel roof. (p. 429)

56:9. In October 1859, Joel Estes (1806–75), a native of Kentucky, following the Little Thompson westward into the mountains on a hunting and exploring expedition with one of his sons, became the first known white man to enter Estes Park. In 1860 Estes decided to use the park as a place to graze cattle and for that purpose built two cabins and a corral on lower Fish Creek Road near its intersection with present-day Route 34, the road from Lyons (a monument erected in his honor in 1926 marks the spot). There they raised cattle and made their home from 1860 to 1866, though how many of the intervening winters they actually spent in residence in the park is somewhat unclear. Estes left the park in April 1866, because the expansion of his stockraising business required a milder climate. William N. Byers, founding editor of the *Rocky Mountain News,* stayed with Joel and Patsy Estes in August 1864, prior to his unsuccessful attempt to climb Longs Peak, and subsequently named the mountain valley for his host. An account of the residency of the Estes couple in Estes Park was written in 1905 by Joel's son, Milton Estes (1840–1913), at the request of Enos Mills. Milton Estes, "Memoirs of Estes Park," *Colorado Magazine,* 16 (July 1939): 121–32.

56:14. The colorful James Nugent (c. 1828–74), better known as "Rocky Mountain Jim," is one of the great legendary figures in Estes Park history. Jim came to the region in 1868 and built a mud-roofed log cabin at the head of Muggins Gulch, southeast of the summit of Park Hill along the road to Lyons (Route 34), strategically guarding the entrance to the park. He earned his living hunting, fishing, and guiding. While hunting in Middle Park in July 1871, Jim ran afoul of a bear, which mangled the right side of his face and cost him an eye. Rocky Mountain Jim is chiefly remembered for two episodes connected with the early history of Estes Park: his relationship with the plucky Englishwoman Isabella Bird (1831–1904), whom he gallantly escorted to the top of Longs Peak in October 1873, and the mystery surrounding his death at the hands of the Welshman Griff Evans in 1874. Bird recorded her adventures in Estes Park in *A Lady's Life in the Rocky Mountains* (London: John Murray, 1879). Of Jim, she wrote:

> His face was remarkable. He is a man about forty-five, and must have been strikingly handsome. He has large grey-blue eyes, deeply set, with well-marked eyebrows, a handsome acquiline

nose, and a very hand some mouth. His face was smooth-shaven except for a dense moustache and imperial. Tawny hair, in thin uncared-for curls, fell from under his hunter's cap and over his collar. One eye was entirely gone, and the loss made one side of his face repulsive, while the other might have been modeled in marble. "Desperado" was written in large letters all over him.

Nugent was a complex, contradictory, and tragic character. Witty, chivalric, and cultured when sober, Jim was also dark and moody, given to periods of drink and violence. The precise nature of the friendship that developed between this improbable couple can only be speculated on. Isabella Bird, for her part, found him both fascinating and dangerous: "He is," she remarked, "a man whom any woman might love but no sane woman would marry." The best account of their relationship and its dynamics is found in Pat Barr's *A Curious Life for a Lady: The Story of Isabella Bird* (London: Macmillan and John Murray, Ltd., 1970), pp. 68–77, 86–95.

Isabella Bird left Estes Park in December 1873. Some six months later, on June 19, 1874, as the final chapter in another, though possibly related, drama that had been playing itself out for some time, Rocky Mountain Jim was mortally wounded by Griffith Evans, a former friend and Miss Bird's host during her stay in the park. Evans had taken over the Joel Estes homestead and with the intention of mixing cattle-raising with the care and feeding of a growing number of tourists added a number of two-room cabins with fireplaces. The exact cause of their fatal confrontation will never be known, and at least five versions, each plausible in its own way, have been put forth over the years. That bad blood had developed between the two is clear, but whether it was over Evans's teenage daughter (as Enos Mills thought) or as the result of Jim's opposition to the Dunraven forces' attempt to take over the park (see below) and their attempt to get rid of a nuisance whose cabin happened to straddle the only way in and out (as Elkanah Lamb and Abner Sprague thought) will never be known. Whatever the motive, it was the second of two shots from Evans's gun on that June evening that put an end to Mountain Jim's romantic career, though he managed to survive for almost three months with a bullet lodged in his brain. Evans was arrested and brought to trial a year later, on July 14, 1875, but the case against him was dismissed because the only witness had disappeared. See Enos A. Mills, *The Story of Estes Park,* pp. 28–37; Lamb, *Miscellaneous Meditations,* pp. 124–33; Buchholtz, *Rocky Mountain National Park,* pp. 69–71.

56:29. The allusion is to Windham Thomas Wyndham-Quin (1841–1926), the fourth Earl of Dunraven, a wealthy Irish lord, who came to the park on a hunting expedition in late December 1872 (not in "the early sixties") and again in 1873 and 1874. Impressed both by the scenery and by the abundance of elk, deer, mountain sheep, and other game, the Earl, as the author indicates, launched with the help of Denver lawyers and a local agent named Theodore Whyte an ambitious (if apparently partially fraudulent) attempt to control the park for his own personal use. What happened in the aftermath is briefly outlined here. Dunraven did eventually succeed in gaining control of some 15,000 acres. When the preserve idea collapsed, Dunraven organized the Estes Park Company, Ltd. (or English Company as it came to be known), which turned to raising registered Hereford cattle and catering to a growing trade in summer tourists, though it never made money at either. Dunraven's ownership lasted until 1907, when Freelan O. Stanley and his partner, Burton D. Sandborn, succeeded in purchasing the Earl's residual interests of some 6,600 acres. The role played by Dunraven in the early history of Estes Park was in many ways fortuitous. "We all began to see," pioneer Abner Sprague noted some years later, "that the holding of so much of the Park by one company, even if it had been secured unlawfully, was the best thing for the place, particularly after it was proven that the place was only valuable because of its location, and its attraction for lovers of the out-of-doors." Quoted in Dave Hicks, *Estes Park from the Beginning* (Denver: A-T-P Publishing Co., 1976), p. 47.

57:17. Earl of Dunraven, *Past Times and Pastimes* (London: Hodder and Stoughton Ltd., 1922). In part, Dunraven's brevity about his Estes Park experiences may be ascribed to the loss of his diaries, which went down with his yacht, *Valkyrie II,* in an 1894 collision with another boat in the River Clyde. The Earl did write an article about his first (1872) visit to Estes Park entitled "A Colorado Sketch" for the September 1880 issue of *Nineteenth Century* [vol. 8, 445–57].

57:21. In 1876 Dunraven decided to build a cottage for himself and a hotel for his friends. That year the famous landscape artist Albert Bierstadt (1830–1902), whom Dunraven had invited to Estes Park on commission to paint Longs Peak, helped to pick out the sites on lower Fish Creek Road because of their magnificent view. The three-story, fifty-room framed English (or Estes Park) Hotel, with its wrap-around porch, artificial lake, and luxurious appointments, opened in July 1877. It was, as Mills notes, the first strictly tourist hotel built in Estes Park. For many years the English Hotel was managed by the English Company. It then passed into other hands, only to burn to the ground on August

4, 1911. Dunraven's cottage, located closeby, still stands. The Earl also built a hunting lodge in Dunraven Glen on the North Fork of the Big Thompson River, where he brought parties of his friends into the late 1880s.

57:28. By the late 1870s and early 1880s a number of the park's pioneer families were taking in paying guests at their "ranches." Elkanah Lamb's Longs Peak House in the Tahosa Valley has been mentioned above. Other guest ranches included those of Abner Sprague (1850–1943), who in 1875 homesteaded in Moraine Park (or Willow Park, as it was then known); Horace Ferguson (1826–1912), who that same year settled in Estes Park for reasons of his wife's health and established a homestead, subsequently known as the Highlands, north of Marys Lake above Beaver Point; Alexander Q. MacGregor (1845–96), another 1875 arrival, who offered cabin accommodations and encouraged tenting on Black Canyon Creek near his homestead; and William E. James (d. 1895), who established the beginnings of the Elkhorn Lodge on Fall River in 1877. Sprague sold his ranch in 1904. It was then operated as Stead's Ranch and Hotel until it was purchased and razed in the early 1960s by the National Park Service. The James lodge, which still stands, gave its name to Elkhorn Avenue, which runs the length of the village of Estes Park. During its early years the James homestead served as a center of entertainment for village residents.

58:15. See 55:15, above. Cleave, as noted, was English, not Scotch.

59:8. Jim Oss has not been identified. An Andrew G. Oss, a carpenter by trade, is listed in the Larimer County directory for 1919. He was then living in Masonville, a small town west of Loveland, and some thirteen miles southwest of Fort Collins. He was still there in 1925 and 1927, the period when Mills's book was written and published.

59:12. Oss had just completed the improvements required to obtain legal title to his land under the terms of the Homestead Act of 1862.

60:5. The present seventeen-mile trail from Estes Park over Flattop Mountain to Grand Lake by way of the North Inlet was blazed in 1901 by Fred Sprague, Abner's brother, and Franklin I. Huntington, a surveyor. It replaced a longer trail that descended to Grand Lake through Big Meadows along Tonahutu Creek.

60:8. Until 1914, when the Bear Lake trailhead came into use, the only trail up Flattop Mountain ascended by way of Mill Creek Basin. The creek received its name from a sawmill operation established by two men named Hill and Beckwith during the fall and winter of 1877–78. It continued to do a brisk business with loggers and woodsmen brought in from Wisconsin until the fall of 1880 when its owners moved the mill to the booming mining town of Teller in North Park. The mill itself was located near where the overflow from Bierstadt Lake enters Mill Creek, and it was in one of the abandoned Hill and Beckwith cabins, whose remnants are still visible, that Mills apparently spent the night.

62:12. Enos Mills describes a similar incident on Flattop Mountain in an article entitled "In the Mountain Snows," which appeared in the May 18, 1905, issue of *The Youth's Companion*. He later incorporated it into his book *Wild Life on the Rockies* (1909; reprint, Lincoln: University of Nebraska Press, 1988), p. 17.

65:1. Because of its isolation and the lingering danger of Indian raids, the area about Grand Lake, across the Continental Divide from Estes Park, remained an undeveloped wilderness known only to hunters and fishermen until the early 1880s. Its sudden growth can be directly attributed to the mining boom along the North Fork of the Colorado and in the Rabbit Ears District in North Park that created the short-lived but lavishly conceived towns of Gaskill, Lulu City, and Teller. By 1882 the village of Grand Lake boasted a growing number of hotels, general stores, and other businesses, as well as a newspaper, the *Grand Lake Prospector*. The mining rush produced more dreams than wealth and the towns it so optimistically spawned were quickly deserted, but Grand Lake survived because it was able to take advantage of a steadily expanding tourist trade, though it would never rival Estes Park. The story of Grand Lake is told in Robert C. Black, *Island in the Rockies* (Boulder: Pruett Publishing Co., 1946) and in two books by Mary Lyons Cairns, *Grand Lake: The Pioneers* (Denver: World Press, 1946) and *Grand Lake in the Olden Days* (Denver, 1971).

65:25. The festivities that Mills describes below are fairly typical of the time and place. Mary Lyons Cairns, in her *Grand Lake: The Pioneers,* devotes part of a chapter (pp. 193–203) to the parties and dances of the early settlers and includes the account of a barn-raising that appeared in the November 18, 1882, edition of the *Grand Lake Prospector:*

> The last of the week Mrs. M. J. Young, of the Fairview House, gave notice of a log raising. At the appointed time the boys commenced to flock in. They came up from the ranches, they came down from the mines, and they came across from the settlements. They came on foot, they came on horseback, and they came in boats. When about forty had arrived they fell to work, some with skids, some with axes, and some with their tongues; these latter were in the majority.
>
> At noon the estimable hostess informed the hungry horde that the fatted venison had been slain, and told them to enter and par-

take thereof. About this time we came and joined the rabble. And such a dinner—rabbits, venison, trout, grouse, cakes, pies, puddings, and everything to satisfy the greedy soul of man and give him dyspepsia. After dinner those who were able went down and finished the barn, which they accomplished by sundown. Then an excellent supper was served, such a supper as only Mrs. Young and her daughter Miss Jennie can prepare.

After doing ample justice to the supper the boys went home, shined their boots, put themselves inside their bib and tucker; then went in search of the fair ones. These they found and hurried them back to the Fairview House, where jolly John Mitchell was waiting, violin in hand. The folding doors had been thrown open, and the dining and sitting rooms thrown into one. And how Mitch did play! Mitch always enjoys these gatherings as much as the boys, he likes to see the boys jump fast to catch up with him. The dance lasted until Old Sol put in an appearance, and it is rumored that the dancers were mad because the night was so short.

66:16. From the 1880s on, there was periodic talk and rumor of the building of a Denver to Salt Lake City railroad across Middle Park. Despite public statements by a number of promoters, and some preliminary work, the hopes of the isolated residents of Grand County remained frustrated until July 1902, when railroad entrepreneur David Moffat (1839–1911) organized the Denver, Northwestern and Pacific Railway Company (which soon became known as the "Moffat Road"). The DNw & P reached Granby and Hot Sulphur Springs by way of Rollins Pass in 1905 and three years later, in November 1908, reached Steamboat Springs. The progress of the Moffat Road into the mountains west of Denver received ongoing coverage in the Denver papers. Robert C. Black, *Island in the Rockies: The History of Grand County, Colorado, to 1930* (Boulder: Pruett Publishing Co., 1969), pp. 255–74; Edward T. Bollinger, *Rails That Climb: The Story of the Moffat Road* (Santa Fe: Rydal Press, 1950); Edward T. Bollinger and Frederick Bauer, *The Moffat Road* (Denver: Sage Books, 1962).

71:13. Both of Joe Mills's parents had Quaker ancestors. His mother's father was Josiah Lamb (1817–62), a millwright and cabinetmaker by trade, who arrived in Linn County, Kansas, with the Mills-Lamb party in the spring of 1857. Josiah Mills, an outspoken and determined free-soiler, served as a member of the Wyandotte Convention, which framed the constitution of the state of Kansas in 1859, and as a member of the first state legislature in 1860–61. That he was also a Quaker minister is far from clear, though his wife and first cousin, Ruth Lamb (1821–62), apparently was.

74:6. Grays Peak (14,270 feet) and Torreys Peak (14,267 feet), named in 1861 after the famous American botanists Asa Gray and John Torrey, and the Collegiate Range, containing Mount Harvard (14,399 feet) Mount Yale (14,172 feet), and Mount Princeton (14,177 feet), are located along the central part of the Front Range. All five are included among the twenty highest peaks in Colorado.

74:20. Tyndall Glacier, named for noted British scientist and mountaineer John Tyndall (1820–93), a pioneer in the study of glaciation, lies in the gorge between Flattop Mountain and Hallett Peak.

CHAPTER 5: "TRAPPING — MOUNTAIN-TOP DWELLERS"

76:7. Joe Mills's 160-acre homestead claim was located on the side of Twin Sisters Mountain just below Cabin Rock overlooking Longs Peak Inn (see the Cooper-Babcock map of 1911 and Ch. 4, 56:8). After Mills abandoned the site in 1909 or 1910, it was filed on by William S. Cooper (1884–1978), who had pioneered in the exploration of Wild Basin and went on to become a leading ecologist at the University of Minnesota. As Charles Hewes recalled, "At the suggestion of Joe Mills, who found himself unable to perfect residence of his homestead on account of his duties at college, I induced Dr. Cooper to secure a relinquishment on his homestead and perfect title to that quarter section under the Timber & Stone act, which he did in 1909 . . . ." Hewes "Autobiography," p. 229. Cooper had spent the summers of 1904 and 1906 observing the plant life at the higher elevations in Estes Park. The results of his study were published in "Alpine Vegetation in the Vicinity of Long's Peak, Colorado," *Botanical Gazette,* 45 (May 1908): 319–37. Some three decades later, in 1941, Cooper built a summer cottage on the property, which he called "Tapiola" after the home of the Finnish god of the forest. William S. Cooper, "Wild Basin in 1904–1908," *Trail and Timberline,* 558 (June 1965): 109.

83:8. The Ute Indians of western Colorado, together with their enemies east of the Divide, the Arapahos, constituted the two major Indian tribes of nineteenth-century Colorado. Both tribes were occasional visitors to the Estes Park and Grand Lake areas. According to Abner Sprague, who homesteaded Moraine Park in 1875, "That the Indians made Estes Park a summer resort, there is no question, as evidence of their summer camps were everywhere throughout the Park when the white pioneer came. . . . it is well established that conflicts between tribes [the Ute and Arapaho] took place in the Park. One battle ground is located without question in Beaver Park and the moraine between there and Moraine Park. There are ruins of a fortified mound at the west end of Beaver Park where the weaker party made their last stand." Abner Sprague, "Estes and Rocky Mountain National Parks: An Historical Reminiscence," p. 2. Typescript ms., Colorado Historical Society. This essay was also published in the April 21, 1922, edition of the *Estes Park Trail*.

83:20. Abner Sprague and other early Estes Park settlers reported seeing Indian lodge poles or "wickiups" in various places in the park in the 1870s, and Frederick Chapin included a photograph of one such remnant in his *Mountaineering in Colorado: The Peaks about Estes Park* (1889). Whether the tepee frames that Mills recalls were authentic, or whether they were the playful work of other early summer visitors, remains to be seen.

CHAPTER 6: "A LOG CABIN IN THE WILDS—PRIMITIVE LIVING"

107.15. Jane Murger Lamb, the second wife of Elkanah J. Lamb. See Ch. 1, 11:13.

109:11. The congressional bill creating the 358.5 square mile Rocky Mountain National Park was signed into law by President Woodrow Wilson on January 26, 1915. The park was formally dedicated on September 4, 1915, with Enos Mills acting as master of ceremonies.

114:11. The allusion, of course, is to the Roosevelt family of New York, which had already produced one president, Theodore Roosevelt (1858–1919), who occupied the White House from 1901 to 1909, and would produce another in Franklin Delano Roosevelt (1882–1945). Teddy Roosevelt was widely known as an outdoor enthusiast and conservationist.

119:25. The novel of 1903 by Jack London (1876–1916) about the adventures of a dog who learns to survive in the hostile environment of the Alaskan Klondike.

CHAPTER 7: "GLACIERS AND FOREST FIRES"

127:12. There are five true or "living" glaciers within the present boundaries of Rocky Mountain National Park: Sprague Glacier, Rowe Glacier, Tyndall Glacier, Andrews Glacier, and Taylor Glacier.

129.5. Arapaho Glacier, located in the Indian Peaks Wilderness Area of the Roosevelt National Forest, south of Rocky Mountain National Park and some twenty miles west of Boulder, is the largest active glacier in Colorado. In 1960 it covered some 62 acres. Between 1900, when it was first studied, and 1960, Arapaho Glacier lost some 22 acres and thinned an estimated average of 106 feet; during the same period its annual movement decreased from about 28 to 12 feet. Henry A. Waldrop, *Arapaho Glacier: A Sixty Year Record,* University of Colorado Studies, Series in Geology, no. 3 (Boulder: University of Colorado Press, 1964).

132:20. The village of Allenspark (now spelled as one word), the southeastern gateway to Rocky Mountain National Park, dates from about 1902. It is named for Alonzo Nelson Allen, who built a prospecting cabin some two miles east of the present town in 1864.

132:21. The fire that Joe Mills describes undoubtedly is the fire of summer 1902, which broke out south of Longs Peak along the headwaters of the St. Vrain River. For a week the fire raged out of control, without any attempt to contain it, thus endangering the water supply of some 38,000 acres of farm land around Longmont. Enos Mills provided photographs for an article describing the fire that was published in the February 4, 1903, edition of the *Denver Times.*

CHAPTER 8: "THE PROVERBIAL BUSY BEAVER"

143:11. The Reverend Lamb's "horde of trappers," like his story of Kit Carson's cabin, is probably apocryphal. As Abner Sprague noted in his essay "Estes and Rocky Mountain National Parks":

> That Estes Park was ever made the trapping grounds by either the Indians or the early white trappers to any great extent, I have my doubts, as the same fur-bearing animals were plentiful at lower altitudes and could be secured with less effort nearer the plains and lines of travel. It is well known that the early trappers and explorers followed the main or larger streams in their travels and explorations. No historical attempt was made to cross the great divide except by way of one of the two Plattes, Arkansas, or the larger streams flowing out of the great divide in Colorado. (p. 3)

144:7. No doubt Tahosa and Cabin creeks.

148:10. Brigham Young (1801–77), as president of the Mormon Church, led his followers to their new home on the banks of the Great Salt Lake in 1848. Young taught and practiced polygamy; he had some two dozen wives and fifty-six children.

156:5. According to tradition, the Cache la Poudre River, which flows northeast out of Poudre Lake to the east of the Continental Divide at

Milner Pass, was named in 1836 by a party of French trappers from St. Louis who over the course of one winter safely deposited some of their supplies, including a quantity of black gunpowder, close by its banks.

157:14. Garden vegetables, usually raised for market.

CHAPTER 9: "MOUNTAIN CLIMBING"

164:1. See Ch. 4, 60:5.

164:17. Hallett Peak (12,713 feet), one of the most photographed mountains in Rocky Mountain National Park, is named after William H. Hallett (1851–1941). Hallett, a native of Massachusetts and an engineer by training, first came to Estes Park in 1878 and was so taken by the place that he returned a year later with his bride. Their honeymoon consisted of a thirty-day camping trip over the Continental Divide to Grand Lake and back guided by Abner Sprague. In 1881, having decided to take up ranching, the Halletts built a summer home, Edgemont, just to the northwest of Marys Lake above Beaver Point. When he was not ranching, Hallett climbed and explored the mountains surrounding Estes Park and guided summer visitors like Frederick Chapin (see below).

169:5. Mount Chapin (12,454 feet), the southernmost peak in the Mummy Range, is named for Frederick Hastings Chapin (1852–1900), a Hartford, Connecticut, druggist who spent the summers of 1886, 1887, and 1888 climbing in Estes Park with several fellow New Englanders under the guidance of Carlyle Lamb and William Hallett. In 1889 he published an account of his adventures entitled *Mountaineering in Colorado: The Peaks about Estes Park* under the auspices of the Appalachian Mountain Club. A new edition, with a foreword and explanatory notes by the present editor, was published by the University of Nebraska Press in 1987.

169:8. In 1886 the *Grand Lake Prospector* asked, "Can't we have a road to Estes Park?" Though it took many years, Fall River Road, which leads from Horseshoe Park up to Fall River Pass where it joins Trail Ridge Road, a distance of 9.4 miles, became the first road across the Continental Divide to Grand Lake. It was begun in the summer of 1913 with the help of thirty-eight convicts from the Colorado Penitentiary, who lived in cabins in Horseshoe Park, and took nearly eight years to complete. When Trail Ridge Road was opened in 1932, Fall River Road, still unpaved, became a one-way road, as it remains today.

175:21. Black Canyon, so named by early visitors because of "its thick growth of pines and black and gloomy shadows," begins to the north of the village of Estes Park.

177:25. The allusion is unclear. The Never Summer Mountains, themselves a part of the Medicine Bow Range, were once known as the Rabbit Ear Range. As Arps and Kingery explain in their *High Country Names*, however, the Rabbit Ear Range was often confused with Rabbit Ear Pass on the far side of North Park. That may be Mills's problem here.

178:9. William N. Byers (1831–1903), the founding editor of the *Rocky Mountain News* and a man whose entire adult life was associated with the growth and development of Colorado, made an unsuccessful attempt to climb Longs Peak in August 1884. "We have been almost all around the Peak," he later wrote, "and we are quite sure that no living creature, unless it had wings to fly, was ever upon its summit. We believe we run no risk in predicting that no man will ever be, though it is barely possible that the ascent can be made." Byers, of course, was wrong. Four years later he was a member (though not "in charge") of the seven-man party led by one-armed Civil War veteran Major John Wesley Powell (1834–1902) that, coming from Grand Lake by way of Wild Basin, reached the elusive summit of Longs Peak on August 23, 1868. Byers wrote accounts of both his 1864 and 1868 climbs for the *Rocky Mountain News.* Another interesting account of the 1868 ascent was written by L. W. Keplinger, a young college student at Illinois Wesleyan who actually discovered the couloir leading to the summit. See L. W. Keplinger, "The First Ascent of Long's [sic] Peak," *Collections of the Kansas State Historical Society,* 14 (1918), pp. 340–53.

178:24. Carrie J. Welton, a wealthy and eccentric native of Waterbury, Connecticut, became the first woman to die on Longs Peak on September 23, 1884. As Mills notes, her guide was Carlyle Lamb (1862–1958). Though the weather that day was bad, Miss Welton refused to turn back. They reached the summit successfully, but Carrie Welton was exhausted. Lamb helped her to descend as far as the Keyhole. It was then midnight and Lamb was forced to go for help. It was five miles to Longs Peak House in the valley below, and by the time that Carlyle returned with his father Carrie Welton was dead. Elkanah Lamb discusses the tragedy in some detail in his *Miscellaneous Meditations* (pp. 78–88).

178:29. On July 20, 1921, eighteen-year-old Gregory Aubuchon of Michigantown, Indiana, defied his parents' wishes and set off alone from the Barthol (now Glacier Basin) campground to climb Longs Peak. His body was found by park rangers on September 16, 1921, buried in the snow at the base of the East Face. He had apparently fallen from the top. Hewes "Journal," September 26, 1921, p. 514.

179:3. Frank Stryker, a young boy from Tipton, Iowa, was fatally injured on August 28, 1889, when a pistol he was carrying accidentally discharged while he was descending the final approach to the summit known as "the Homestretch" in the company of three other members of his family. Carlyle Lamb once again was the guide.

179:4. The allusion is to Jesse E. Kitts of Greeley, Colorado, who was struck and killed on the summit by a bolt of lightning on July 1, 1922.

179:5. Agnes Vaille (1890–1925), a resident of Denver and member of the Colorado Mountain Club, having reached her goal to be the first woman to climb the sheer East Face of Longs Peak in winter, became exhausted on the summit and froze to death in fourteen-degree-below-zero weather on January 12, 1925. Her climbing partner, Walter Kiener, an experienced Swiss mountaineer, was more fortunate. Though he suffered severe frostbite, Kiener managed to reach Enos Mills's Timberline Cabin, located below the Boulder Field in Jim's Grove, from where he attempted to mount a rescue effort. One of those to respond was Herbert Sortland, the caretaker of Longs Peak Inn, who started up the trail, became lost in the storm, and perished, after falling and breaking a hip, as he tried to return to the Inn. His body was found on February 27, 1925, near the Inn stables, within a hundred yards of his own quarters. In 1927 the Vaille family built a rescue shelter just below the Keyhole in memory of their daughter. Accounts of the Vaille tragedy have been left by two members of the rescue party: Jack C. Moomaw, *Recollections of a Rocky Mountain Ranger* (Longmont, Colo.: Times-Call Publishing Co., 1963), pp. 34–39; and Carl A. Blaurock, "Tragedy on Longs Peak," *Denver Westerners Roundup,* 37 (September-October 1981): 3–12. The official report of the incident by Roger W. Toll, superintendent of Rocky Mountain National Park, was subsequently republished in *Trail and Timberline,* 77 (February 1925): 4–9.

CHAPTER 10: "MODERN PATHFINDERS"

181:2. James Bridger (1804–81), trapper, fur trader, scout, and frontier explorer, in 1824 became the first white man to visit the shores of the Great Salt Lake. In 1843, with the fur trade on the wane, Bridger established Fort Bridger in southwest Wyoming as a way station on the Oregon Trail catering to the needs of emigrants streaming west. Later he served as an army scout and guide, using his invaluable store of geographical knowledge and knowledge of the Indians to further the cause of westward expansion.

181:3. Buffalo Bill was the nickname of William F. Cody (1846–1917), whose extraordinary career as Pony Express rider, buffalo hunter for the Kansas Pacific Railroad, chief of scouts for the Fifth Cavalry, and entrepreneur of the "Wild West" show, came to epitomize for many what life in the frontier West was all about.

182:19. The allusion, of course, is to the famous mail-order company, which sent out its first catalog (a one-page price list of "Merchandise at Wholesale Prices") in 1872.

184:13. Proteus, the wise old man of the sea of Greek mythology, was known for his ability to assume many guises.

185:26. Storm Pass (10,250 feet) is located between Estes Cone and Battle Mountain, at the head of a trail that begins in Glacier Basin.

185:27. The Keyhole, alluded to above, is the jagged opening, framed by two overhanging ledges above the Boulder Field. Once through the Keyhole, with its spectacular view of the lakes in Glacier Gorge below, the climb to the top of Longs Peak begins in earnest.

187:8. Chasm Lake (11,760 feet) lies in a glacial cirque at the foot of the sheer East Face of Longs Peak.

188:5. Elkanah Lamb's Longs Peak House was purchased by Enos Mills in 1902 and renamed Longs Peak Inn. The Inn burned in 1906, after which Mills rebuilt it to his own specifications. It burned again in 1946.

193:17. Specimen Mountain (12,489 feet) is located above Poudre Lake and Milner Pass. Though they once were believed to be an extinct volcano, geologists have now determined that Specimen Mountain and the adjacent Crater to the southwest are formed of ash and other volcanic material from an eruption that took place elsewhere. Early tourists, including Frederick Chapin and his friends, noted the sheep trails leading over into The Crater, and the area still remains perhaps the best place within Rocky Mountain National Park to watch out for the elusive big horns.

194:30. Troublesome Creek lies to the west of Grand Lake.

197:29. Thunder Pass (11,331 feet), which early settlers knew as Lulu Pass, connects Middle Park and North Park. It lies on the Continental Divide to the north of the site of Lulu City and just west of Lulu Mountain.

199:9. C. R. Trowbridge, serving as "acting supervisor," was appointed on July 1, 1915, to organize Rocky Mountain National Park and given a budget of $10,000 to accomplish the task. Trowbridge was replaced some fifteen months later, on September 18, 1916, by L. Claude Way, a former army captain and ranger, who served as "chief ranger in charge" until October 24, 1921, when he resigned and was, in turn, succeeded by Roger W. Toll. The popular Toll (1883–1936), a civil engineer by training but an avid mountain climber and outdoorsman, was serving as superintendent at the time of the book's publication.

201:20. Mills Moraine.

201:22. Columbine Falls, which lies between Chasm Lake and Peacock Pool below the East Face of Longs Peak.

210:24. Victoria Broughm or Brougham, a socially prominent young woman from Michigan, had been staying at Enos Mills's Longs Peak Inn and it was Mills's famous dog, Scotch, who accompanied her to the summit. Mills tells the story of her ascent and near-fatal ordeal in his *Wild Life on the Rockies* (1909; reprint, Lincoln: University of Nebraska Press, 1988), pp. 138–41, and in *The Story of Scotch* (Boston: Houghton Mifflin, 1916), pp. 17–22.

211:20. William S. Cooper (See Ch. 2, 15:25 and Ch. 5, 76:7), Carl Piltz, and Joe Mills were guiding for Enos Mills that summer. Enos Mills in his account of the incident noted above says that he sent four guides in search of Miss Broughm; Joe Mills indicates only three. Piltz (186?–1926), a mason by trade, built the stone fireplace in Longs Peak Inn; he also set the foundation for the memorial plaque marking the site of Joel Estes's cabin, which was erected by the citizens of Estes Park in 1926.

215:16. On September 2, 1915, the Rev. Thornton R. Sampson, a Presbyterian minister and a friend of Woodrow Wilson's, left Grand Lake for Estes Park over Flattop Mountain to attend the dedication ceremonies for Rocky Mountain Park, planning to descend by way of Odessa Gorge. His remains were discovered by a trail crew working near the Fern Lake trailhead on July 8, 1932 (six years after the publication of Mills's book) and were reinterred closeby at the base of the cliff.

215:16. Walden is a village in North Park, Jackson County. The episode described, however, has not been identified.

219:17. A euphemism for the devil.

221:17. All were famous nineteenth-century Colorado mining towns.

222:11. No doubt one of the abandoned cabins at the Eugenia Mine (see Ch. 3, 47:2).

227:13. Heavily wooded Forest Canyon, whose northwest slopes provide the source of the Big Thompson River, was and still remains one of the most inaccessible and seldom visited areas within Rocky Mountain National Park. It is best viewed from above at the Forest Canyon Overlook on Trail Ridge Road. Joe Mills wrote an account of a trip through Forest Canyon, beginning at Forest Canyon Pass above Poudre Lake and ending at the Fern Lake trail below the Pool, for the May 1921 issue of *Trail and Timberline* (no. 32, pp. 2–5).

229:1. Ypsilon is the Greek word for the letter *Y*. Ypsilon Mountain (13,514 feet) was named in 1887 by Alice Chapin, the wife of Frederick Chapin, because of the unmistakable snow-filled *Y* in its side. "So it went forth," Chapin wrote two years later, "and the name was accepted by the dwellers of the valley and by visitors to the ranches."

229:15. Dust or small nuggets washed away from an outcropping by the action of water. To strike it rich one must, of course, trace the float to its originating vein or load.

CHAPTER 13: "THE CITY OF SILENCE"

243:14. Teller, named in honor of Henry M. Teller (1830–1914), one of Colorado's first senators and a staunch supporter of the new state's mining interests, was located on a tributary of the Illinois River across the Continental Divide in North Park. Following the initial discovery of paying ore in 1879, Teller grew rapidly, and at its height boasted a population of some 1200 to 1300 residents, 400 buildings, and its own newspaper, the *North Park Miner*. Like the other mining towns in the region, Teller's history was short. By 1885 the boom was over and Teller, once the largest mining camp in Grand County, became just another ghost town. According to Mary Lyon Cairns (*Grand Lake: The Pioneers,* p. 185), "when Teller was over and done with and deserted, the people just walked out, most of them leaving much of their furniture, many leaving dirty dishes on the tables."

243:24. The mining claims listed are apparently Mills's invention. See, for example, Robert A. Corregan and David F. Lingane, *Colorado Mining Directory: Containing an Accurate Description of the Mines, Mining Properties and Mills, and the Mining, Milling, Smelting, Reducing and Refining Companies and Corporations of Colorado* (Denver: The Colorado Mining Directory Co., 1883), which lists several thousand contemporary mines.

244:11. Joe Mills's own parents had moved from Iowa to Kansas in 1857. See Ch. 1, 1:2.

245:17. The lack of a processing mill was a frequent complaint voiced by the miners of Grand County.

248:16. North Arapaho Peak (13,502 feet) and South Arapaho Peak (13,397 feet) surround Arapaho Glacier in the Indian Peaks Wilderness Area south of Longs Peak (see Ch. 7, 129:5).

CHAPTER 14: "BEARS AND BUGBEARS"

254:4. Davy Crockett (1786–1836), who served two terms in Congress and died defending the Alamo, was one of the most colorful frontiersmen in American history.

260:8. The famous expedition under the joint command of Meriwether Lewis (1744–1809) and William Clark (1770–1838) was dispatched by Thomas Jefferson in 1804 to investigate the newly acquired Louisiana Purchase. Their trip westward to the Pacific Ocean provided the first description of the Rocky Mountains, which they crossed north of Colorado.

264:5. Mount Meeker (13,911 feet), which stands just to the southeast of Longs Peak, is the second highest mountain in Rocky Mountain National Park.

278:16. Mr. Hill is Alfred E. Hill (1850–1918), who worked for the Denver Zoo from 1890 to 1912, the greater part of the time as superintendent. Enos Mills gave two bear cubs, a female named Jenny and a male named Jack, to the Denver Zoo in 1903. The two grew to maturity in a large compound known as the "stockade," which housed wolves, coyotes, and bears. Johnny died in 1925; the six-hundred-pound Jenny lived until 1936. Enos Mills tells the story of Johnny and Jenny without mentioning his brother Joe in *The Spell of the Rockies* (Boston: Houghton Mifflin, 1911), pp. 207–19, and in *The Grizzly: Our Greatest Wild Animal* (Boston: Houghton Mifflin, 1919), pp. 101–15. Both accounts are accompanied by pictures of the two bear cubs; the latter by a picture of Johnny and Jenny "At the Age of Fourteen" and of Johnny as a mature bear. How or why Jack became Johnny is unclear. A picture of "Johnny, My Grizzly Cub" also appears in Enos Mills's *Watched By Wild Animals* (Garden City, N.Y.: Doubleday, Page & Co., 1922), opp. p. 196. Joe Mills had already told the story of the two bears, again without mentioning his brother, in "My Friends the Grizzlies," *St. Nicholas,* 41 (February 1914): 294–97.

The truth of the matter, undoubtedly, is that the capture of the bear cubs originally was a joint enterprise in which both brothers participated. Only later, following their quarrel and estrangement of 1908, did the story of Johnny and Jenny come to take on a decidedly parochial cast. In this respect, the writer for the *Denver Post* who on July 22, 1936, noted Jenny's death probably came close to the truth:

Jennie [*sic*] was born in the wilds of what is now Rocky Mountain National park in January 1903. The late Joseph and Enos Mills, longtime residents of the region and Colorado naturalists, had a string of traps out for coyotes. Jennie, a cub, was caught.

What became of the mother is a mystery, but Jack, her brother, refused to desert her and was captured with her. He died ten years ago. Both bears were sold to the zoo, and, according to the late Joe Mills's story of the catch, as told to Hill [Clyde E. Hill, superintendent of the Denver Zoo and Alfred Hill's son], the $225 they brought went toward Mills' education at the University of Colorado. (p. 16)

The *Rocky Mountain News,* July 22, 1936, p. 7, also carried the story of Jenny's death, but attributed her capture to Enos Mills without mentioning Joe or his role.

CHAPTER 15: "ROCKY MOUNTAIN NATIONAL PARK"

282:20. This was the wagon road that Elkanah Lamb and his son Carlyle cut in the fall of 1875 and the spring of 1876 to allow access to their home in Longs Peak Valley. See Ch. 3, 35:7.

285:21. As is noted in the Introduction, the issue of concessions within the National Park was one on which Joe and Enos Mills parted company. Enos Mills argued vehemently that the concessions granted by the National Park Service, particularly as they affected transportation within park boundaries, constituted a monopoly that discriminated against local hotel owners.